OPENING UP HUNGARY TO
THE WORLD MARKET

Opening up Hungary to the World Market

External Constraints and Opportunities

Jochen Lorentzen
Assistant Professor at the
Prague College of the Central European University
Czech Republic

Foreword by Susan Strange
London School of Economics
and Political Science

St. Martin's Press

337.439
L860

First published in Great Britain 1995 by
MACMILLAN PRESS LTD
Houndmills, Basingstoke, Hampshire RG21 2XS
and London
Companies and representatives
throughout the world

A catalogue record for this book is available
from the British Library.

ISBN 0–333–62813–6

10   9   8   7   6   5   4   3   2   1
04   03   02   01   00   99   98   97   96   95

Printed and bound in Great Britain by
Antony Rowe Ltd
Chippenham, Wiltshire

First published in the United States of America 1995 by
Scholarly and Reference Division,
ST. MARTIN'S PRESS, INC.,
175 Fifth Avenue,
New York, N.Y. 10010

ISBN 0–312–12408–2

Library of Congress Cataloging-in-Publication Data
Opening up Hungary to the world market : external constraints and
opportunities / Jochen Lorentzen.
p. cm.
Includes index.
ISBN 0–312–12408–2 (U.S.)
1. Hungary—Foreign economic relations.   2. Hungary—Economic
policy—1989–   .   3. Hungary—Economic policy—1968–1989.
4. Industrial policy—Hungary.   5. Investments, Foreign—Hungary.
I. Title.
HF1542.L67   1995
337.439—dc20
                                        94–32257
                                          CIP

Contents

List of Figures

List of Tables

Foreword

Some two or three years before the Berlin Wall came down the Soviet Union sent three of its top economists to Italy to discuss with Italian economists the role of credit in a socialist economy. The Italians were obviously considered to be more sympathetic, politically and intellectually, to Soviet ways of thinking than the Germans or the British, let alone the Americans. One of the three Soviet economists was Abel Agenbegyan, a close adviser to Mikhail Gorbachev, so that the outcome of these discussions might be expected to have some bearing on the course of economic reform in the USSR. By accident and through a good friend, the late and sadly-missed Ricardo Parboni, I was invited to come down from Bologna to Naples to listen.

What I best remember about the occasion was how, again and again, an Italian would press the Russians to comment on what was being attempted in Hungary. There was talk of issuing government bonds and of letting people buy and sell them. There was even discussion of how state banks could be freed from total subservience to the Planning Ministry. What did the Soviet economists make of these developments? And time after time, the Russians, visibly bewildered, replied that they neither knew nor were interested in what went on in Budapest. 'Hungary', they said, 'is a small country. What they do there has no importance for the Soviet Union.'

They were wrong, of course. It was the Hungarians who opened their borders to refugees from East Germany. And once they did that, the fate of the Soviet Empire in Central Europe was sealed. The avalanche of political and economic change gathered speed. Gorbachev himself was swept away; so far as I know, Agenbegyan was too.

The point of the story is plain. We can all learn from each other's successes and each other's failures, and it becomes more than ever necessary to study the experiences of others now that every country is engaged in a worldwide competition to sell on the world market. Superpower snobbery, like the snobbery of the old imperialist great powers, belongs to the past. The Russians and Ukrainians have much to learn from the Poles, the Hungarians and even the Slovenes. The Hungarians themselves would be wise to overcome their European self-esteem and pick up some ideas from Taiwan, Malaysia or even Brazil.

This book seems to me to be an important contribution to that learning process. Of course, every country is different. Of course, its assets and its handicaps – intellectual and historical as well as purely material – are peculiar to itself. But all – from the Philippines to South Africa, from Australia to Finland – are having to adjust to the same structural changes in the world economy and world society. Technology knows no frontiers, and the common problem for everyone is to gain access to it – and to international finance – and to make good use of both.

This is also a highly critical book: more so, probably, than if it had been written by a Hungarian. No punches are pulled. The Hungarians are criticised, not so much for borrowing from the West as for failing – like the Brazilians – to realise how vulnerable they were to the failures of others (the Poles for Hungary, the Mexicans for Brazil). They made the mistake of believing that the system would reward virtue and punish vice, that paying up on time and in full on past debt was no guarantee that more credit would be forthcoming. They failed to understand that the real objective of policy – as in the 1930s – was to preserve the credibility of the banking system, to look after the interests of the creditors, not the debtors, and to bend the rules accordingly. To that extent, the study is implicitly critical of the International Monetary Fund (IMF) for its narrowness of vision and the shortness of its policy horizons.

Neither does Dr Lorentzen spare the European Community (EC), as it then was, first for failing to respond to the whole of ex-socialist central Europe with a coherent strategy for the economic and political transition; second, for actually hindering that transition with short-sighted measures of trade protection which failed to solve the problems of those it pretended to protect while putting obstacles in the path of the private enterprise struggling to get started.

For policy-makers west and east, south and north; for students of development and survival in the world economy; for business leaders and teachers of management seeking to understand the difficulties of host governments, especially in Central Europe; for political economists intrigued by the two-way relation of theories to practice and of practical experience on theory, this is a good, worthwhile read.

London School of Economics and Political Science

SUSAN STRANGE

Preface

One of the most influential international bankers, William Rhodes of Citibank, predicted in April 1994 on CNN's Business Report that Poland would be able to access international capital markets by the end of the year. Meanwhile, analysts who have criticised the restrictive trade policy of the European Union *vis-à-vis* the countries of Central and Eastern Europe for some time increasingly worry about protectionist tendencies in the capitals of the more advanced transition economies themselves, namely Warsaw, Prague and Budapest. People in these capitals seem to worry about something else. In early 1994, the Czech Prime Minister, Klaus, and the Hungarian Minister of International Economic Relations, Kádár, issued statements to the effect that there was too much foreign investment coming into their countries. All of this is happening as the European Union Commission in Brussels and the Central European governments named above are busily trying to prepare the ground for membership negotiations that are to begin sometime in the next couple of years.

The research for this volume was completed in April 1993. At that time the European Union was still the EC and had not yet offered membership, *de facto*, to the Associated Countries; populist tirades against foreign direct investment (FDI) were confined to the political right; the new, liberal trade regimes in Central Europe were taken for granted; and the Polish government was far from raising credit from private creditors. In sum, the world in April 1994 is a little different from a year earlier. Writing a preface at a year's distance affords authors the opportunity to judge how well their arguments hold up in the light of new evidence; where their attention was perhaps misdirected or unduly limited; and whether the conclusions of their work have any claim to a longer shelf-life.

The book discusses two areas of Hungarian economic policy: the management of external debt, and the management of international competitiveness. The analysis of the first as well as the policy recommendations it implies appear, in the light of recent developments, defensible. I am not aware of any evidence that would question the analysis of the second topic; however, there are serious grounds to dispute my recommendations. Both sides of the story are illustrated below. It is then up to the reader to pass judgement on the durability of this work's conclusions.

THE MANAGEMENT OF EXTERNAL DEBT

> *Claim*:   Uninterrupted and complete debt service did not buy the
> Hungarians privileged treatment on international capital
> markets compared to other, less well-behaved debtors. There-
> fore, it did not pay to repay (Chapter 1).

Some people could not disagree more. In line with Hungarian official
thinking, an analyst at an influential think-tank reviews debt management
in Eastern Europe and quotes straight from the catechism: 'The consequence of a debt default is the decreasing credibility of the indebted
country, a loss of confidence by bankers, capital flight, a declining or dis-
appearing chance of obtaining new loans ..., and worsening conditions for
new borrowing, leading to an increasing debt burden' (Kiss 1993, 18).
Kiss's evidence for 'worsening conditions' is, for example, the higher
interest rate Bulgaria was made to pay on new money after its 1990 moratorium. Yet the rate was higher by a mere 0.2 percentage points (ibid, 18–
19). Whether this signals worsening or improving conditions can only be
judged by comparing the debt service saved from default and the value of
interrupted future credit flows due to the moratorium. But Kiss does not
do that. Instead, she warns against rescheduling because it bothers creditors, foreign investors and domestic holders of capital alike, and would
consequently lead to lower capital inflows and capital flight: 'So it is self-
evident that this kind of debt management endangers the external financing of economies struggling in any case with a shortage of internal
resources of finance, leads to the depletion of international reserves, and
curbs vitally important imports' (ibid, 19). The recourse to self-evidence
is the privilege of true believers. Kiss would be hard put to explain the tre-
mendous increase in portfolio investment into Latin America since 1989;
how is it that Brazil, a defaulter, managed to float two international bond
issues by the time she published her paper; why is Mexico, a frequent
rescheduler, the only debtor country that successfully engaged in sovereign borrowing; what about the rally in Brady bonds in 1993, or the funny
story of Vietnam which, in 1994, is in a position to repay its arrears but
does not, and has lots of official and private capital coming its way
anyway? By Kiss's definition, these countries have all been engaged in
'destructive' debt management but, bad guys or not, they apparently have
relatively good to very good growth prospects, which is what excites
investors. Hence, if a country's growth prospects brighten by rescheduling, defaulting or obtaining debt relief, then it should start doing its calculations: does it pay to repay?

Consider Poland. In the spring of 1993, Poland managed to get its commercial creditors to resume discussions about debt relief, despite some $1 billion in interest arrears.[1] In March 1994 the country struck a deal with the banks' advisory committee which will reduce the value of its outstanding obligations by about 45 per cent and also give it a big discount on its interest arrears. Quite definitely, this was not 'destructive' debt management but tough and successful bargaining, which is what this book argues Hungarians should have done also. In the light of the Polish deal, the only thing that can save the Hungarians from asking themselves whether it would not have been better to have bargained for some type of debt relief in the past is the sort of faith in a *code d'honneur* Kiss exposes and which defies rational analysis: regardless of the circumstances, repayment is good – everywhere and to all eternity.

Why did the Polish deal work out? The theoretical literature on debt management suggests, for example, that an unanticipated increase in world interest rates will help debtors to exploit the impatience of creditors who are eager to invest their money elsewhere (see Armendariz de Aghion 1993, 472). Empirical studies find that creditworthiness improves with an increase in the per capitum gross domestic product (GDP) growth rate (Lee 1993).[2] At least the second condition holds in the Polish case.

However the really convincing explanations come from insiders who describe both sides to the deal: 'This was a game of chicken and the Poles won. The London Club blinked' (David Hunter, head of Asea Brown Boveri (ABB) Poland, quoted in Valencia and Simpson 1994, 13). The London Club was chaired by Dresdner Bank which 'took a long-term view, looking at the money their banks, investors and traders could make in Poland' (Letitia Rydjeski, analyst with Chemical Bank, quoted ibid). Rumour has it that the German government offered its banks financial incentives to agree to the deal. Actions by the Polish government thus resemble what this book argues the Hungarians should have done in 1989/ '90 namely:

- take an impassionate view of the rules of international financial management
- bargain for an alternative to full repayment
- try to ensure support for your action from friends in high places

There is no way of knowing whether it would have worked. But the Polish deal, if anything, certainly suggests that it might have been worth trying.

THE MANAGEMENT OF INTERNATIONAL COMPETITIVENESS

Claim: Some Hungarian firms were successful at selling their products to Organisation for Economic Cooperation and Development (OECD) countries in the 1980s (see Chapter 2). Western, and especially EC, protectionism was partially responsible for Hungary's declining shares on world markets. Hence, it does not make sense to charge that Hungary, as a country, was not competitive, and blame its dismal economic performance exclusively on its economic system (Chapter 3).

Academic observers have come to recognise the worldwide divergence of productivity of individual industries. There is less talk of 'invincible Japan', 'sclerotic Europe' or 'declining America'. Instead, following a trend which was perhaps set by journalists, more attention is being paid to the competitiveness of individual firms and industries: US-produced laptops, high-fashion textiles from Italy, software produced in India and so on. If this had happened earlier, maybe people would have studied how and why Hungarian firms managed to register 131 patents in the USA in 1989 while the Hungarian economy at large was demonstrably not in good shape at all.

Past EC protectionism, this book argues, has contributed to the deterioration of Hungary's shares in the OECD markets. In the same vein, Rollo and Smith (1993) illustrate that, at present, EC protectionism in agriculture, textiles and steel is totally disproportionate to the absolute volume of imports from the East and to their share in total EC imports of goods in the sensitive sectors. If the disputes between the EC and Central Europe – as after the outbreak of cases of foot and mouth disease in Croatia which led to a complete ban on imports of meat and dairy products from all over Eastern and Central Europe in the spring of 1993, or after alleged Czech dumping in steel – are any indication, this unhappy story is likely to continue. On the other hand, the 1993 EC Summit in Copenhagen undoubtedly gave Central Europe a more prominent place on the EC's agenda which makes it easier, in the medium- to long-term, to resolve these conflicts. I express scepticism (in Chapter 4) on the Community's willingness to engage in closer association and am glad to have been proven wrong by events.

Claim: The Hungarian government should have helped its exporters to understand demand in foreign markets and to adjust to OECD protectionism (Chapter 3). Likewise, it may be necessary to exempt individual firms, notably in investment-intensive branches, temporarily from import competition if costs associated with the transition process or managed trade practices in important export markets make it difficult for these firms to remain viable (Chapter 4).

Small countries do not make the rules of international trade, and it is unwise to trust big countries always to stick by theirs. Chapters 3 and 4 suggest two lines of action. The more aggressive one consists of trade promotion and assistance for firms to adjust to protectionism. The more defensive recommends select import protection. In line with the former, the Hungarian government established in late 1993 an Investment and Trade Development Agency which is intended to provide Hungarian exporters with a better understanding of foreign markets and what it takes to compete in them. Good luck to their efforts!

My recommendation to undertake select and temporary import restrictions neglects what many observers consider Central Europe's biggest recent problem, namely a creeping establishment of managed trade practices. Édes (1992–93) goes to great lengths to detail what kind of import restrictions Hungary could impose in line with its international commitments, but he cautions against their application for fear of abuse (see also Sapir 1994). Ostry (1993) is more straightforward. Trade restrictions – even if imposed in response to managed-trade practices by OECD countries – are to be avoided by all means because they endanger the very essence of the reform process. Messerlin (1994) sees these tendencies strengthening and has the same worries. If the developments Ostry and Messerlin foresee materialise, then my argument in favour of select import restrictions was made too lightheartedly. At any rate, the two score a point in the debate because of what was a truly unlucky selection of a firm to argue my case, namely General Electric's Tungsram operation. Tungsram, I argued, in the absence of a devaluation of the forint, should be ensured a protected domestic market for as long as inflation caused it to run up losses due to higher input costs. Although the government devalued the forint only in September 1993, General Electric reported profits of some $12.5 million for 1993 and is very upbeat about prospects for 1994 without, to be sure, being afforded any protection.

Claim: Foreign investments appear to have made an above average contribution to Hungary's export revenues. Also, big foreign business helps to modernise the Hungarian economy. Therefore, the environment for FDI should be continuously improved although it appears unnecessary to offer fiscal incentives to this effect (Chapter 4).

A recent publication on FDI in Hungary reports somewhat inconclusive evidence on the export performance of foreign firms (Marton 1993, 126–7). While exports by foreign affiliates apparently increased faster than those by domestic companies, the importance of sales in international markets is only slightly higher for foreign companies. However, their import propensity appears to be much higher. This may spell problems because of Hungary's precarious balance of payments situation. Once the latter is overcome, the narrow look at individual firms' trade balances will have to be substituted by a more comprehensive view of the manifold effects of FDI on the Hungarian economy.

Survey results reported by Wang (1993) as well as others undertaken for the OECD and by the European Bank for Reconstruction and Development (EBRD) (see Meth-Cohn *et al.* 1994) indicated that foreign firms aimed at the longer-term prospects of enlarged markets and were willing to accept a lower rate of profit for the time being. Alas, a long haul, rather than the quick buck, is the dominant expectation. This takes much wind out of the charge, still fashionable with some political groups in Budapest that foreign investors primarily cream off the countries' jewels and then run.

FDI comes with trade, and inward investment will increase as (or if) more trade barriers are removed (Thomson and Woolcock 1993). In principle, FDI is potentially a no less important mechanism to integrate Central Europe with the European Union than trade. Future surveys of foreign firms in Central Europe should try to find out to what extent further integration through inward investment is impeded by trade obstacles; and case studies could show the trade effects of FDI, especially large-scale FDI.

This book, in short, is about the international constraints on opening up. It does not dispute the salience of domestic policy but underlines the importance of the external environment. Much current writing in comparative political economy addresses this concern: 'we have a situation in the 1990s where economies are more open to international forces but analysts pay less attention to their impact. As a consequence, theorists and policy makers are ill-prepared to understand or cope with many of the problems that now face us' (Stallings 1992, 48). Most of this literature looks at (South)East Asia, Latin America, Africa and the European newly industrialising countries (NICs). Very little has been written about Central and Eastern Europe, and virtually nothing about Central Asia. It is an important task to address this shortcoming and integrate insights, findings and relevant policy recommendations.

* * *

Research and writing for this book were done between late 1990 and early 1993 at the European University Institute in San Domenico di Fiesole outside Florence. It is difficult to convey the beauty of this place to anyone who has never been there. Suffice it to say that it provided a splendid setting, and that it is indeed a site worth visiting.

An invitation to the Europa-Intézet, Budapest, in late 1991 enabled me to conduct interviews with officials of the National Bank, the Ministry of Finance and the Ministry of International Economic Relations and at various research institutes and private banks. In early 1992 I had the opportunity to talk to current and former officials at the IMF, the World Bank and the Institute of International Finance (IIF) in Washington. They generously fitted me into their tight schedules and helped with much technical detail.

Preliminary versions of this work have been presented at the 1992 convention of the International Studies Association, the Johns Hopkins University Bologna Center and, of course, the European University Institute. Participants in these seminars made useful comments and gave me the impression that there was an interesting story to tell. For the encouragement that came with the latter I am most grateful. Throughout, I benefited from a grant given by the German Academic Exchange Service.

Much of what follows is owed to the simple idea that opening up the Hungarian economy to the world market has had a lot to do with external constraints and opportunities: in other words, the 'world environment' matters. This is no less true for the present work. It benefited from advice, comments, suggestions and criticism by Tamás Bácskai, Tilman Ehrbeck, David Henderson, Edurne Iraizoz, Patrick Messerlin, Peter Møllgaard, Louis Pauly, Susan Strange and Robert Waldmann. They were a marvellous 'external opportunity'. None of them, of course, are responsible for any remaining errors. Two are positively exempted from this disclaimer: Susan Strange and Peter Møllgaard. Their input, support and friendship far transcended 'opportunity'; in fact, if this were a plate of spaghetti rather than an academic dish, it would not be *al pomodoro* but be served *ai tre! formaggi*. To all of the above – and my fellow cooks in particular – many thanks.

Prague   JOCHEN LORENTZEN

Abbreviations

BIS	Bank for International Settlements
CCCN	Common Customs Classification Nomenclature
CDPs	Central Development Programmes
CEO	chief executive officer
CEPR	Centre for Economic Policy Research
CETRA	China External Trade Development Council
CMEA	Council for Mutual Economic Assistance
CMS	constant market shares
COCOM	Coordinating Committee on Trade with Communist Nations
CPE	centrally planned economy
DDSR	debt and debt service reduction
DME	developed market economy
DRCs	domestic resource costs
EBRD	European Bank for Reconstruction and Development
EC	European Community
ECE	Eastern and Central Europe
EEA	European Economic Area
EFF	extended financing facility
EFTA	European Free Trade Association
ERP	effective rate of protection
FDI	foreign direct investment
FTC	foreign trade company
GATT	General Agreement on Tariffs and Trade
GDP	gross domestic product
GNP	gross national product
GSP	general system of preferences
HCSO	Hungarian Central Statistical Office
HSWP	Hungarian Socialist Workers Party
HUF	Hungarian Forint
IFI	international financial institution
IIF	Institute of International Finance
IMF	International Monetary Fund
IT	Information technology
LDC	less developed country
Libor	London interbank offered rate
MFA	Multi-Fibre Arrangement

MFN	most favoured nation
MIMIC	moderately indebted middle-income country
MNB	Magyar Nemzeti Bank (Hungarian National Bank)
MVA	manufacturing value added
MYRA	multiyear rescheduling agreement
NAFTA	North American Free Trade Agreement
NEM	New Economic Mechanism
NFI	new forms of investment
NIC	newly industrialised/industrialising country
NTB	non-tariff barrier
OECD	Organisation for Economic Cooperation and Development
OMA	orderly market arrangement
QR	quantitative restriction
R&D	research and development
RCA	revealed comparative advantage
RER	real exchange rate
SAL	structural adjustment loan
SDR	special drawing rights
SIMIC	severely indebted middle-income country
SITC	Standard International Trade Classification
SME	small and medium-sized enterprise
TFP	total factor productivity
TNC	transnational corporation
UNCTAD	United Nations Conference on Trade and Development
UNECA	United Nations Economic Commission for Africa
UNECE	United Nations Economic Commission for Europe
UNIDO	United Nations Industrial Development Organization
UNTCMD	United Nations Transnational Corporations and Management Division
VER	voluntary export restraint

Introduction

Since 1989, Hungary has been trying to integrate its economy fully with the world market. Two crucial tasks have accompanied the transition:

- coping with one of the highest per capita debts in the world
- achieving international competitiveness for goods *Made in Hungary*

The legacy of external debt and the requirement of international competitiveness are, in short, the topics of this analysis. To be sure, many more problems have been encountered during the transition. The decade-long economic crisis of the 1980s still burdens the country in more than one way, and the establishment of a viable market system depends not just on how good or bad goods produced by Hungarian firms are. However, given the size of Hungary's external debt, its small domestic market and hence the high trade dependence of the country, debt management and the achievement of international competitiveness are the key ingredients for a strategy of successfully opening up its economy to the world.

This introduction zooms in on the topic by considering, first, what the causes of Hungary's contemporary problems are generally perceived to be and why there is reason to doubt the authority with which diagnoses are cast and treatments recommended by Western institutions involved in the transition. Second, a historical overview of Hungarian industrialisation is given as a backdrop to the country's present attempt to become a member of the EC. Readers familiar with Central European economic and political history may want to skip this section and go straight to the outline which presents the plan of the work and briefly sketches its conclusions.

OPENING UP AND EXTERNAL CONSTRAINTS

Transition in Central Europe and Western Advice

The reforms associated with the transition to a market economy address, loosely speaking, past policies that, by the late 1980s, had led to a situation in which the production of wealth proved insufficient to cover the social welfare system to which the Hungarians were accustomed. The unsustainability of muddling through the economic crisis provoked a crisis of legitimacy for Hungary's reform communists. A new political arrangement – a government-opposition round table followed by multiparty elections – was

1

supposed to provide a solution to the economic crisis and to restore legitimacy in the form of a new government (Swain 1992, Ch. 1). In other words, the idea was to remedy today mistakes committed yesterday. To do something about yesterday's mistakes presumed an understanding of their origins and effects. This concerned not only the Hungarian administration but also the Western governments and international organisations that took an active interest in the transition. Unfortunately, very few people outside Hungary had any knowledge of the former planned economies. Anybody leafing through books and articles published on the member countries of the former Council of Mutual Economic Assistance (CMEA) before 1989 comes across the same small group of authors whose surnames often suggest the reason for their interest in Eastern Europe and the Soviet Union, but who were also largely unknown outside their field.

By 1989, the experts had been joined by an army of well-meaning academics, foreign government officials and a large number of consultants eager to swarm into the Mecca of Inefficiencies now that the green light had been given to remove most or all characteristics of a planned economy. It is of no small importance that eastern policy-makers actively sought their help. Advice was asked and given on how to disassemble the old system of central planning, and how to establish a market system in its place.[1] Past policy mistakes were held responsible for the (then) current predicament, and the remedy prescribed accordingly: 'change your way of doing things and that will resolve most – if not all – of your problems in due course.' 'In due course', in 1989, meant at most a few years. Only die-hard ideologues would find anything wrong with the implication of the first part of this assertion concerning the need to completely overhaul the old economic system.[2] What is problematic, however, is to suggest that all of Hungary's contemporary problems are due exclusively to its past domestic policies. The quarrel here is with the word 'all'; in what follows, the external constraints on integrating a former CMEA member with the world economy, alongside the pitfalls that result from ignoring them, are illustrated.

Homemade Problems?

The assumptions generally underlying the above remedy and applied here to external debt and then to international competitiveness, are variations of the following premises.

Premise No. 1:   Hungary has a high external debt because it borrowed too much, and it suffers from a debt crisis because the borrowed funds were either squandered on consumption or unwisely invested in projects that never realised a return, in foreign exchange, above the rate of interest to be paid on the loans.

Certainly, there is much truth in this. But is this the whole story? How was it, for example, that the Hungarian National Bank easily managed to contract funds from private sources on the international credit markets until 1987 at rather favourable conditions? Bankers all over the world were taken by surprise when Poland (in 1981) and Mexico (in 1982) defaulted on their obligations but have become extremely cautious in extending new credits ever since. Why did they resume lending to Hungary if it was apparent that the country's leadership was making such poor use of the money? It could not have been because they did not know; the sustainability of Hungary's foreign borrowing had been questioned both inside the country and by (a few) outside observers. And why did the banks abruptly change their country risk assessment in the late 1980s? Not because they were tired of lending to communist regimes; on the contrary, one of the most severe withdrawals of foreign deposits with the National Bank took place after the old leadership decided to take 'market socialism' off the agenda and the new government had declared its commitment to a market economy, Western style.

Premise No. 2:   Meaningless prices and a system of perverse incentives prevented Hungarian firms from producing anything technologically acceptable to world markets.

Again, this is a good description of forbiddingly high profit taxes, informal but painstaking export regulations, artificially high prices for non-tradeables and so on. And again, it is an incomplete description. Throughout the 1980s, Hungary was the West's darling. It was lauded for its courageous reforms that started earlier and went further than anywhere else in the former Soviet Bloc;[3] among centrally planned economies (CPEs), only China overtook Hungary in the late 1980s in the speed and depth of its economic reforms. As anybody who has visited the area would know, Hungary was different not because of its higher level of development – per capitum income in Czechoslovakia, for example, was higher – but because things were managed differently. A few Hungarian firms were world leaders in their product range. Commuters in some Californian cities rode to work in Hungarian-made buses. Tungsram light bulbs were no less known in many parts of the world than those of competitors Osram and Philips. Furthermore, when Hungarian exporters lost outlets for their products in the former CMEA following the introduction of hard-currency settlements in 1991, they rapidly expanded their exports to the West, particularly to the EC. Competitiveness, especially if based on quality and not on price, is not something a firm is likely to acquire overnight,[4] so how was this export surge feasible? Is it possible that the commercial policies of its main trading partners, notably the EC, had an influence on what and how much Hungary exported?

Finding the missing elements to the story is important if one believes that only a thorough understanding of the various reasons for past performances – successes, failures and anything in between – can lead to appropriate policy prescriptions. It is all the more important because officials of the international financial institutions (IFIs) most deeply involved in the transition have been among those who were happy to base their recommendations on the partial stories suggested above.

Small Samples, Big Lessons, No Consensus

In 1990 the World Bank organised a conference on the transition in Eastern Europe that gave rise to a publication outlining the Bank's approach to reforms in the transition economies (Corbo, Coricelli and Bossak 1991). Though acknowledging that it had no blueprints because there were no historical precedents for such a transition, the Bank's officials still claimed that they could make use of the experience accumulated elsewhere in many years of structural adjustment in developing countries.[5] They, too, had typically suffered from pervasive distortions in whose removal the Bank and the Fund had been involved. Applying these experiences to Central and Eastern Europe would entail similar measures to stabilise the economy, institute and codify property rights, rationalise prices, privatise state property, and create a banking system and financial markets. In general, all these reforms would be necessary if the maximum output was to be extracted from existing resources. By such means the Bank would eliminate what it was convinced were the main evils of the old system: 'many years of distortionary trade, regulatory exchange rate policies and an expansion of the state's role in the allocation of resources' (Corbo 1991, 27).[6]

There are at least three fallacies in the conclusions which the Bank draws from the earlier structural adjustment experiences. First, adjustment was successful only in a handful of countries; hence, the sample generating the purported lessons is rather small. In fact, prominence is given to three 'strongly-outward oriented' countries, namely South Korea, Hong Kong and Singapore,[7] and to their superior growth performance. The last two are, as two authors who had good reason to know have argued, 'hard acts to follow' (Koh and Lee Tsao Yuan 1992).[8] What worked in South Korea, in other words, is supposed to apply to Eastern Europe, too. But *what* worked in these countries? Their success is due to the virtual absence of trade controls, so the Bank argues, and 'they got their prices right'. Not so, reply a large number of experts on East Asia, and that is problem no. 2: while most observers agree that the East Asian tigers are worth studying, there is wild disagreement about the necessary and sufficient conditions for East Asian success.

Colin Bradford (1987), for example, concludes that the East Asian NICs managed to underprice investment goods in the 1970s. This facilitated capital formation and structural change. Compared to the Latin American and European NICs, manufacturing export growth was speeded up. He thus disclaims the linkage which posits that low price distortions equal high economic growth. Bradford's article is part of a literature that emphasises the importance of long-run capital formation over short-run efficiency concerns as an engine of structural change without which 'manufacturing miracles' would not work.

> Rather, the evidence here suggests that a supply-push development model with government playing a key role in stimulating capital formation through macropolicies and in accelerating structural change through sectoral strategies affecting the output and export mix may provide a more accurate framework for capturing the causal elements explaining rapid transitional growth. (Bradford 1987, 314)[9]

There is disagreement, too, on the importance of trade policies followed by the East Asian NICs. A trade regime is balanced (or 'neutral', in World Bank parlance) if, on average, the effective rate of protection (ERP) for importables equals the ERP for exportables. This then qualifies as free trade in the sense that there is no overall policy bias towards the production of any particular product within the tradeable sector. Free trade is commonly associated with export promotion and that, says the Bank, promotes growth.[10] By contrast, sectoral industrial policy does not qualify as free trade in that it favours particular products within the tradeable sector. Hence, it is inferior in terms of achieving high growth. Evidence for this is provided by South Korea and Taiwan where export promotion plus competitive real exchange rates, or RER (through inflation control, in Taiwan; through devaluation of the nominal exchange rate, in South Korea), have been the basis of success (Lin 1989; see also Collins and Park 1989).

Another strand of the literature based on evidence from the very same countries concludes exactly the opposite. Both Amsden (1989) and Wade (1990) argue that South Korea and Taiwan 'made it' because governments intervened to direct investments to strategic industries where new technologies soon translated into actual production.[11] The governments availed themselves of tools that are nobody's idea of free trade: incentives, subsidies, controls, protection, mechanisms to spread risk for investors and so on. This, and exposure of the firms to international competition in foreign (but not necessarily in home) markets lay behind their success in world markets. More precisely, the governments used their knowledge of externalities and of differential growth potentials of different industries (in line with shifting world demand) to help their firms exploit economies of scale or learning when their asset base was too low to try on their own; to provide credit where promising entrepreneurs could not get it for lack of reputation; and to promote long-term investments.[12]

In sum: (1) evidence for what facilitates successful adjustment is drawn from a rather small sample of countries; (2) there is pervasive disagreement as to just what the ingredients to success are. The debate often resembles medieval theological disputes more than reasoned arguments.[13] Where the controversy is going is not clear. Optimists cite the *World Development Report 1991* and the Bank's insistence on 'good governance' as well as the prominence of some interventionists in neoclassical quarters as evidence for a new reflectiveness. As an example of the debate that is going on one may take *The Economist's* review of Colclough and Manor's *States and Markets: Neo-liberalism and the Development-Policy Debate* ('The Left, the Right and the Third World' 1992) and the ensuing comment by Robert Wade, also in *The Economist* (1992). Colclough (1991), in a volume reflecting much current thinking of critical development economists, acknowledges the failure of the 'old' development economics to analyse the effects of prices and recognises insights from neoliberals in this field. Less emotional analyses also appear elsewhere. Clute and Turner (1992) find that a series of African countries is better off than it would be without SALs; but they add that without debt forgiveness and massive foreign aid healthy economies will not materialise (for a more sceptical view, see Bradshaw and Tshandu, 1990). The policy prescriptions of the Bank and the Fund, however, remain for the most part squarely rooted in neoclassical theory. Although their proponents are 'probably a minority' (among all those concerned with development policy and aid management), as John Lewis concluded, the conventional neoclassical wisdom 'has the louder voice' (1986, 5; see also Biersteker 1990).

The third and last problem with evaluations of structural adjustments by the IFIs is that they almost totally ignore the global context and reduce results to outcomes of essentially domestic policies. Some external shocks, such as changes in interest rates or terms of trade as well as the availability of private capital flows, are mentioned. But, these apart, it is assumed that all countries face the same world environment. This is a prime example of a heroic assumption turned kamikaze: big debtors, small debtors, neighbours of the USA or Japan, landlocked Central European countries, banana exporters and chip producers all show up in the same alphabet beginning with Albania and ending with Zimbabwe. What is more, this condition is supposed to be valid over time so that one may compare Korea in 1983 with Poland in 1989. South Korea's and Taiwan's rise from the periphery of the world economy clearly did not begin with their liberalisation policies in the early 1980s: Historical timing was an essential element in their export-led growth. From the Korean War onwards, both countries received massive US assistance. At that time, aid monies were used to finance import substitution.[14] The termination of the aid flows in the late 1950s provoked policy reforms encouraging manufactured exports in the 1960s, at a time when the US and West European markets were liberalised and world trade was expanding (Haggard 1989, 9–10).[15] This does not *per se* exclude that they did not also 'get their prices right', but it certainly suggests that an inside-out, domestic-only explanation cannot possibly be the whole truth.

External Linkages

For debtors especially, there are crucial insights in the alternative outside-in analysis. For example, Hungary faced a different environment from, say, the Philippines or Mexico. All three countries developed external debt problems, underwent adjustment programmes and tried to meet the challenge to overcome their economic crises somehow. But their debt composition (official to private credit) differed, as did the countries of origin of the banks holding their debt. European banks behave differently from Japanese banks, as do the Japanese in comparison to US banks. Even the same creditors – for example, the IMF – did not deal with them all alike. Mexico and the Philippines were treated as candidates for international debt relief schemes; Hungary was not. They exported to different markets and competed in different products. Exporting Mexican fruit or beer to the USA is not the same as selling Hungarian chemicals in the EC. In addition, the three countries differ in their significance as import markets. Mexico's northern border is with a country that has the means and the will to assure – in tandem with the IFIs or alone – that economic crises south of the Rio Grande do not translate into widespread instability. Instead, the superpower nearest to Hungary's north-eastern border had no interest in the 1980s in stabilising actual or potential economic crises elsewhere because it increasingly lost the ability to keep its own house in order. In sum, the political, financial and commercial environment for countries is never the same below a rather high level of abstraction. And it is below this level that policies are designed and implemented or where, in other words, policymakers react to and deal with external constraints and where, likewise, they can seize or (fail to seize) a variety of opportunities.

Constraints should not be thought of as gunboats steaming down the Danube to collect debt payments. Instead, they emanate from the 'political and economic arrangements [that make up the international political economy] affecting the systems of production, exchange and distribution, and the mix of values reflected therein' (Strange 1988, 18).[16] These arrangements define notions of what is regarded as good behaviour (for example, timely debt service) and what is not (for example, delays in repayment or default), and divide acceptable solutions to problems (such as rescheduling) from rule violations (such as unilateral moratoria). Small countries such as Hungary are less likely to influence these arrangements than countries that are economic heavyweights. This does not mean that small countries are the only ones subject to external constraints, or that the constraints may not still leave them choices from which a government can pick what it deems best.[17] But the range of choices will not be the same for all. If, say, Brazil and Hungary both want to export meat to industrialised countries one would guess that, of the two, Brazil is more likely to strike the more advantageous bargain and, also, less likely to give in to pressure to alter its negotiating position (cf. Strange 1988, Ch. 2).

Paying attention to external constraints does not mean that everything is determined by structures. If two similarly endowed countries, both heavily dependent on the export of a particular product, are hurt by trade restrictions, their different reactions may depend to a large degree on how policymakers in each country think they can 'make do' under the new regime: perhaps through aggressive diversification, complaints lodged with GATT (General Agreement on Tariffs and Trade) or aid to the industry in question. In sum, in every case the specific impact of external constraints needs to be examined. In some, the constraints may restrict policy options; in others, the constraints may actually appear as opportunities. To understand their effect fully one must consider in each case how, and why, policymakers have dealt with them.

On Methodology

Analysing Hungary's attempt to open up to the world economy, to explain the domestic and external causes of the outcomes and to denote whether policies have been successful or not requires some basis of comparison. The availability (at least in principle) of options to policy-makers implies that events could have taken a different turn and that things might now look very different. *What* they might have looked like opens the question of the relevant counterfactual. I have argued above that it is problematic to draw sweeping generalisations from samples which are too small. On the other hand, no country is so special that it cannot – in principle – be compared to others; what counts are the criteria one uses to establish certain comparisons and the level of generality to which one restricts one's conclusions.[18] For example, it would be fallacious to argue that country X followed a certain type of industrial policy and was successful with it, and that therefore Hungary should have done the same. But one can carefully compare key determinants of – in this case – the management of external debt and international competitiveness among various countries, and similarities and differences in dealing with both (cf. Gereffi and Wyman 1989). For example, if country X tries to sell a product without brand recognition in a foreign market and assists its exporters in the pre-sale phase by introducing samples to potentially interested importers through a well-functioning network of commercial representations, while another country, Y, under similar conditions, only employs a commercial affairs attaché in its embassy, this difference in institutional handling may help to explain X's relatively more successful export performance.

The present work is a case study. As such, it is not its goal to say anything much in general about the risks and rewards of opening up, not even for other transition economies in Central Europe. Case studies are frequently derided as anecdotal (a charge I can live with). An often quoted volume on national development experiences, put together in the early 1980s, argued the methodological matter as follows.

> we do so not in abstract theoretical terms, but by examining actual strategies and policies of governments in concrete historical settings. We do not strive to formulate or even to 'test' causal laws; the complexity and diversity of experiences forbid both at this juncture. Rather, our hope is to produce situationally valid generalizations, which will better equip both scholars and practitioners to resist the temptation of axiomatic substitutes for thought and struggle, while, at the same time, providing some systematic basis for picking and choosing among plausible and possible policy options. (Ruggie 1983, 15–16)

Ten years later, this seems just fine as a research programme (and as an aspiration). If the current disenchantment with grand theories and universal truths in research on development (cf. Menzel 1991) leads to carefully structured comparative studies of country (or industry or sector) experiences, relevant theoretical insights may actually emerge. Until that day, there is much to be gained by refraining from too sweeping generalisations.

Insofar as perceptions of the past influence the way we look at contemporary problems and their possible solutions, Hungary's opening-up today is part of its much older attempt to catch up with the more developed economies of Western Europe. Viewing Hungary's economic difficulties of the past decade only as the result of the system of economic planning is simplistic and wrong: simplistic, because there have been gaps in the level of economic development between East and West in Europe for more than a century and a half, and wrong because the differences in level of industrialisation narrowed in the 1950s and 1960s so that some catching-up actually occurred when central planning was at its extreme. During the period from about 1830 to the end of the Second World War the gap widened. The same happened over the last two decades. Taken together, this is the problematic legacy.

In a sense, 'joining the EC' has many parallels with escaping from backwardness during the late nineteenth century. Then, as now, the level of national income decides more than anything to which part of Europe a country belongs. The transition in Central and Eastern Europe is primarily aimed at instituting the principles, rules and operating procedures of a market economy. As things stand, this process looks set to succeed. But establishing a market economy is only a necessary condition for EC membership; it is not sufficient. On current evidence, the prime obstacle to membership will be the difference in welfare levels between the Central European countries and the EC average or, more precisely, the distributional conflicts this is going to give rise to among the Community's current members. Hence wealth, and a country's skills and fortunes in obtaining it, matter a great deal in the context of European integration. This is briefly considered in the next section.

CHALLENGE AND RESPONSE IN HUNGARIAN INDUSTRIALISATION

In 1860, the industrialising countries of Western Europe had managed to reach a level of per capitum GNP only 20 per cent lower than Britain's. In contrast, the periphery around the core industrialising countries – Scandinavia, the Mediterranean countries and Eastern Europe – were still almost 50 per cent below Britain's per capitum income. By this measure, Eastern Europe was the least developed part of the periphery; its GNP levels were no higher than that of pre-industrial Europe. The eastern half of the Habsburg Empire was better off than the neighbouring areas, especially compared to the Balkans. But Hungarian per capitum GNP was about 25 per cent lower than the European average (Bairoch 1976). For Europe's backward areas, the challenge was to close the technological gap between themselves and the leading industrialising countries. Some regions were more successful than others in taking up this challenge. Half a century later, by 1910, the Scandinavian countries had almost reached the average GNP per capita of Western Europe. Eastern Europe as a whole lagged behind the Mediterranean countries. But Hungary's GNP per capita was higher than that of Italy and Spain, the two most advanced countries of the southern periphery. While its per capita industrial production around the turn of the century was still some 30 per cent below the European average (and 3.5 times lower than in Britain) it had managed, with Italy, to draw away from the rest of the southern and south-eastern periphery (Bairoch 1982). Its specific response to what was happening in Western Europe brought it closer to the industrialised core, though it still fell far short of what other small, agricultural economies such as Denmark succeeded in doing. Why the country ended up where it did resulted from the interaction between external and domestic constraints and opportunities and the response to both by Hungary's elite. By way of a brief review, this is illustrated below.[19]

The rapid industrialisation of the Western European economies led to increasing demands for food and raw materials which needed to be imported, either from the new lands of America, Argentina and Australasia or from the neighbouring, less developed countries of Europe. The flow of goods and also of capital between the core and the periphery intensified. The pull into Western Europe's orbit implied different options for the backward regions: either they could resign themselves to dependence on these new markets, shipping raw materials for processing to the industrial centres, or they could take advantage of an export-induced economic boom to develop a more or less integrated industrial structure, featuring not just, say, foreign-built, modern railways in an otherwise rural economy but also an indigenous manufacturing sector. Which outcome prevailed – whether a country developed like Denmark or remained hopelessly backward, such as Romania – depended in part on the interests of the West which constrained policy choices in these countries. But it also depended, next to geographical location and resource endowments, on the prevailing political and institutional framework in the periphery: that is, whether land reform had done away with serfdom; whether children were given schooling; whether entrepreneurs could get credit to purchase machines and so on. Which of the different options came to bear is best illustrated by looking at the external influences and the effect they had on Hungarian economic and social development.

International Trade and Finance before the First World War

The Habsburg Empire was a protected free trade area. The main market for Hungarian agricultural products and minerals, such as coal and iron, lay in Austria and the Czech part of the Habsburg monarchy. To facilitate the extraction, processing and transportation of these commodities, Austrian financiers invested mainly in railway building.[20] The capital inflow was sizeable; in the second half of the century it represented 40 per cent of total investment. Very little of this was in the form of actual working capital. Hence, FDI as such was no direct boost for industrial development. But foreign investment did accelerate domestic accumulation: in 1867, foreign capital accounted for three-quarters of all investments made in Hungary, while after 1900 this diminished to 25 per cent.[21] Since the demand for capital throughout the area exceeded supply, the creditor nations' banks charged hefty interest rates and fees on their loans and profited rather well from the early phase of Hungary's development.

Did Hungary benefit also? By 1913, the country possessed one of the densest railway networks in Europe. In Western Europe, traffic and domestically financed transport lines had developed together and the latter helped to explore ironworks and coal mines. In Eastern Europe, lines were built by foreign capital and in some way preceded indigenous traffic whose volume was lower due to the generally lower level of industrial activity. There was then the danger, of course, that foreign competition imported by the railways would destroy local infant industries and, furthermore, create debt problems (Pollard 1986, Ch. 3). However, this appears to have been much less of a problem in Hungary than in, say, the Balkan countries where the arrival of the railway essentially ruined small, local handicraft industries and also contributed to these countries' accumulation of debt and subsequent default on their foreign obligations.

In the four decades before the First World War, exports tripled. Grain, along with animal products, was the major export commodity, and grain prices tended to rise. Thus, Hungary did not suffer from deteriorating terms of trade. Even after the depression of the 1870s, Hungary still managed to make a profit on its grain sales because the high external tariff of the monarchy, especially after 1906, kept foreign competitors out of the market. From the late 1860s, Hungary exploited the industrial potential of grain exports by developing a world-class milling industry. As such, it was the only country in the area that succeeded in transforming part of its grain exports into the export of food products, notably flour.[22] Cheap raw materials combined with higher productivity, occasioned by a skilled labour force, and an innovative technology – the cart rolling mill – led to lower production costs. Investment in the milling industry came mostly from reinvested profits from exports of food products and were almost entirely domestic. Profits from the milling industry, in turn, were invested in further industrialisation activities. This industrial graduation was reflected in the composition of Hungarian exports; by 1913, only 50 per cent of its exports were still agricultural. In this sense, the economy responded well to external stimuli and developed a competitive food industry. At the same time, investment goods replaced consumer products as Hungary's most important manufacturing imports (Berend and Ránki 1980).

The benefits of Austro-Hungarian protection against competitive Russian or US grain imports contrasted with the free trade regime that prevailed within the monarchy in the 1850s and 1860s. In fact, Hungarian industry initially did not stand much of a chance against Austrian or Czech imports; and unrestrained competition probably retarded its indigenous industrial development. Structurally, the country was lucky in several respects. It had immense agricultural resources; geographic proximity to Western European markets; an easy, flat terrain for railway development; and the ability to adopt foreign technology. Thanks to this last item, spin-off effects resulting from external influences could be exploited. But the results were scattered among very few industrial sectors, notably engineering, and did not add up to a genuine economic transformation. Milling remained the only real export industry. By 1900, domestic industry supplied the largest part of the domestic market in machinery, textiles and paper and leather goods.[23] But overall industrialisation did not take place, which is why Berend calls Hungary a case of semi-success/semi-failure (1986a, 12). The process of large-scale industrialisation was only initiated by the time the First World War broke out. Hungarian historiography refuted as early as the 1960s that Hungary's backwardness was primarily due to the exploitation by the western part of the monarchy (Ránki 1968).[24] On the whole, the judgement of the challenge manifested by Western Europe's and Austria's industrial development is positive:

> we find foreign capital investment to have tapped the national income, and to have led to imbalanced development, to distortions in the economic structure that developed. Nevertheless, in Hungary, it was the impetus that foreign investment gave to economic development that must be considered the more significant: it got the economy over its period of stagnation and helped start a period of sustained economic growth. (Berend and Ránki 1982, 131)

What, then, was the reason for Hungary's 'semi-failure'? Was there not enough 'tension between the preindustrialization conditions and the benefits expected from industrialization [to] become sufficiently strong to overcome the existing obstacles and to liberate the forces that made for industrial progress', as Alexander Gerschenkron put it when summing up the heterogeneous national experiences in the nineteenth century (1966, 11)? Such a conclusion begs the question, why not? Contemporary Hungarian economic historians suggest a variety of reasons, social and political. Berend, for example, argues that the transformation of an economy is unlikely to go far unless it is accompanied by radical changes in the social structure. He thus reconsiders the partial success of some of the backward countries in making progress on the road to full-scale industrial development. 'Even if the gross national product per head increased considerably, the heads which owned it did not change to any great degree' (1986a, 14). Andrew Janos argues that the emphasis on the processes of industrialisation and commercialisation means that too many studies fail to appreciate the bureaucratisation of political life as a key determinant for retarded development (1982). In the periphery, changes in the institutional structure were emulated on the basis of the experiences of the core countries. But whereas in these core countries technological progress and the diffusion of a capitalist way of life led to the creation of a strong and modern state, it happened the other way round in Hungary. Instead of bottom-up, the state was formed top-down. Its structures were in place long before a modern economic and social structure existed. They slowly crowded out the commercialisation of land and labour, and the upwardly mobile, instead of becoming budding entrepreneurs, invested their careers either in professional politics or made it as pariah entrepreneurs (Janos 1989). Agricultural management remained decidedly conservative: as, for example, in Prussia and Poland but unlike in Sweden or the Basque country (Pollard 1986, Ch. 5). The image of the society was thus one where scattered manifestations of modernity – symbolised by the system of transportation and education and also some factory activity – coexisted with largely unaltered patterns of economic activity and reproduction.

> In part, at least, the premature rise of the state is the result of the desire of elites to create a modern economy. The problem is that the costs of maintaining a modern state apparatus are likely to become a serious drain on scarce resources, which tends to diminish the purchasing power of the public and to prevent a measure of economic development. But the transfer of surplus from the public to the state, from the economy to the polity, may well have been far more substantial than any transfer of surplus from the country to the more developed sectors of the world economy. (Janos 1982, 322)

'It's all been there before': Crises After the First World War

The reduction of Hungarian territory after the First World War and the loss of the large, protected imperial markets increased the country's dependence on foreign trade at a time when the growth of international trade was slowing down. With the loss of territory by the Treaty of Trianon went also significant natural and mineral resources; hence the country required raw material imports for every industry as well as machinery and components.[25] Markets for agricultural exports needed to be found. But increased protectionism in Austria and Germany made this more and more difficult (at least initially). Later, as Germany built up its war economy, selling agricultural products became easier. During the inter-war period, Hungary applied what Berend termed the 'two-market formula' (1980, 11). On the one hand, export-oriented industries turned out fairly modern, competitive products targeted at the world market. On the other hand, the state created the potential for a domestic market by encouraging wide-scale import substitution, thereby preserving old production patterns.

> [This] resulted in regressive structural changes in ways partly inconsistent with the new postulates of world economy and provided for growth and relative equilibrium ... in the old frameworks. But in the meantime both ... turned out to be extremely expensive as the lag of the Hungarian economy increased. Its production patterns and technological standards fell more and more behind the modern requirements of world economy. (Berend 1980, 11–12)

That said, import substitution was not without logic. Since competitive successes in foreign markets typically provoked an increase in all-round protectionism, the attempts at autarchy were poor but reasonable alternatives to international trade. The post-war economic crisis affected primarily countries with open economies that exchanged primary products for industrial goods. It had become much more difficult to sustain this type of exchange; the Hungarian government needed to reconsider the country's position *vis-à-vis* the industrial core. The lack of capital in the economy remained pervasive; domestic accumulation was for a long time below the pre-war level. Hungary's main pre-war creditors, namely Austria and Germany, were no longer available as investors. The foreign money flowing into the country until 1924 was insignificant although it represented half of cumulative savings. Loans from the League of Nations were more of a confidence-building, symbolic character (Nötel 1974). In addition, the League insisted that Hungary proportionally repay its pre-war debt.

Domestic bank credits to the government made up for the insufficient amount of foreign credit flows and the very low level of taxation. The creation of liquidity in the absence of an adequate supply response – in 1920, Hungarian industrial and agricultural production was at 40 per cent of the pre-war level – led to inflation. In June 1924, the foreign exchange quotation of the crown was at 0.006 per cent of the original parity. In December 1924, the cost of living was 18 000 times higher than before the war. Agricultural production, which had been most decisive for pre-war development, stagnated. Capital accumulation in agriculture was too low to generate continuing industrial development. This was partly due to the lack of a significant land reform:[26] latifundism kept the efficiency of the agricultural sector down (Berend and Ránki 1972, 174). Exports fell and productivity did not increase. Balance of payments problems soon came on top of the budgetary difficulties. Although Hungary had gained political independence with the Treaty of Trianon, the country was not allowed to introduce an independent tariff line until 1924; this aggravated the problems for the largely non-competitive industry.

Around 1925, financial stabilisation had brought inflation under control. A new tariff was introduced. This, and the general economic upturn in Europe, helped Hungary to reach the pre-war output in agriculture and in industry. But it remained difficult to find markets for its agricultural products; furthermore, capital accumulation in agriculture continued to remain low, and it was not easy to attract foreign finance for industrial investments. Unlike the pre-war period, credit was predominantly short-term and rates had become expensive; also, poor use was made of the credits (Nötel 1986; see also Berend and Ránki 1965). They did not go into investments but were instead used to cover the balance of payments deficit. In 1929, debt service was higher than new loans. The depression came, and hit the country with a fall in commodity prices and further shrinking markets (Aldcroft 1977, Ch. 9). Again, industrial output fell drastically. The eventual drying-up of foreign funds led Hungary, along with many others, into a debt crisis in 1931. The debt:service ratio had risen to 48 per cent. International payment imbalances were not remedied by higher imports and home prices on the part of the surplus countries as the operation of the gold standard in principle mandated; instead, the latter simply accumulated the inflowing gold. The financial collapse that followed was part of a worldwide monetary turmoil which eventually made Britain abandon the gold standard. Faced with the alternative of engineering a severe deflation, many countries followed suit, devalued their currencies and introduced exchange controls (Aldcroft 1977, Ch. 7). The Hungarian government announced a moratorium on foreign transfers. From then on, the financial needs of industry were met primarily from domestic accumulation. Eastern governments searched for agreed settlements and Western governments forced investors to halve the costs of assets they had supplied to Eastern Europe. Hungary's creditors knew that the country would never meet its obligations unless it was allowed to sell its agricultural products on Western markets. The value of outstanding debt was reduced through redemption below par and because of devaluations of the pound sterling and the dollar compared to the currencies in which Hungary's external debt was primarily denominated (Kaser 1985). The creditors accepted this because Hungary's service record was considerably better than that of the other East European debtors. On the whole however, 'rare, and politically motivated, inflows of new credit were, at this stage, greatly counterbalanced by outflows' (Nötel 1986, 171). The settlement with the creditors in 1937 ended the financial emergency. During this period, Hungarian industry, thanks to the break it got from competition through import restrictions, recovered. Notwithstanding its poor performance – relative to the pre-war growth pattern and relative to that of other latecomers in the 1920s – Hungary's industrialisation continued. Industry accounted for roughly 25 per cent of GNP (much lower than, say, in Austria, Denmark or Norway but higher than in the Balkans). Hungary had reached an intermediate position, although it was closer to that of the less developed than to the industrialised countries.

Subsequently, the country was drawn into the German *Großwirtschaftsraum*. The Germans guaranteed prices which the Hungarians could not have realised on the world market, which made trade between the two attractive for Hungary. But trade was based on barter, and the Germans never paid for the growing Hungarian surpluses; essentially they received an increasing part of their imports for free. Hence, the Hungarians unwillingly extended commercial credits to a much richer country. What began bad, ended worse: in 1945, Hungary was one of the most devastated countries in Europe.

Post-war Reconstruction

Despite the enormous setback caused by the Second World War, post-war Hungary achieved a high rate of industrial recovery. That was not easy: Hungary hardly received any Western assistance and had to put up with heavy reparations. Since there was no prospect for the collection of taxes, the government resorted to money creation to finance reconstruction. The ensuing hyperinflation was the worst recorded in history. Taking the price index in July 1945 as 1, the cost of living a year later was 10 599 989 000 quintillion (Siklos 1991). In 1946, the introduction of a new currency, the forint, successfully stabilised the economy. By 1948, employment, industrial output, productivity and real wages exceeded the 1938 level. The rapid recovery meant that many opportunities actually to build greenfield factories and renew the technological equipment were missed. But by comparison with reconstruction elsewhere in Europe, the Hungarian recovery was a remarkable achievement (see Wszelaki 1951; Paulat 1954).

On average, industrial production grew annually by 7 per cent until the 1970s. In the late 1960s, Hungary had all the characteristics of an industrialised country. Per capita industrial production resembled that of Japan, Italy and Finland. Investments were concentrated on heavy industry : first coal mining and basic industries, and later electric power generation, engineering and chemical industries.In that, the structural development of Hungarian industry, although biased towards the heavy branches, resembled the general world pattern (which does not mean that industrial products were internationally competitive). For the first time in modern economic history, Hungary significantly reduced the degree of underdevelopment that had still characterised its agricultural-industrial economy when the Second World War broke out (Hare 1988; see also Wszelaki 1951, Paulat 1954). A drawback was the lack of specialisation at the national and even at the firm level; each firm and the country as a whole wanted to be as self-sufficient as possible. The emphasis on mining and basic industries led to an enormous demand for energy. By the late 1960s, a third of the country's energy needs were imported. As long as cheap Soviet oil was available, this was less of a problem, but it became a big problem when the Soviets followed world prices upon the first oil price hike in 1973.

The engineering and chemical industries, which had received much investment and, since the 1960s, Western technology, became important sources of national income. Their problem was the low quality requirements of the CMEA markets into which most of their exports went; the lack of competition within CMEA largely prevented successful innovation. But throughout the 1970s, productivity increased and plants became more modern. Agriculture, also, was thoroughly industrialised. Growth rates of agricultural output were second only to those in the Netherlands.

The rate of growth of foreign trade 1950–80 was significantly higher than that of production and national income. By this measure, Hungary was becoming an increasingly open economy, although primarily in the context of the CMEA. There, Hungary exported mostly machinery and industrial consumer goods. The country had thus taken a big step away from the agricultural exporter it still was before the Second World War. To Western countries, Hungary exported mostly raw materials and semi-finished goods. The terms of trade loss of these commodities translated into increasing trade deficits after 1973. As in many other countries, the deficits were financed through foreign credit. Debt accumulated rapidly; the belated reckoning, in the 1980s, with what turned out to be an unsustainable economic strategy gave a new impulse to reforms in Hungary. *Opening up* is one aspect of this and the topic of what follows.

Since the last century, Hungary's level of development has been in the neighbourhood of the countries that are now the EC's poorer members. It was ahead of Greece, Portugal and Spain until the late 1940s (and in some sense until the late 1960s). In the 1990s, its per capita income is much lower than theirs and likely to remain so for many years to come. What is decisive for Hungary's future is whether the country is visibly and credibly moving up toward the lower end of the welfare level in the EC. If history is any guide, the outcome of the current transition will depend both on domestic social and economic policies and on the conditions prevailing in the wider external environment, notably EC trade policies. After the First World War, the admiration Central and Eastern Europeans had traditionally felt for the Western European path to modernisation gave way to increasing discontent with the post-war settlement. Rejection replaced emulation. This suggests that there is nothing inevitable about the attractiveness of the EC as a model of integration for its eastern neighbours. If the EC disappoints the aspiration of the Central and Eastern Europeans (that is, to become part of European integration), they may eventually turn to other, and possibly less attractive, alternatives.

OUTLINE

The four chapters that follow are about opening up Hungary to the world economy. The time period considered is generally the 1980s. The exact cut-off point varies and, on occasion, extends into the early 1990s. Chapter 4 falls somewhat out of line with this in that it treats the period 1989–92.

The chapters are fairly self-contained, although 2 and 3 should be read together. Chapter 1 focuses on the key issue of Hungarian debt and its management by the IMF, the commercial banks, the creditor governments and the Hungarian government. Chapter 2, on industrial policy and trade promotion, discusses the performance of firms, both in production and exports. It shows that the heritage of the 1980s is not all negative. The chapter also prepares the ground for an evaluation of Hungary's international competitiveness, undertaken in Chapter 3: is it true that Hungarian firms never turned out products that successfully competed in international markets?

And if so, what has this to do with the commercial policies that characterise Hungary's main export markets, and with its own trade promotion policies? Chapter 4 is the 'youngest'. It considers a distinctly post-1989 phenomenon, namely the management of FDI. Thus, it is concerned with transition policies but none for which lessons exist from the 1980s. It addresses the Hungarian record in attracting foreign capital and discusses the effectiveness of the government's incentive policy.

Throughout I have attempted to answer the following questions:

● what did the external constraints look like?
● how did Hungarian policy-makers react to them?
● were there alternative courses of action?

The focus on external constraints and opportunities implies a certain bias – in terms of pages, if not in conclusions – in the analysis. This is not to suggest that external constraints have been more important than domestic policies in determining Hungary's successes and failures in opening up: it simply follows from my intention to underline the significance of the 'world environment'. Where this concern appears exaggerated, it may be taken to compensate for the lack of attention it enjoys in much related work on the transition and transformation in Central Europe. Apart from that I would like this work to resemble the spirit within which one of the most eminent scholars on the Hungarian economy has remarked:

> We must try to put forward our idea with due modesty. What if the idea we favour is inapplicable? What if it is inadequately adapted to local circumstances with which we are insufficiently familiar? Let us not be aggressive, pushing our own ideas through at all costs, for that may rebound by discrediting the work of advisors as a whole. Let us draw inspiration from Erasmus; it is good to retain a little irony about ourselves. (Kornai 1993, 63)

With this in mind, three major conclusions result from the analysis. First, Hungarian debt management, based on undelayed debt service even under difficult conditions, did not buy the country a favourable treatment by its official or commercial creditors: on the contrary. Compared to the majority of middle-income debtors, Hungary does not enjoy privileged access to world financial markets; in addition, the country is suffering from rising net resource outflows at a time when debtors with a severely disturbed debt service record have managed, with the help of IFIs, to contain outward capital transfers. Second, some Hungarian firms have been better at selling their products in competitive Western markets than generally acknowledged. The country's overall export performance has not been more impressive because – among other reasons – Western protectionism prevented Hungarian goods from reaching their markets and because Hungarian planners proved unable to find ways and means to circumvent trade barriers in the OECD. Third, Hungary's post-1988 management of FDI has been fairly successful in attracting some highly-capitalised and technology-intensive firms without leading to a 'sell-out' of national assets to transnational corporations. However, the viability of these (as well as of purely domestic) operations is constrained by a combination of the rapid trade liberalisation since 1989, the relatively high inflation accompanying the transition and, again, managed trade in Hungary's major export markets.

All told, the rewards of opening up are not guaranteed. Risks exist when small countries such as Hungary attempt to join the world market relying on international monetary conventions or trade arrangements that are designed more by and for those who are well established in the world economy rather than for newcomers. To avoid the risks – while not missing the rewards – of opening-up entails a creative use of political and economic assets, including *new ideas*, in the area of credit and trade management that may occasionally violate some of the written or unwritten rules of international economic exchange. Default on external debt and select import restrictions are two such examples.

1 The Management of External Debt

The debt crisis of the 1980s means different things to different people. To some, it is the ultimate form of exploitation of developing countries by the debt-holding north. Others see it as a problem of portfolio management whose temporary aberrations during the 1970s have been largely overcome in a decade of restructuring. Treatments of the debt crisis easily fill not just bookshelves but entire libraries. While it is relatively easy to explain its origins, it proves more difficult to agree on remedies. Structural adjustment programmes, administered by the IFIs, distributed the costs of adjustment between creditors and debtors; hence, different groups stood to gain or lose from how deals were struck between official creditors, commercial banks and debtor governments. 'Rescheduling' was the buzzword during the first five years of the crisis; since 1989, 'debt relief' has been added to the vocabulary of what, in the USA, might be termed politically correct language. In 1992, ten years after the outbreak of the crisis in Latin America, Citibank's principal troubleshooter, William Rhodes, sang the post-mortem: 'the disaster that didn't happen' (1992, 17).[1] Meanwhile, Third World leaders such as Julius Nyerere, chairman of the South Commission, worry that the 1990s will witness a yet more drastic submission of developing countries to the north's financial prerogatives (South Centre 1992a). In short, interpretations and outlooks differ.

What has received relatively scant attention in the literature is a comparison of how debtor countries have dealt with the crisis once it had arisen. Undoubtedly, different debtors got different treatments from the creditors. The result is due in part to their debt management strategy. In their dealings with creditors, any debtor can pick from a bundle of choices which one may imagine on a continuum from full and timely debt service and principal repayment to outright default. To some degree, a debtor's future access to the capital markets depends on the chosen strategy. In theory at least, a track record of timely debt servicing guarantees the availability of new money. Default, on the other hand, makes for a bad reputation and will bar debtors from being considered by lenders. In practice, the situation is a lot more complex. One feature of the debt crisis in the 1980s was that debtors sent more money to the creditors than they received in return: that is, the servicing of external liabilities led to a net capital outflow from debtor countries because the creditors did not provide new funds in any meaningful measure. Net capital transfers from developing to developed countries do not defy logic, but they stand everything on its head that has ever been said about capital accumulation in the context of development. Of course, this was not lost on debtor governments. Should they compress domestic demand and run current account surpluses if that did not lead to new external financing?

There is a precise answer to this question. They should, to the point that the costs of lost new credit exceed the benefits of default on old debt. Put differently, debt service is rational as long as the present discounted value of future flows of private credit (minus adjustment costs) is greater than the present discounted value of debt service the country saves if it defaults (minus the losses incurred through sanctions). After that point, *ceteris paribus*, they should not. Of course, judging these costs and benefits is not easy. For example, there is no straightforward method to estimate the future availability of financing because bankers behave in no more linear fashion than other human beings. In fact, they sometimes get caught in the dynamics of herd instinct and behave like sheep (Bouchet 1987, Ch. 2). Throughout the 1980s, most debtor countries had built up arrears, at first mostly on principal, then also on interest payments. In part, these arrears simply reflected an inability to pay, but countries also consciously decided payments moratoria that expressed their unwillingness (rather than inability) to go along with further outward capital transfers. They judged, in other words, that the present value of future credits was lower than the present value of income forgone through resource transfers abroad.

Hungary belongs to the exclusive club of debtors that always paid up on time.[2] Given this record, the country, in theory, should enjoy privileged access to international capital markets, relative to debtors elsewhere (notably in Latin America). In practice, it does not. The question of why not is one this chapter seeks to answer. If a country behaves like a model debtor and does not get much in return, it presumably follows a suboptimal strategy. Evidence suggests that one can also get 'not much in return' for behaving like a bad debtor. In other words, if Hungary could be where it is today without having always honoured all its liabilities on time, it should not have done so. With hindsight, this is easily concluded but not to much avail. The really interesting question is this: in the light of bargaining strategies exercised by other debtor countries *vis-à-vis* their creditors, could the Hungarians have done better?

ALL ROADS LEAD TO WASHINGTON

This chapter first reviews Hungarian debt management and highlights its problems, and then it analyses how other major debtors, primarily in Latin America, helped to bring debt relief from the fringes of the vocabulary of the international financial community to centre stage by objecting to continuous capital outflows. Finally, I discuss debt management in the context of transition and reform.

Join the Club

Hungary had piled up debt in the 1970s for much the same reasons most other LDCs and NICs did (cf. Tyson 1986). Credit was cheap: it financed the acquisition of investment goods imported from the West and thus relaxed the foreign-exchange constraint on growth.[3] It also allowed the government to delay or avoid adjustments to the first oil-price hike. Since little of the foreign finance was used to build capacity to export to the West, the level of outstanding net debt rose throughout the 1970s, from $0.8 billion in 1970 to $7.7 billion in 1980. Deteriorating terms of trade, sluggish demand for Hungarian exportables in the recession-struck OECD, another oil-price induced change in the level of world prices, a rise in interest rates and, as a result, worsening balance-of-payments disequilibria all made a continuation of the debt-cum-growth strategy infeasible (cf. Zloch-Christy 1987). Consequently, the leadership of the Hungarian Socialist Workers Party (HSWP), in the late 1970s, decided to renew the push to integrate the country into the international division of labour and go ahead with reforms.

The political situation within the party was not one of unanimous support of introducing more market elements in the economy. Influential figures also disagreed with a policy geared towards outward-orientation at the cost of weakening CMEA cooperation (Berend 1990). The party leadership tried to enlist international support for its reform policies by becoming an IMF member. Credit markets had largely dried up for the CMEA; Eurocredits had become prohibitively expensive. It was hoped that the IMF, through its own funds and by granting its seal of approval to the conduct of Hungary's pro-reform policy, would help the country to regain access to sovereign borrowing. The leadership of the HSWP let the reformists in the National Bank (MNB) handle the dealings with IMF personnel, thus indirectly strengthening them against hardliners in the party.

When Hungary applied for membership in the Fund in 1981, the only other CMEA member of the Fund was Romania.[4] The West differentiated among the CMEA countries; Poland's application, filed at the same time as

Hungary's, was rejected. The domestic political crisis had made Poland an unlikely candidate for some time to come; but influential members of the Fund considered Hungary's advances a welcome opportunity to support a country whose explicit Western orientation in matters economic and commercial could only strengthen, at a time of deteriorating East-West relations, the West's clout *vis-à-vis* the Eastern Bloc. In sum, in November 1981 a reform-minded Hungarian leadership intent on remedying its external imbalance through an overhaul of its domestic economic mechanisms asked to join a club whose speciality was just that: helping members to achieve a sustainable balance of payments position. The club conceded to accession, which was not a surprising result. The more interesting question is whether Hungary had any policy alternatives to choose from; could it not have restored some form of external equilibrium without becoming an IMF member?

Liquidity and Creditworthiness: First Act

Although the initial flirting and eventual engagement boded well for the future, the honeymoon had to be cut short. The reason was a serious liquidity crisis which threatened trade flows between Hungary and the world and brought the country to the brink of default. The outbreak of the debt crisis in Eastern Europe was expected by the international financial community no more than that in Latin America. In 1981, the year when Poland's debt service difficulties became apparent, the *Financial Times* carried only four articles on Hungary, praising the scope and success of the reforms. Not one featured balance of payments difficulties, possibly due to the improvement in the current account since 1979 plus a small surplus in 1981.[5] None discussed debt, either.[6]

However after the Poles had announced repayment difficulties in March 1981, Hungary was suddenly unable to borrow medium-term money from the international capital markets. The commercial banks began to doubt that the USSR would act as a lender of last resort for CMEA and foresaw further débâcles (for example, 'International Credit Market Developments', 1982, 8). Their subsequent actions ensured that mere – and, in the case of Hungary, unlikely – possibilities became self-fulfilling prophecies. Resistance to extending medium-term Eurocredits spilled over into the short-term money and precious metal markets. During the first four months of 1982, the banks withdrew some $800 million. In March, Hungarian reserves covered barely one month's worth of imports.

Thus, it was the fall-out from Poland's solvency crisis, and not domestic economic mismanagement, that led to Hungary's liquidity crisis.[7] The country was in urgent need of cash to finance its imports. In addition, of course, it needed to re-establish its creditworthiness on the international capital markets. Short of waiting for a divine miracle, joining the Fund was the only reasonable choice. As *The Economist* put it: 'There will then be the advantage that the West will not be treating an east European country that is moving in the right economic direction as harshly as those moving in the wrong one' ('Hungary's Case', 1982, 16).

Hungary signed the Fund's Articles of Agreement in May 1982 (de Fontenay 1982). Since IMF financing was not going to be available before the autumn, the Bank for International Settlements (BIS) – of which Hungary, like most other CMEA countries, was a member – organised a number of short-term and bridging loans to help Hungary finance its ongoing operations. Apart from this direct assistance, the BIS and especially the Bank of England also tried to facilitate Hungary's return to the international capital markets. In July, Manufacturers Hanover led a club deal over $260 million with three years' maturity. The participating banks were for the most part heavily exposed to Eastern Europe, with much to lose in case of default. But some of the British banks, less inclined to continue to do business with Hungary, participated in the deal only after the intervention by Gordon Richardson, Governor of the Bank of England. Some observers argue that the Hungarians exaggerated the seriousness of the liquidity crunch. Csaba (1989), for example, says the issue never has been having or not having a couple of hundred million US dollars. It may be true that the crisis was exploited politically by the government. Nonetheless, it was serious, so much so that the National Bank did not know where to get enough hard currency to pay for its quota upon becoming a member of the IMF. Ironically, it was the National Bank of China that secretly seconded Hungary with a two-year loan over $200 million. Needless to say, the Fund did not know anything about this.

In December, Hungary received a stand-by credit plus additional finance from the Compensatory Finance Facility over special drawing rights (SDR) of 475 million from the IMF. The credit was used to pay off the outstanding short-term drawings from the BIS. International reserves had risen to over $700 million. Hence, due to a concerted effort by the BIS, individual Western central banks and the IMF, the first liquidity crisis was over. In fact, by 1983 major international banks had resumed lending to Hungary.

The crisis had been triggered by private creditors. Its solution was organised through public intervention; official, (especially Western European) creditors, mobilised credit not in order to bail out commercial banks but to help the debtor. Table 1.1 shows the composition of credit flows during and

Table 1.1   Disbursed credits to Hungary 1980–90 ($ million)

	1980	1981	1982	1983	1984	1985	1986	1987	1988	1989	1990
Total	1552	1880	1440	1878	3538	4513	4105	3364	2787	3436	2746
Euromarkets	600	591	483	567	1146	1642	1315	1951	1016	1708	990
IMF	0	0	237	355	436	0	0	0	222	64	173
Other official	187	546	99	201	184	269	387	338	590	365	728
Other*	765	743	621	755	1772	2602	2403	1075	959	1299	855
Official/ Euromarkets	0.31	0.92	0.70	0.98	5.4	0.16	0.29	0.17	0.80	0.25	0.91

Notes: Some small double accounting is involved between Eurocurrency loans and other official credits because of World Bank cofinancing schemes.
*For example, from banks not reporting to the BIS, unpublished bank-to-bank operations, etc.
Sources: OECD, Financial Market Trends; World Bank, *World Debt Tables*.

after Hungary's liquidity crisis. The share of official credit is unusually high between 1981 and 1984. Expressed as a share of convertible currency imports, official creditors regularly covered roughly between one and two months' worth of imports. What these figures express is that without the IMF's involvement, Hungary's situation would have been much worse. In conclusion, Hungary was helped by IFIs. Decision-makers in Budapest knew that Western governments appreciated their reforms. The impression they were given, in turn, was that you can count on your friends when you are in need. They also learnt that good behaviour – exemplified by an unmarred debt service record and reform-mindedness – does not help much with the banks once they start running.

Adjustment Programmes

Between 1982 and 1991 the IMF initiated and completed four programmes under its stand-by and compensatory financing provisions. Afterwards, Hungary was drawing on a medium-term (1991–93) loan from the extended financing facility (EFF). The IMF programmes can be divided into two phases: one lasted from 1982 to early 1985; the second began in 1988 and continued until 1991. What happened in the intermittent years, 1985–87, is covered in the next section. Broadly speaking, the Fund's attention was focused on the restoration of liquidity until 1984. Only in the second phase did it begin to recommend reform policy options. Designing adjustment programmes for a CPE was a novel challenge for the IMF.

Institutional experience with administered rather than incentive-driven economies was scarce. Yugoslavia had entered a stand-by arrangement with the Fund in 1980. In 1982, the IMF published a comprehensive review of the literature on adjustment in CPEs (Allen 1982).

For the design of IMF programmes, the relationship between the particular country suffering from payment imbalances and international financial markets is critical. The country's access to these markets determines the volume of freely available foreign capital and, hence, how much and how fast its current account position must be improved. Unless output increases, domestic absorption (that is, total final consumption and gross capital formation over GDP) has to give. In other words, the expenditure items in the national accounts must fall. What is more, expenditure reduction is typically accompanied by expenditure-switching programmes intent on boosting exports and curbing imports. The stabilisation of expenditures is achieved through tight monetary and fiscal policies; exchange-rate management, on the other hand, is geared toward expenditure-switching (IMF 1987).

The IMF was of course aware that adjusting a CPE was an altogether different job from doing the same thing to a market economy. For example, how do you get enterprises to invest less if firms have a soft budget constraint? Tightening credit will obviously not do by itself. Even if there is a limit to aggregate net credit, firms may simply resort to extending intra-firm credits, thus circumventing central bank policy. Or, how do you manage to increase the price of tradeables relative to non-tradeables if prevailing pricing practices effectively fix the RER? Neither is it clear how, under the conditions of highly regulated foreign trade, the attainment of an equilibrium RER will have much impact on the volume of imports (Wolf 1985a,1985b).

In what follows, an attempt is made to compare IMF targets with what was actually achieved. The interesting question of whether the targets were achieved because of the IMF is, in the absence of a counterfactual, obviously not answerable. Likewise, when targets were missed, the inappropriateness of an adjustment programme might account for that; but so may a number of other possible factors, such as deficient programme implementation by the Hungarian planners. In addition, letters of intent being confidential, targets are often not even publicly known and relevant data need to be retrieved through interviews with negotiators and so on. However, these serious methodological problems should not prevent one from looking for indirect evidence (cf. Tyson, Robinson and Woods 1988). Revealing at least the basics of an adjustment package helps to determine the relationship between the Fund and the debtor, namely whether or not the requirements to obtain a loan contradicted the debtor country's policy preferences.

Table 1.2 gives reference numbers for a series of macroeconomic indicators. For 1983, the year of the first stand-by programme, the Fund's targets for GNP growth (target: 0.5–1.0 per cent; actual: 0.7 per cent) and limiting the budget deficit to one per cent of GDP were achieved. The reduction of real wages approximated the target (–4 per cent; actual: –3.2 per cent). But for fixed investment (target: –10 per cent; actual: –3.4 per cent), the size of the current account surplus (target: $600 million; actual $71 million)[8] and the reduction of real personal income, the development was off track. The buoyancy of the second economy was partly responsible for missing the adjustment target of real income decline (Buchan 1983, 2).

In 1984, output growth was somewhat higher than projected (target: 1.5–2.0 per cent; actual: 2.7 per cent), while consumption rose instead of falling (target: –1 to –2 per cent; actual: 1.2 per cent). Industry output increased a little more than planned (target: 1.5–2 per cent). Convertible currency exports rose only by 1.7 per cent after no increase at all in 1983. This was partly due to a severe drought. Projected output growth was supposed to offset the drop in consumption, while in fact they increased together. In line with the improving liquidity position, Hungary phased out import restrictions it had imposed in September 1982.

The Fund was involved in attempts to reform the system of public finance and reduce the budget deficit. In fact, subsidies were cut and in 1984 the budget turned into surplus. But it remained difficult to estimate what a sustainable budget position would be because the Hungarian finance officials never relayed the exact data to the IMF. For example, the Fund never knew about the HUF 300 billion (HUF = Hungarian forints) of domestic debt accumulated in the early 1980s. In sum, in the course of the first two years of stand-by programmes, domestic absorption was reduced largely through a squeeze on investment and real wages. At low rates of output growth, the adjustment burden on consumption was minimal. By the end of 1984, the international reserve position covered six months' worth of imports.

Hungarian policy-makers placed a strong emphasis on avoiding a severe income differentiation among social groups in the country, and hence they were not fond of cuts in price subsidies and real wages. Instead, they set their bets on short-term relief through hitting investment. Except for wage levels, which the government would have preferred to remain higher, the Fund accommodated these preferences. Reformist policy-makers tend to support this interpretation. Available evidence from the first round of IMF-sponsored adjustment packages lends support to the claim that the Fund never forced its views on Hungary when priorities diverged (Mendelsohn 1983; Zloch-Christy 1987, 123; Tyson, Robinson and Woods 1988). On the

Table 1.2 Macroeconomic indicators, and their annual rates of change

Item	1980/1	1981/2	1982/3	1983/4	1984/5	1985/6	1986/7	1987/8	1988/9	1989/90
GDP	2.9	2.8	0.7	2.7	-0.3	1.5	4.1	-0.1	-0.2	-4.0
Consumption	2.9	1.2	0.5	1.2	1.7	2.4	3.3	2.8	0.7	-4.0
Fixed investment	-4.3	-1.6	-3.4	-3.7	-3.1	6.5	9.8	-9.1	4.3	-9.0
Domestic absorption	1.4	-0.1	-1.7	0.3	0.4	3.9	3.2	-2.9	-0.3	-5.0
Producer prices	6.3	4.8	6.2	5.0	5.0	2.1	3.5	4.7	15.4	20.9
Consumer prices	4.6	6.9	7.3	8.3	7.0	5.3	8.6	15.5	17.0	28.9
Real wages	1.1	-0.7	-0.2	-2.3	1.3	1.9	-0.4	-4.9	0.9	-5.1

Sources: Hungarian Central Statistical Office (HCSO), Statistical Yearbook 1990; National Bank of Hungary, Annual Report 1990.

contrary, the Fund has traditionally held that consumption should bear the brunt of austerity programmes for, if investment is crowded out, the conditions for future growth are undermined. Clearly, this principle was not reflected in the design of the first two packages. It is difficult to explain this in purely economic terms. Of central importance was Hungary's exotic status: it was the IMF's only reformist socialist customer at the time.

The programme was atypical also in another respect. Expenditure switching effectively did not take place. Slight improvements in the trade balance resulted more than anything from import reductions. Exports stagnated (see Table 1.3). Shifting resources from non-tradeables to tradeables is not always possible when the latter is associated with low quality, technological backwardness and so on. Existing distortions make it difficult to know one's comparative advantages; promoting saleables within tradeables may thus lead to losses. Given the high degree of import-substitution, the scope for shifting demand from imports to import substitutes was limited. Western inputs were crucial for saleability. So when imports fell, Hungary tended to lose market shares and experience deteriorating terms of trade. The bilateral trade balance significantly improved in the early 1980s only with the Middle East and North Africa (Kaminski 1988). Was an outcome conceivable that would have scored better in expenditure reduction and achieved something in expenditure switching? Some suggest not (Winiecki 1988). Excess demand on the producer goods market was not a temporary phenomenon but a systemic feature based on soft budget constraints and exacerbated through investment cycles. Investment cycles accompany planning in CPEs. They typically begin with built-in distortions of underestimated cost and overestimated capacity, leading eventually to internal imbalances. In the following year's plan, adjustment takes place through cuts in investment outlays. Since it is easier to save costs on imported capital goods and raw materials, there is subsequently a shift in

Table 1.3　Convertible currency trade, current account, international reserves ($ million)

Item	1982	1983	1984	1985	1986	1987	1988	1989	1990
Exports	4 831	4 832	4 916	4 188	4 186	5 050	5 505	6 446	6 345
Imports	4 163	4 059	4 025	4 060	4 668	5 014	5 016	5 910	5 998
Trade balance	668	772	891	127	−482	36	489	537	348
Current account	−299	71	67	−847	−1 495	−876	−807	−1 437	127
Reserves	942	1 577	2 026	2 793	3 053	2 159	1 976	1 725	1 166

Source: National Bank of Hungary, *Annual Report 1990*.

the composition of investment towards consumption-related projects. That of course translates into an even higher excess demand on the producer goods market. Hence, firms' behaviour does not change at all; cost considerations remain elusive. Perhaps an increase in exports in the short term could have been achieved had Hungary not respected the Fund's aversion to export subsidies (Tyson, Robinson and Woods 1988, 94).

Between 1985 and 1987, the Fund did not administer any programmes in Hungary, but it continued to give technical advice to the country, especially with respect to a reform of the system of public finance. During this period, the current account balance deteriorated massively and remained negative. In the long run, this could only weaken Hungary's bargaining stance *vis-à-vis* the Fund.

In more than one way the situation from 1988 onwards resembled that of 1982. Hungary again found it difficult to borrow from international financial markets. Terms of syndicated loans deteriorated. On two occasions, foreign deposits were withdrawn in large volumes. One was the announcement of Bulgaria's repayment difficulties. The other was when the Democratic Forum, which was perceived as somewhat less reform-minded than the contenders from the Free Democrats, emerged as the strongest party in Hungary's first free parliamentary elections. Creditworthiness suffered. Again, official creditors intervened, for both economic and political motives. The West German government, for example, leant on West German banks to provide fresh money. The BIS organised bridging loans. Western governments in general, in conjunction with the Fund and the Bank, teamed up for assistance in the newly formed G-24 (comprising the OECD member countries), coordinated by the EC Commission. In contrast to the first period of official creditor intervention, external financing was now much more closely linked to detailed policy requirements embodied in adjustment packages. Beginning in 1987, the Hungarian leadership had renewed its reform drive. It instituted a two-stage programme of austerity measures and reform which the Fund supported, in 1988, with a stand-by loan to cover refinancing needs and provide some assurance to the international financial markets. The programme placed great emphasis on institutional changes, such as company independence and restructuring of industry. That included the reduction of subsidies, which amounted to roughly 20 per cent of GDP. Cutting price-support schemes for inefficient industry meant that some companies were no longer able to produce contracted exports to the other CMEA countries because essential inputs were missing. This led, in turn, to energy and raw-material shortages for Hungary. Likewise, the hard-currency shortage discouraged subsidy cuts because not much home production could be replaced by imports without incurring higher levels of debt. At the end of 1988 it became clear that Hungary had run up a budget deficit twice as high as that agreed with the Fund (target: HUF10 billion). The current account deficit was $307 million higher than projected. Consequently, in early 1989, the Fund suspended the fifth tranche of its credit. It did not accept the mid-year budget revision, and neither did it offer a new agreement in 1989. To unblock the tranche the Fund demanded reduced public spending, higher interest rates and unemployment, a lower balance of payments deficit and a rouble surplus with the USSR. In addition, it advised the government to take social security and housing expenditure out of the budget.

In March 1990, after many months of negotiations, a new IMF loan targeted a current account deficit of $550 million. Trade with the West was supposed to become more important. When the collapse of trade with the CMEA subsequent to the introduction of world prices exacerbated the budget deficit, the government announced an emergency package to meet the Fund's targets. The IMF's leverage was high. The 1990 debt service was scheduled at $1.5 billion, which Hungary did not have. Without support from official creditors, the country risked insolvency. The announcement of the package freed the next two tranches of its credits, bridged over by a BIS credit. The effect on the capital markets was limited; the investment rating firm Moody's downgraded Hungarian bond issues below investment grade. But the National Bank, thanks to a World Bank guarantee under its Expanded Cofinancing Operations, managed to launch a ten-year Eurobond issue in Japan (Gelb and Gray 1991, Ch. 4). Compared to the first adjustment period from 1982 to 1984, Western official creditors were more differentiated in their responses to Hungary's financing problems. The Bank of England, instead of coaxing commercial banks into credit operations, did the opposite: it ordered British banks to undertake prudential provisions on their loans to Hungary. The same was true for the French banks (Financial Research Ltd 1991). This hardly encouraged banks to keep on lending. The West German government, on the other hand, guaranteed up to 90 per cent of commercial bank loans to Hungary. The IMF got tougher. By late 1989 considerable disagreement emerged over what pace of reform was appropriate. The Hungarian government's gradualist approach contrasted with the Fund's frontloading (that is, target-setting). Also, the Hungarians opposed too large a forint devaluation for fear of increasing or accelerating inflation. In a sense, the relationship normalised. The extremely polite *tête-à-tête* of the earlier period was replaced by a no-nonsense exchange more characteristic of how the Fund deals with its clients. Better information enabled the Fund to assess the situation more realistically. In some respects, Hungary was in worse shape than many had believed. In 1989, the Németh government revealed that, due to consistent underreporting, the country's debt stock had appeared $2 billion lower than it actually was. On the whole, however, the relationship lacked the politicised controversies often surrounding negotiations between the IMF and Latin American creditors. The Fund rallied to Hungary's support when the country suffered a run on its deposits in 1989. Both the Fund and the government reckoned they saw light at the end of the tunnel when they agreed on the current 1991–93 EFF loan, predicting a resumption of real GDP growth of 1–3 per cent by 1992. In a memorandum accompanying the respective letter of intent, the Hungarian government predicted that the country's precarious financial situation would be resolved by 1993:

> it is the government's objective ... to maintain Hungary's traditional access to capital markets by halting the growth of external indebtedness within three years, while fully observing its debt obligations. ... The target of stopping accumulation of external debt by 1993 implies a current account deficit which, in that year, cannot exceed what can be financed by foreign direct investment. (Hungary – Memorandum of Economic Transformation and Medium-Term Policies 1991, 11)

Unfortunately, things did not quite turn out that way.

Liquidity and Creditworthiness: Second Act

Hungary reduced its liabilities in current dollars to commercial banks between 1980 and 1984 by 15 per cent; it paid $3.3 billion in interest during this time. Net debt fell. In January 1984, *The Economist* concluded: 'The region's financial problems now look less serious' ('East–West Traders Raise the Curtain', 1984, 64). The magazine did not carry another article on Hungarian financial problems until October 1987. The statement certainly reflects how the banks felt about Eastern Europe. Convinced that the CMEA's remarkable ability to adjust to balance of payments difficulties – as evidenced in the turnaround of the region's current account balance – protected them against future losses, they dashed back into the area. Increased competition among suppliers in the capital markets made the CMEA an attractive borrower. Except for Hungary which had some experience with launching bonds, Eastern European countries mostly used syndicated loans on which banks realise higher returns than they do in the Euronote market ('Renewed Appetite', 1984, 90). The change in risk assessment was remarkable. Hungary, despite its high debt, raised various credits at just 0.25 per cent over Libor (the London interbank offered rate); even OECD countries did not do better. Hungarian bond issues and syndicated Euroloans were frequently oversubscribed. European, US and Japanese banks scrambled to get a part of the action (Fairlamb 1987). Inevitably, since the new disbursements did not translate into an export offensive, all available debt indicators worsened (see Table 1.4). Net foreign debt rose on average by 25 per cent each year. Hungary's international liabilities roughly doubled in only three years. A large part of the increase was due to genuine new lending, but other factors contributed as well. The fall of the value of the dollar increased the value of roughly 50 per cent of Hungarian debt, denominated mostly in deutschmarks, yen, Swiss francs and French francs. What made the situation worse was that the MNB had speculated on a continued strong dollar. Hence, the volume of business and the terms on which credits were offered had little to do with Hungary's economic performance or, if it did, the banks clearly overrated the country (cf. Gajdeczka 1988).

The situation was obviously unsustainable, but it took all participants a couple of years to realise that. Then, Moody's and the Japanese rating agency downgraded the credit rating on Hungarian international bonds (United Nations Economic Commission for Europe (UNECE), 1990, 71; McDougall 1990, 23). Terms on new credits generally toughened. Hungarian sovereign debt also appeared in the secondary market. While the discount was low and the market actually very thin, it did reflect concern by some banks that they would not be able to recover their loans. The first warning calls provided only *ex-post* rationalisations for essentially inconsistent behaviour on the part of the banks. According to the Economist Intelligence Unit, bankers, by 1988, had come to worry about Hungary's ability to increase its hard-currency exports (Kerpel and Young 1988, 76). For this explanation to make sense, one needs to believe that, from 1984 to 1987, there was ever reason to

Table 1.4   Debt indicators

Item	1981	1982	1983	1984	1985	1986	1987	1988	1989	1990
Net debt/X	160	148	143	147	275	352	358	331	302	343
Net int./X	24	18	13	13	18	20	22	24	26	35
Debt service	42	37	36	45	58	67	52	57	49	65
Reserves/M	20	18	33	41	56	47	30	27	20	28

Notes: X = hard-currency exports.
    int. = interest payments.
    debt service = int. + principal (re)payments over X.
    M = imports.
Source: OECD, *Financial Market Trends* Nos. 45, 48.

assume the contrary. As illustrated in the discussion of the adjustment programmes, investment bore the brunt of administered austerity. While that changed temporarily in 1985, investments put into operation in 1982 were no higher, in constant volume terms, than in 1975, and fell during the 1980s. Hence, it is not clear where increased exports were supposed to come from. The US bank, Morgan Guaranty, argued in 1990 that the 'Eastern economies are not *yet* prudently bankable on commercial terms, and certainly not for general-purpose balance of payments funding' ('Eastern Europe: A Cautionary Note', 1990, 13; emphasis added).

To make the argument a sound one, they would need to explain why the region ever was prudently bankable since 1984, and what had changed all of a sudden. The OECD (1991) concluded that it was the slow progress of the reforms which led to the reduction of credit lines and deposit withdrawals by Hungary's major creditors. Whatever the speed of reform in 1989 and 1990, it was certainly much faster than anything the HSWP dared do before Kádár's fall from power. Paradoxically, Hungary's relation with its creditors between 1984/85 and 1987 had been based on the understanding of *We-pretend-to-reform-and-you-pretend-to-believe-it.* In other words, if reforms were the critical ingredient to loan agreements, the banks had more reason to lend in 1989 than ever before. Since Hungary remained current on its debt service, realised a current account surplus in 1990 and reduced virtually all expenditure items in its national accounts, the banks' behaviour must ultimately be explained by other factors.

Case-by-Case Approach?

Both official and private creditors have always held that there is no global solution to the debt crisis. Each debtor faces a different set of problems that needs to be dealt with individually rather than within some grand scheme. Remedies, appropriate in one case, so the argument went, might not do any good at all in another case. Also, consciously or not, this assumption helped prevent debtor cartels from forming and exerting increased bargaining power in rescheduling operations.

In fact, given the considerable differences between indebted countries, differentiation (while obviously hiding politically charged motivations) might be in order. However, rules of this sort do not always govern behaviour. The case-by-case rule was not applied much to Eastern Europe. When rain was reported in Poland (in 1981) and Bulgaria (in 1990) – that is, when the two countries admitted payment difficulties – banks expected bad weather all over Eastern Europe and started a run on their short-term deposits. Their expectations almost became a self-fulfilling prophecy; the induced liquidity crisis cast doubt on Hungary's ability to continue to do business and, alas, endangered its creditworthiness. Similarly, official debt reduction for Poland by the Paris Club (in 1991) affected Hungary's credit standing, although the government had always been very vocal about not wanting any debt relief. In sum, banks do not always differentiate among their debtor-clients.[9] Presumably, this entails costs (either in terms of loan losses or forgone opportunities). Who bears them?

Lender of Last Resort for Whom?

First and foremost, liquidity crises are a problem for the affected country, but they are no fun for its creditors either. If a country faces a situation where its financing requirements exceed its own resources it has no choice – barring a mobilisation of credit to bridge the gap – but to stop paying its bills, and then everybody takes losses. Thanks to official creditors, especially the IMF and the BIS, this did not happen in Hungary. IFIs intervened whenever a liquidity crisis occurred and saved the country from default. But they also socialised part of the risk commercial banks had initially agreed to underwrite in a private credit deal. Because of this, official exposure in Hungary's liabilities has been on the rise since 1987. In sum, banks believe in the validity of a case-by-case approach only under sunny weather conditions. Second, they can afford to ignore the case-by-case rule because the lender of last resort protects them against losses provoked by their own behaviour.[10]

VIA DEBITI: FROM RESTRUCTURING TO REDUCTION

If somebody had predicted in August 1982 that ten years later an internationally sponsored debt-relief and reduction programme was going to affect almost 70 per cent of all private bank loans to highly indebted countries, few bankers would have believed it. The other major players – governments in their triple capacity as official creditors and bank overseers and regulators, and debtor governments – would not have believed the prediction, either. Perhaps historians, remembering the treatment of Germany's reparation/debt problems in the 1930s and 1950s, would not have been surprised (Bareau 1983; Faber 1990). But historically inspired suggestions of how to solve the debt crisis entered the policy debate only later (for an example, see Eichengreen and Lindert, 1989). In general, it is true that 'the international financial community has often preferred to repeat the past rather than study it' (Lindert and Morton 1989, 225). A remarkable exception is the first edition of Kindleberger (1989), published in 1978, which effectively predicted the debt crisis of the 1980s. In general, both debtors and creditors thought that they were facing a temporary liquidity problem which, pending some fiscal and monetary restraint, would go away. Consequently, debtors were intent on repaying principal and servicing interest. In return, they expected that reschedulings would save them from unbridgeable bottlenecks. This consensus – on the remedy if not on the cause of the problem – lasted roughly four years and helped to avoid a major disruption of the international financial system.

By the mid-1980s, debtor governments realised that the end of the tunnel was more distant than originally assumed and began to object to the terms of debt management. These terms, in the words of an English diplomat stationed in São Paolo, had come to be 'The more you pay the more you owe', and 'The more you export the less it's worth'. With some years' delay, creditor governments slowly realised that, in the absence of growth, the debt crisis would never come to an end and that, in turn, upholding the myth of full repayment was detrimental to resuming growth. Banks also began to recognise the inevitability of losses. The consensus between debtors and creditors during the first period of adjustment had given way to an increasing disarray among the major players, who now openly disagreed about the causes of and the remedy for the protracted crisis. Debtors' interests diverged and, more importantly, so did those of creditors. In an extreme simplification, one might view the two phases of the debt crisis as a shift and change of coalitions.[11] From 1982 to about 1986, official and private creditors insisted on full repayment (a demand to which debtors acquiesced). In 1987 and 1988, some official creditors began cautiously to think about alternatives to full repayment. The Miyazawa Plan, named after the then Japanese finance minister, is one example. When the Japanese delegation proposed it at the G-7 summit in Toronto in 1988, the USA rejected the plan in part because it resembled a bank bail-out. Banks tried to limit their losses. The position of official creditors shifted away from the banks and moved closer towards the debtors. In 1989, the coalition changed. Official creditors promoted debt reduction and debtor countries subsequently bargained for good deals in the ensuing relief operations. Commercial banks, in contrast, objected to the new debt management strategy, especially to the toleration of interest arrears by official creditors. In what follows, this shift and change of strategy is illustrated in detail.

Creditors versus Debtors

When the debt crisis broke in 1982, private and public debtors in the LDCs, especially in Latin America, owed US banks a sum equivalent to 280 per cent of the banks' combined equity capital. This was fine as long as everybody believed that the servicing of the debt would not pose a problem. But when it did, individual banks became highly vulnerable and were in danger of bankruptcy. Due to their exposure in the interbank market, this implied potentially disruptive repercussions for the USA and the world banking system. The banks were not braced for the crisis; contingency plans to deal with a crisis of such dimensions did not exist (Bouchet 1987). 'Rescheduling' was not an unknown term but, of the 80 or so reschedulings that had taken place prior to 1982, about 70 had been arranged between governments. The only private debt reschedulings undertaken since the mid-1970s concerned Turkey, in 1979, and Poland, in 1982. Hence, experience with this kind of debt management was scarce among bank boards (Mendelsohn 1983). In addition to sovereign debt, banks also experienced problems in their corporate loan portfolio. Stagflation, high interest rates and erratic exchange rate movements made interest and amortisation payments difficult for a growing number of firms (Bell 1982). Later in the decade, take-overs and leveraged buy-outs increased corporate debt levels further.

In retrospect, the international financial system proved sufficiently flexible to ensure, apart from some exceptions, that problem debtors could more or less remain current on their obligations, thus avoiding a run on bank deposits. The IMF got the banks to expand their loan portfolios and the debtors to agree to adjustment programmes. The rationale of the IMF operation – to protect the system against a collapse – meant that IMF funds were allocated to the potentially most destabilising cases. These were not necessarily synonymous with countries in need or with those exhibiting the soundest economic policies, but this has been the Fund's practice throughout its history (Strange 1974, 272). Officially, the myth that equates the availability of credit with sound economic policies is kept alive. In a recent study on private market financing of developing countries the authors claim that 'some countries – particularly in ... Eastern Europe ... – succeeded in maintaining normal market relations *owing largely to the pursuit of sound economic and financial policies*' (Leipold *et al.* 1991, 1; emphasis added). This assertion makes one wonder just which countries they have in mind.

Since the banks were rather in the mood to curtail operations in the debtor countries, new lending was often referred to as 'involuntary'. This was reflected in the very expensive terms banks asked for in the restructurings. Initially, the debt crisis was good business for the banks. Consequently, Robert Devlin likens the rescheduling terms to monopoly rents: 'The additional income [above the administrative cost of rescheduling] was a superprofit and created the anomaly that banks could report robust profits from Latin America in the middle of their worst financial crisis since the 1970s' (1989, 207). In successive rounds of reschedulings, the terms softened. Interest rates fell and maturities were expanded. Below is an illustration of why that happened. By 1986, multiyear rescheduling agreements (MYRAs) had been signed with ten big debtors. At the same time, banks strengthened their capital ratios in an attempt to reduce their vulnerability and to insure themselves against the consequences of their retreat from problem debtors by refusing to grant new credit or accept new bond issues. Due to different levels of exposure in terms of capital adequacy and geographical concentration as well as different tax regimes in their home countries, banks emerged in different shape from these exercises (see Figure 1.1). In continental Europe, bank reserves against problematic loans reached up to 50 per cent. Unlike in the USA where only general provisions count as primary capital, banks were allowed to make specific provisions. In Germany, for example, banks can fully deduct provisions from taxable income. US banks enjoy that privilege only once a loan is actually written off. In addition, European regulators often required their banks to set aside reserves against problematic loans, while all US banks were free to practise what comes down to interest rescheduling: extending new loans (without improving reserves) just to ensure the servicing of old loans. By the mid-1980s, the debtor countries received no more new lending from the banks. One of the two pillars on which crisis management had

Figure 1.1   Bank provisions and after tax profits as percentage of net income

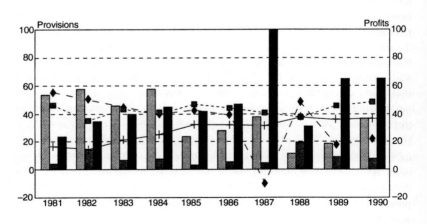

been based collapsed. But until early 1987, the banks insisted that they expected full debt service on their outstanding loans.

Theoretically, increased debt service does not need to be financed from increased export proceeds. It can also come, at least for some time, from expenditure reduction. To banks, the difference does not matter. To debtor governments, it does. Adjustment without new money meant continuing recession and forgone growth in the future. It also meant that it became more difficult to sell adjustment programmes to electorates or, more generally, to master the necessary political support for their implementation (Haggard and Kaufman 1989; Nelson 1989). This was true in Latin America, although the democratic transitions had generally brought economists with orthodox credentials and beliefs to the finance ministries and central banks. The first phase of the debt crisis ended when a number of debtor countries lost their earlier held confidence that they would somehow grow out of the crisis. By 1986, they had run up some $40 billion in arrears to private creditors.

When strains in the debt management strategy became visible, creditor governments promoted essentially two initiatives to avoid the formation of debtor cartels (Devlin 1989, 221–6) and restore consensus. Both initiatives remained squarely embedded in the principles that had guided the management of the crisis from its onset: restructuring yes, reduction no. The 1985 Baker Plan promised both public and private funds; 'adjustment with growth' was the new catchphrase. The idea was to get the banks to continue involuntary lending in an environment made more attractive by IMF and World Bank funds. But the exposure of private banks continued to fall both in Latin America and in Africa, and the IFIs' exposure also rose less than envisaged. Indeed, the IMF's exposure had been declining since 1985. To the banks, therefore, the Fund was a free rider. To debtor countries, it became just like the banks in terms of taking money out of their countries. Since 1986, the Fund has been a net recipient of money. Only in 1991 did it disburse more than what was repaid. The plan did not manage to restore any lasting consensus in international debt management, but debtor cartels did not form, either. Two years after Baker I, Baker II was announced. Instead of betting on private capital, it promoted non-lending options such as converting discounted bank loans to equity or securitising sovereign debt. Banks had engaged in this for some time already but the market for debt trading was initially very thin.[12] It grew fast but remained small compared to the total volume of outstanding debt and current debt service. It was clearly not an all-out remedy to the crisis.

The earlier consensus was never restored. Perceived interests between all participants differed increasingly. The IMF campaigned for a doubling of its capital but found governments hostile to the plan ('Can We Help You, Sir?', 1988). It aroused the anger of banks over its willingness to lend to debtors in arrears with their commercial creditors. Banks also had enough of pleas by creditor governments to continue involuntary lending; instead, they resorted to corrections of the value of their outstanding loans. All banks wanted to get out of the sovereign loan business; but those, mostly small ones, that had already managed to shed their bad loans did not care that other, mostly large banks found it difficult to follow suit at the same speed. There was no transatlantic or transpacific bank solidarity (cf. B. Cohen 1989, 20–3). Finally, debtors had begun to question the terms of the deals they had agreed to in the first rounds of reschedulings. In the words of a Mexican official, the willingness to acquiesce to creditors' demands was exhausted.

> With respect to the internal problems that the Latin American countries have to face, it must be stressed that the whole process of adjusting our economies has really left no more room for maneuvre. There are some cases in which one could truly say that the government has reached the bottom line. These are cases in which the political cost of abandoning altogether the international financial system is less then carrying on trying to abide by the present rules of the game. (Olea 1989, 74)

Through a variety of actions short of default the debtors had begun to extract concessions from their creditors. The banks' behaviour in the crisis had demonstrated that the central determinant of new loans was the probability of default of the debtor, not how cooperative it had been in designing adjustment programmes, or how successful in carrying them out. Seemingly paradoxically, cooperative behaviour did not result in voluntary lending. Instead, it gave rise to the banks' pull-out from the area. The dynamic was perverse.

> Not only have 'model' debtors lacked worthwhile rewards, but in some cases 'bad' debtor behaviour has extracted concessions from the creditors – at least in the short run – that might otherwise have been unavailable. Some major debtor governments which seem on the brink of an uncontrollable crisis (perhaps even caused by their own mismanagement) may be in a position to frighten their creditors into otherwise undesirable concessions. Bankers try not to admit this reality (which they call 'moral hazard'). (Whitehead 1989, 237)

Hence, countries that go by the rules are punished. Benjamin Cohen called this a 'tax on a country's effort to adjust its economy' (1989, 27). One debtor after another began to engage in what had been virtually absent from the early debt negotiations: bargaining. It became, in the words of the then chief economist at the World Bank, the 'key question' (Fischer 1989; see also Krugman 1989).

Mexican Poker and Other Games

Mexico was the first country to obtain concessions from its creditors this way. In 1986, the country obtained commitments of $12 billion of new money over two years. A novel feature of the rescheduling agreement was that it included a growth and oil-price guarantee: that is, the Mexican negotiators had succeeded in inserting a clause in the agreement that provided for extra money from the banks should the country not meet its 3–4 per cent growth target or suffer from a decline in oil prices below $9 per barrel. The deal might never have got wrapped up had it not been for US pressure. Mexican negotiators, in turn, while remaining closely in touch with the banks' steering committee, threatened unilateral action of limiting debt service. Peru had already decided unilaterally in mid-1985 to limit debt service to 10 per cent of the proceeds from its exports. Argentina, since 1984, had accumulated arrears and insisted on liquidation through new loans rather than through its own reserves. Venezuela did not want new money but simply a restructuring of its principal. A strong international reserve position enabled it to reject terms suggested by the IMF and the banks. Chile and Uruguay, too, tried to obtain terms similar to the ones that characterised the Mexican deal. The Philippines had managed to establish a linkage between their privatisation programme, the stabilisation of democracy and far-reaching financing requirements. The IMF went along, but the banks did not (Boschmann 1991). In January 1987, Ecuador declared a moratorium. In February of the same year, Brazil followed.

The Brazilian case is very interesting. Brazil had twice before defaulted: once around the turn of the century and again in the 1930s. In 1985, the country needed to reschedule $45.3 billion of debt service due in 1985–89. At the time, it enjoyed high growth and had accumulated a substantial trade surplus. Indeed, Brazil insisted that growth be regarded as an essential ingredient to adjustment. While it was willing to talk to the commercial banks it objected to the monitoring of an agreement by the IMF, thus effectively challenging the established package deal between an IMF-prescribed adjustment package and new lending. President Sarney's negotiators felt that they could afford to bargain because the country, due to its export boom, was not in any immediate need of new credit.

In 1986 the banks gave in and lent Brazil some money so as to avoid technical default. Domestically, economic reforms embodied in the Cruzado Plan failed to work and the Sarney government ran into an increasing opposition to its adjustment policies. By the end of the year, international reserves had fallen sharply. In January 1987 – the IMF had just issued a favourable report on the country – the Paris Club consolidated Brazil's $2.8 billion official obligations despite the absence of an IMF programme to which Brazil continued to object. A month later, Brazil halted interest payments to commercial banks in order to avoid import controls which would have been necessary to protect rapidly falling reserves (Carneiro 1988; Cardoso and Fishlow 1989). The banks reacted by curtailing short-term, commercial and interbank credits and doubled the spread on trade finance loans. These measures hurt the country, especially its industrial importers. Of course, the banks took substantial losses as well. Nine months into the moratorium Brazil resumed interest payments in exchange for new lending. A final agreement was reached in June 1988, after an IMF loan which did not specify any targets or establish a formal link to the agreement with the banks.

The World Bank concluded in 1991 that running up arrears has been costly to Brazil (1991, 37). 'Costly compared to what?' one must ask. Until 1987, the external adjustment had contributed to higher inflation, public sector disequilibria and so on. It is ultimately impossible to say whether the country would have been better off without the moratorium (which was followed by an even larger one that commenced in July 1989 and lasted through December 1990). One of the most important insights gained by debt watchers observing the Brazilian gamble was that the country in effect did not get cut off completely from short-term financing used to keep trade going. Of course, after the moratorium voluntary lending was not available to any great extent; but that had already been the case since long before the announcement of the moratorium. The conditions of the agreement rather seem to reward Brazil for its tough bargaining; $62 billion was rescheduled over 20 years at a lower-than-average spread and with improved exit bond subscriptions. Also, the banks provided $5.2 billion of new money. Thus, the agreement came to resemble the Mexican deal in that it acknowledged the need to look for long-term solutions.

Whatever the conclusion, 'debt crisis management was never to be the same after Brazil's action' (Griffiths-Jones 1988a, 32). The big Latin American debtors and the Philippines now received terms on interest payments on long-term debt that they previously had been refused. The creditors' idea was clearly to isolate Brazil and ensure that its behaviour would not be copied elsewhere, but Peru, Brazil and Ecuador did not experience any legal action by the creditors. The banks' rather defensive stance was to cut short-term credit lines. However, it was not too difficult for the debtors to replenish those through other banks.

Some authors have tried to develop a taxonomy of resources debtors can bring to bear in negotiations. Haggard and Kaufman suggest the size of the debt; the debtor's strategic significance to the creditor country's foreign policy; the availability of non-conditional resources; and the existence or absence of debtor cartels (1989, 264–7). In sum, large debtors, geo-strategically important countries and, for example, oil exporters can strike relatively better deals. Griffiths-Jones also developed criteria along which the potential bargaining power of debtors can be measured (1988a, 1988b). All of these elements make sense. But these attempts should be seen as no more than *ex-post* rationalisations. They do not provide conjectures about, say, Hungary's potential bargaining strength had the country ever tried to renegotiate its obligations. Neither Haggard and Kaufman nor Griffith-Jones say anything about the relative influence of the determining elements, yet that is the crucial point for a tentative 'theory' of debt bargaining. For example, it would seem impossible for Hungary to receive debt relief to the tune of the Paris Club and, possibly, London Club arrangements with Poland. Does that suggest that Poland's debt is higher (true only in absolute terms) or that its strategic significance is more salient? Of course, bargaining has to do with power, but there are always 'born losers' in negotiations. Not always are they the weakest participants, however. Griffiths-Jones additionally points to the importance of clear objectives in the bargaining stances taken by the debtors. Conciliatory language, symbolic payments and willingness to threaten unilateral action all make it more likely that bankers take the debtor seriously, without antagonising communication to the point of breakdown. In short, do it the Mexican way, not the Peruvian way (1988b, 355). Even the declaration of a moratorium should be designed as part of a larger strategy and not simply a desperate and inevitable default. For example, Brazil's moratorium was meant to resolve the conflict between debt service and the government's priority on growth. If the action had been taken in 1986 when reserves were still high and the Cruzado Plan still drew positive comments, the country's bargaining position would have been enhanced. Toughness alone is no good: 'debtor governments have achieved better results when they have taken the initiative and put forward clear, specific proposals to the creditors. Though not always all their suggestions have been accepted, a *clear initial position* by the debtor governments can serve as a basis for the package adopted' (ibid, 371; emphasis in original). Devlin advises that countries planning to default should continue to pay interest on short-term credit lines to avoid being cut off from trade finance. They should also hide their reserves and present non-monetary 'carrots' to the banks, namely the domestic liberalisation of the bank sector and so on (1989, 269–71).

Lehman and McCoy (1992) argue that the strength of a debt negotiator has two faces: one *vis-à-vis* the opponent in the negotiation, the banker (level I), and the other towards the domestic constituency (level II). They complain that bargaining models limited to level-I dynamics neglect the fact that international debt agreements typically require domestic ratification, either formally through the legislature or informally through a coalition of interest groups whose political support is essential for the government in order to push through an adjustment package. This neglect may lead to wrong predictions of negotiators' behaviour. For example, a one-level game would predict that a government with sizeable international reserves could simply stonewall against creditors' demands; because of its strength, it would probably engage in tough bargaining. Similarly, a government vulnerable to interruptions of credit flows would readily give in to creditors' demands; because of its weakness, it would probably be willing to make concessions. Not so, say Lehman and McCoy. If the vulnerable government is at the same time weak at home – that is, not in a position to see unpopular adjustment packages through – it may use its domestic difficulties as a bargaining chip at level I: 'If you force this agreement on us, we will get thrown out of office and then you can forget about debt service for a long time to come'.

Likewise, if the government which is strong at level I is also strong at level II, it may use this latter strength to impose a politically difficult adjustment policy if it really wants an agreement. Thus, although a strong negotiator, it does not engage in tough bargaining but rather makes concessions. Which of the two options it chooses would depend on the costs of non-agreement: the higher they are, the more likely concessions become. If applied, Lehman's and McCoy's model would probably explain the outcomes of many international debt negotiations, but not the Hungarian. Governments that are domestically weak, the model predicts, will not make concessions, regardless of their position at level I, for they simply could not afford to do so for fear of losing power. The Antall government, and much less the preceding transition government, was in anything but a strong position in Hungarian society, yet both made concessions. The failure of the model to explain the Hungarian case may have a simple explanation: the domestic level was less important because all significant groups in Hungarian society were aware that adjustment was coming their way. They had accepted this as the price for introducing a market economy, and debt service raised this price by only so much. Thus, the issue lent itself less to politicisation.

Following the Brazilian moratorium, Argentina, Brazil and Mexico arranged rescheduling deals with the banks that featured so-called exit bonds. These bonds are issued by debtors to creditors, effectively substituting a bank credit. They are called 'Exit' because the purchasing institution is not obliged to participate in future rescheduling operations. Inasmuch as the face value of the bond was below the denomination of the original credit, debt reduction slowly made its way into international debt management. High provisions increased the room for multilaterally agreed deals because the banks' solvency would not be in danger any more. But the menu approach of Baker, the US Secretary of the Treasury, failed to resuscitate the business-as-usual spirit of the early 1980s. By late 1988, 49 countries had accumulated arrears on their debt. The United Nations Conference on Trade and Developement (UNCTAD) argued that debt relief – not a big increase in new lending – was needed ('A Debtor's Dream', 1988).

Baker goes, Brady comes: with a speech by the new secretary of the treasury in March 1989, a shift in strategy was made official. Debt reduction and debt service reduction became its central elements. The Brady Plan acknowledged the simple yet crucial insight that the benefits of the reform programmes lay in the future, while the cost of their implementation was current. The continuously high debt service payments endangered the sustainability of adjustment. To allow growth to resume, net capital outflows had to be reduced (cf. Borensztein 1989, 1991). This could be achieved either through new money or through debt relief. Since the former was unlikely to materialise, debt relief remained the only feasible solution.

In a nutshell, the plan was simple.[13] The World Bank and the IMF would provide funds to the debtors that they could use to acquire guarantees (for example, US zero coupon bonds) for bonds swapped against some old debt. For the banks to be happy with this, they needed to believe that the expected net present value of the newly issued bonds was higher than that of the old credit. Overall debt reduction depended on the amount of guarantees available, in that banks obviously expected some incentive to agree to the swaps (Kuczynski 1989). How much debt reduction was required depended on the estimation of the financing gap (debt service due, minus available resources); a large gap increased the pressure on the banks to grant larger reductions. There is some evidence that the IMF saw the Brady Plan as a green light implicitly to favour the debtors and corner the banks (Vernon, Spar and Tobin 1991, 99).

The year 1987 marked the highest exposure of banks to debtor countries. Since then, debt stock to private creditors has been falling. Hence, governments had ensured the stability of their banks during the first phase of the debt crisis without having the favour returned. On the contrary, the banks' pull-out from the area complicated the management of the crisis for creditor and debtor governments. The US government was clearly determined not to let the banks get off for nothing; in May 1989, the Internal Revenue Service issued a tax ruling eliminating lucrative foreign tax credits that rather heavily reined in the banks' business reports. For an account detailing the abuse of foreign tax reporting practice, see Lissakers (1991, Ch. 5). In 1990, the estrangement between official and private creditors over debt management increased. The banks were dismayed at the toleration of arrears by the IFIs. In effect, this epitomised most clearly that the creditor coalition no longer existed. Neither did the banks fancy official debt forgiveness programmes (Schulmann 1990a). That banks should be bullied by regulators into supporting the Brady Plan was proposed by Sachs (1989b, 16). By contrast, Louis Pauly (1990) has explained how stricter capital adequacy standards, loan disclosure rules and a number of other regulatory devices effectively imposed higher operating costs on banks in the USA. In order to avoid US banks being put at a disadvantage *vis-à-vis* foreign competitors, the Reagan and Bush administrations successfully lobbied for similar regulatory and supervisory standards in all capital market countries. As a result, the banks' retreat from lending to developing countries was reinforced.

Mexico, again, was the test case for the Brady Plan. A comprehensive summary of the Mexican deal is given by Sweder van Wijnbergen (1991). He argues that the country managed to reduce the value of the banks' claims by almost the full amount of the resources that the IMF, the World Bank and the Japanese government had contributed. This suggests a very efficient use of official funds. The banks, on the other hand, were not worse off than before because the market value of the outstanding claims after the credit enhancement more or less corresponded with the debt relief granted. Hence, the deal worked as projected by the IFIs: the benefits accrued to Mexico and not one-sidedly to the banks. This would not have been the case if the value of the claims against Mexico had risen by more than the extent to which debt was actually reduced. Much academic literature had predicted that this would happen (a bank bail-out rather than assistance to the debtors).[14]

By 1992, eight Brady agreements had been negotiated, mostly with Latin American debtors, covering some 70 per cent of all bank loans. This prompted *The Banker* to claim that the debt crisis was finally a thing of the past ('Crisis? What Crisis?', 1992, 11). In fact, in 1991 some $7 billion in foreign capital was invested in Latin American stocks; total capital inflow amounted to about $ 40 billion. Banks began to underwrite Eurobonds and equities. For the first time in ten years, the resource transfer was positive, a fact that made the Inter-American Development Bank hail the beginning of Latin America's long-awaited economic revival ('Virtue Rewarded', 1992).

Everybody, it seemed, was happy. Debt reduction under the Brady Plan led to a rise in the value of debt traded in the secondary markets. Prices began to rise in 1990 and turned into a rush in 1991. This divided banks into three different groups: First, banks that had begun to specialise on trading debt made big profits; second, banks which sold their debt when the market was very depressed (for example, some US regionals and also a few European banks) lost most; third, the banks who got rid of their loans after the secondary market developed, when discounts were still low, and those who hung on to them, did better (Westlake 1991). The value improvement plus higher interest receipts in developing-country loans made banks look much better than they had expected a year earlier.

This cursory summary of negotiation practices of major debtor countries provides the backdrop against which Hungarian debt management can be judged.

The Vice of Being Nice

Throughout the 1980s Hungary has insisted on servicing and repaying its debts on time. The only thing Hungary ever did in the 1980s was to renegotiate the terms of a bankers' acceptance fee. Originally contracted in 1984 at over $ 210 million, Hungary's central bankers managed to more than halve the acceptance commission, reduce the margin over Libor by a factor of 4.5 (from 110 to 25 basis points on advances) and extend the maturity. The renegotiation reflected an improvement in market rates that Hungary took advantage of; it had nothing to do with payment difficulties (Montagnon 1986, 30).

Some observers question the merits of this policy (for example, Young 1989, 230; Hare and Révész 1992). Others assert that the repayment policy was adequate, and that the country should go on doing this (Riecke 1992; Storf 1992) In contrast, Gábor Oblath maintains that the country has no alternative to repayment but that the debt burden potentially harms the reform process today (1992; see also Rácz 1993). The different opinions reflect more than the authors' detached judgement. The first two are academics; Riecke is with the Hungarian National Bank; Storf is senior economist with Deutsche Bank; Oblath is a Hungarian policy analyst; Rácz is an investment banker with CSFB Credit Suisse First Boston in Budapest. George Soros, the Hungarian-American financial manager known for his sponsorship of education projects and civic activities in Eastern Europe, in 1990 supported a debt-per-equity scheme (Denton 1990, 3). Naturally, what is best for one may be bad for another participant in the debt crisis. This section attempts to clarify whether the Hungarian authorities, in comparison to other middle-income debtors, managed to get a good deal for the country.

When Károly Grosz replaced János Kádár as general secretary of the HSWP in May 1988 and reformers like Imre Poszgay and Rezsö Nyers got

promoted to the politbureau, the party quickly considered a series of micro-
and macroeconomic reforms. The trade-off involved in pursuing both debt
service and a policy of opening up led to some mutterings about rescheduling. *The Economist* recognised that as a 'muddled and probably unserious
threat' ('So Have We Learnt our Lesson?', 1988, 78) and, in fact, nothing
ever came of it. A year later, following the G-7 summit in Paris which
launched the Western assistance programmes for Hungary and Poland, the
Hungarian government submitted a document detailing requests for assistance. The recourse to debt relief was categorically dismissed.

> Hungary doesn't raise a claim on the debt relief offered by the Brady-
> Plan, but asks for participation in the actions attached to the Brady-Plan
> aiming at enlarging of the financing sources... ..... we believe it is import-
> ant to avoid a scenario, whereby the Brady proposal be implemented
> countries fulfilling their debt service obligations in time would fall into a
> less favourable situation than those which have already rescheduled their
> debts. Regarding the debt strategy of the Western countries we urge the
> support of these solutions, which appreciate the efforts carried out by
> those countries, which repay their debts in time in spite of their consider-
> able difficulties. ('Initiatives by the Hungarian Government concerning
> the negotiations with the Group of "24"' n.d., 24)

In short, the government was saying to its official (and, indirectly, also to its
private) creditors that it intended to maintain its debt management practice.
In turn, so the plea went, Western governments should ensure that Hungary
would not get a worse deal than the rescheduling Brady countries. In effect,
this was an appeal to morality. Morals, however, are an unreliable feature of
relations between creditors and debtors. In a sense, the Hungarians defied
the logic of markets; if debt relief in a Brady country made it seem worthwhile investing in the country because it had a promising future, then that is
where the finance capital would go. The government's position paper left
unclear how it expected Western governments to intervene. It suggested
state guarantees in case banks were not sufficiently forthcoming with new
money (ibid, 35). Yet to the degree that loans are a question not only of risk
but also of returns, the scope for action by Western governments was
obviously limited.

Debt relief, on the other hand, can be effectively organised because
governments, through their regulating agencies, have the means to influence their banks' portfolio management. This insight is no less valid
because it is often forgotten. Karen Lissakers summed up numerous interviews with bankers as follows:

The history of sovereign lending suggests that potential lenders care more about the relative level of outstanding indebtedness and economic outlook of a country than they do about its past payment performance. At the end of the day, even bank managers tend to be more concerned with prospective new business than about the losses their predecessors may have incurred. The attitude of the market can change quickly once there is a firm settlement of outstanding debts – even a settlement that is highly favorable to the debtor. Indeed, the more favorable the settlement to the debtor, the more attractive the debtor may seem to the next lender. (1991, 261–2)

In the campaign leading up to Hungary's first free elections in early 1990, most of the better-known reformers outside the HSWP had supported the Free Democrats, who lost the election. The winners, a conservative coalition, had run a populist campaign; banks became worried about the implications and withdrew credit lines in April 1990. The mood changed when the new Antall government ruled out rescheduling, keeping in line with its predecessor and in agreement with the opposition ('Off the Leash', 1990). The change from campaign rhetoric to government policy was less smooth than it appeared in newspaper accounts. Antall, after winning the election, went to Washington and met, among others, senior World Bank and IMF officials. Asked whether they would support a Hungarian moratorium, they successfully dissuaded the new prime minister from entertaining this idea any further. They could have advised him differently only if an influential IMF member had declared Hungary a candidate for the Brady initiative, despite its past payment performance.

Hungary not only heeded the advice of its official creditors but also followed the commercial banks' demands. An IIF team visited Hungary in May 1990. At that time, as pointed out above, banks were wary of committing new money; in addition, they had begun to withdraw short-term inter-bank deposits following the Bulgarian moratorium. The IIF argued in a confidential report that to restore normal financing patterns Hungary had to do much better than was required in the ongoing programme with the Fund: that is, a current account deficit of $550 million (IIF 1990b). The IIF raised the target to a $200 million deficit. Instead of availing themselves of the Fund's authority to stay with the easier conditions, the Hungarians took the IIF's requests at face value and, in the end, even outdid the banks' expectations. The banks have no reason to be unhappy with Hungary's performance. Daniel Cohen calculated that the commercial banks, from 1983 to 1989, managed to recover 54 per cent of their loans to Hungary in 1982 (1992, 6–10). This compares with an (unweighted) average of 44 per cent

Table 1.5 Debt/GNP: the Baker 15, Hungary, Poland, South Korea and Turkey

Year	Argentina	Bolivia	Brazil	Chile	Colombia	C.d'I	Ecuador	Mexico	Morocco	Nigeria
1982	83.8	114.7	34.8	76.7	27.0	111.4	66.9	53.4	84.9	17.2
1983	81.4	151.2	50.6	98.8	30.1	124.8	77.5	66.6	100.4	21.0
1984	67.5	164.9	52.3	113.8	32.3	133.1	89.2	57.3	116.9	20.2
1985	84.2	176.6	49.0	143.3	42.9	154.6	77.4	55.2	136.5	22.2
1986	70.5	156.0	43.7	141.6	46.0	127.8	90.1	82.5	111.3	51.7
1987	76.4	144.1	42.3	124.5	48.9	143.1	106.8	82.1	116.7	133.9
1988	66.5	117.9	34.3	97.1	45.2	148.3	115.2	60.4	99.5	113.2
1989	119.1	96.9	25.6	76.8	44.7	187.3	120.5	47.2	101.2	119.1
1990	61.7	101.0	22.8	73.6	44.3	203.9	120.6	42.1	97.1	117.9
Memo item: average annual per capitum growth rates										
GDP	−0.3	−0.9	3.0	2.7	3.5	1.2	1.9	0.7	4.1	−0.4
Investment	−7.8	−11.6	0.7	2.7	0.3	−12.1	−3.2	−5.0	4.5	−12.9
Population	1.4	2.7	2.2	1.7	2.0	4.1	2.7	2.1	2.6	3.4

Notes: C.d'I = Côte d'Ivoire.
Sources: World Bank, *World Debt Tables*; *World Development Report 1991*.

for the twenty most indebted countries. Although total arrears, mostly from severely indebted middle-income countries to private creditors, added up to $110 billion in 1990 (compared to only $40 billion in 1986), banks in 1991 received on average 64 per cent of due interest, compared to only 55 per cent in 1990. If one did the same exercise for a time period into the early 1990s, taking account of the liquidation value of the debt in the secondary market, the figure would even rise considerably.

When the new Hungarian government decided to continue to honour its external obligations fully, commercial banks had just concluded, under the Brady Plan, a debt and debt service reduction (DDSR) agreement with Mexico. Also in February 1990, the Paris Club had consolidated $9.4 billion of long overdue and previously rescheduled Polish debt. By that time, Hungary was in its fourth year as a net capital exporter. Mexico was the first country to receive the Brady treatment; in Poland, Western governments saw the need to remove the debt overhang in order to start the transition to a viable market economy. In a sense, Mexico's past adjustment and reforms were given credit with the DDSR package. Poland, in contrast, was given credit to render possible its future reforms. Both initiatives were thus motivated by the political interest (creditor) governments had in guaranteeing the success of ambitious reform projects in two strategic countries. Could Hungary have qualified for this sort of treatment?

Tables 1.5 and 1.6 show that Hungary's debt burden, measured as debt and debt service ratios, is comparable to that of a number of the original Baker 15. Noteworthy is the rapid increase of the debt service ratio in 1990

Table 1.5   *cont.*

Year	Peru	Philippines	Uruguay	Venezuela	Yugoslavia	Hungary	Poland	S. Korea	Turkey
1982	45.0	66.9	29.6	–	31.5	46.3	–	52.3	38.2
1983	63.4	71.6	68.7	48.4	43.8	52.3	–	50.8	40.9
1984	65.8	77.1	68.2	63.8	44.4	55.6	–	48.4	44.8
1985	90.8	83.9	89.7	59.1	48.2	70.2	48.7	52.5	50.5
1986	70.0	94.6	70.0	58.2	33.3	74.0	51.5	45.5	58.0
1987	71.1	87.2	60.8	74.3	34.6	77.9	69.9	31.0	61.6
1988	104.3	74.3	52.6	59.6	35.0	69.5	64.0	21.1	59.3
1989	73.5	64.3	50.4	77.8	26.0	73.7	66.7	15.6	53.6
1990	60.1	65.4	46.9	71.0	23.7	65.6	82.4	14.4	46.3
Memo item: average annual per capitum growth rates									
GDP	0.4	0.7	0.1	1.0	1.3	1.6	2.5	9.7	5.1
Investment	–4.5	–7.8	–7.9	–3.8	–0.4	–1.2	2.1	11.6	3.7
Population	2.3	2.5	0.6	2.8	0.7	–0.2	0.7	1.2	2.4

when Hungary paid almost half of its export proceeds on interest and repayment of principal. According to the World Bank classification, Hungary has graduated from SIMIC (severely indebted middle-income country) to MIMIC (moderately indebted MIC) in recent years. In other words, the severity of its indebtedness has decreased. This is based on a three-year average of four debt indicators, namely debt/GNP, debt/exports, debt service/exports and interest/exports. Since three of these indicators deteriorated markedly in 1990 while only one (debt/GNP) improved a bit, it is not clear why Hungary's situation has supposedly improved (World Bank 1991, 17).

Of course, how heavy a debt burden is depends on growth; nothing in the table indicates that Hungary should be in a group with, say, Korea and Turkey rather than with the rest. Hence, the essential difference between Hungary and the original Baker 15 remains the accumulation of arrears. No arrears, in short, also means no relief. Does it mean easier access to new funds, or at better conditions? Among middle-income countries, Hungary has traditionally been a major borrower on the capital markets, along with South Korea, Malaysia, Thailand and Turkey. In 1990, Hungary still managed to borrow roughly $1 billion, mostly through bond issues. But in the first half of 1991, new international lending dropped to $300 million; Mexico, in contrast, raised $1.25 billion. Average terms of new commitments are shown in Table 1.7; it is evident that countries with a record of arrears do not necessarily get stiffer treatment than Hungary. Note that Poland, the debtor with the worst debt service record of all the countries in

Table 1.6 Debt service/exports ratios: the Baker 15, Hungary, Poland, South Korea and Turkey

Year	Argentina	Bolivia	Brazil	Chile	Colombia	C.d'I	Ecuador	Mexico	Morocco	Nigeria
1982	50.0	59.2	81.3	71.3	29.5	46.0	78.4	56.8	43.2	16.2
1983	69.7	51.3	55.1	54.5	38.3	49.6	29.6	51.7	38.9	2
1984	52.4	63.2	46.3	59.9	30.0	40.6	37.7	52.1	26.8	33.8
1985	58.9	49.5	38.6	48.6	41.9	44.7	33.0	51.5	33.3	33.8
1986	76.2	36.6	47.0	41.5	32.4	48.5	43.4	54.2	36.8	32.7
1987	74.3	33.5	41.9	36.5	35.1	43.3	34.0	40.1	31.7	13.4
1988	44.5	49.1	48.2	23.5	41.6	39.2	40.2	48.0	27.2	29.4
1989	36.2	31.0	29.8	27.1	46.0	40.8	36.4	37.9	33.3	23.2
1990	34.1	39.8	21.8	25.9	38.9	38.6	33.2	27.8	23.4	20.3
Memo item: average annual per capitum growth rates										
GDP	−0.3	−0.9	3.0	2.7	3.5	1.2	1.9	0.7	4.1	−0.4
Investment	−7.8	−11.6	0.7	2.7	0.3	−12.1	−3.2	−5.0	4.5	−12.9
Population	1.4	2.7	2.2	1.7	2.0	4.1	2.7	2.1	2.6	3.4

Notes: See table 1.5.
Source: World Bank, *World Debt Tables 1990–91.*

the table, in 1990 paid more than half a percentage point less on new commitments than Hungary. So the answer is no: a good repayment record is less decisive for the availability and terms of new credits than other factors which affect the expected returns on the loans. This conclusion is supported by other analysts. Peter Lindert has regressed a series of variables, generally held to be determinants of the accessibility of credit markets, on the terms on which new loans from official creditors were given. They included the absolute nominal public and publicly guaranteed debt in 1981; the share of the former held by official creditors; debt service/GNP in 1981; reserves/imports in 1981; GDP/capitum in 1985; money stock growth; defaults (pre-1929; in 1930s; anytime 1940–81); rescheduled anytime 1979–85; years since first rescheduling. The dataset consisted of 51 debtors (of which Hungary was one); regressions were run for 1985. Lindert examined interest rates charged on new official loans as well as the level of new loans from private and official creditors. He found that the past payment record had no significant influence on either the interest rate or the level of official credit; in fact, the sign was negative except for pre-1929 defaults. Strongly significant were only the absolute debt size and per capita income (1989, 238–45).

The expected returns on the loans, as pointed out before, directly depend on the existence of a debt overhang. This is also reflected in price developments on the secondary market. Hungarian debt entered the market in 1989, at a negligible discount. Prices went down to almost 75 per cent until early 1990 and remained there for about a year. This coincided with the

Peru	The Philippines	Uruguay	Venezuela	Yugoslavia	Hungary	Poland	South Korea	Turkey
48.7	42.6	30.5	29.5	20.9	24.9	–	22.4	29.5
39.3	36.4	27.6	26.8	21.9	22.7	–	21.2	33.2
32.4	33.5	36.4	25.2	27.0	25.3	–	21.3	27.9
30.2	31.8	42.7	25.0	19.4	36.8	15.5	27.3	34.8
24.3	34.6	32.0	45.3	21.0	37.9	12.8	26.7	35.5
11.9	38.0	37.4	37.8	19.4	31.1	14.2	32.3	36.0
6.4	32.0	38.9	43.8	16.8	28.9	10.6	14.8	38.0
6.8	25.3	29.4	24.5	14.8	27.6	9.4	11.8	32.3
10.8	21.2	41.0	20.9	13.7	48.7	4.9	10.7	28.0
0.4	0.7	0.1	1.0	1.3	1.6	2.5	9.7	5.1
−4.5	−7.8	−7.9	−3.8	−0.4	−1.2	2.1	11.6	3.7
2.3	2.5	0.6	2.8	0.7	−0.2	0.7	1.2	2.4

election campaign and Antall's ruling-out of debt renegotiations. Over 1991, the value fell further to the lower sixties. In contrast, as already alluded to above, secondary market prices of debt held against actual or potential Brady countries, especially the larger ones (Venezuela, Mexico and, within limits, even Brazil), recovered. By 1991, the discount was reduced as follows: Chile, 10–15 per cent; Venezuela, 30 per cent; Mexico, 40 per cent; Brazil, 65–75 per cent. Citicorp, a major creditor of Argentina, expected to collect 100 cents on the dollar after the April 1992 DDSR agreement with the country. This is because the bank acquired very profitable companies in debt-for-equity operations.

None of the countries discussed here has ever received debt relief without having asked for it first. What counted was (next to obvious factors such as how important the debtor was to governments in the capital market countries) how persistently the debtor pursued its request for debt relief. As Charles Kindleberger put it in his history of financial crises: 'There is ... a political dimension to all rescue operations that are not generalised in the way that open-market operations are: who is helped, and who not' (1989, 241). In this respect, it may be more appropriate to use Poland rather than the Brady countries as a basis for comparison. After two reschedulings in 1982, Polish negotiators antagonised bankers by demanding that their outstanding liabilities be rescheduled over 20 years, starting with an eight-year grace period ('Turning the Screw', 1983). At that time, bankers considered reschedulings over eight and grace periods of four years as long. The country got less than it had asked for (ten years' maturity and four-and-a-half-years' grace), but that was still

Table 1.7 Average terms of new commitments: the Brady countries, Hungary, Poland, South Korea and Turkey

Year	Mexico	Venezuela	Costa Rica	Uruguay	The Philippines	Argentina	Brazil	Hungary	Poland	South Korea	Turkey
1982	14.2	15.9	5.2	12.6	10.8	11.1	12.6	11.3	–	11.3	9.9
1983	10.6	11.5	8.1	12.0	8.5	11.9	11.0	9.9	–	9.5	8.9
1984	11.4	9.7	6.8	10.4	7.5	10.6	12.5	10.6	–	9.5	9.1
1985	9.4	8.6	7.6	11.4	8.5	10.2	9.1	8.4	5.0	8.5	8.6
1986	8.6	7.9	7.9	8.0	5.3	8.0	8.3	7.3	6.3	7.6	7.2
1987	7.6	8.0	6.8	8.2	5.4	8.3	7.8	7.2	6.9	7.1	7.0
1988	8.1	8.4	8.4	9.5	4.8	7.8	9.4	7.1	6.6	7.6	7.6
1989	8.5	8.7	6.5	8.4	4.3	8.5	8.6	8.9	9.3	8.3	7.8
1990	8.6	8.3	6.9	9.2	6.0	8.5	8.5	8.9	8.3	7.1	8.9

Source: World Bank, *World Debt Tables 1990–91.*

substantial in comparison to other rescheduling deals. The EC was afraid to let Poland slip into default because that would have brought losses to Western European trade and banking. In the OECD, the EC obtained a softening of the position of the Reagan Administration on the Jaruzelski government by agreeing, in exchange, to higher interest rates on export credits to all CMEA countries. The USA, in turn, was then willing to consider the stretching of Poland's maturities ('The Bear Necessities', 1982). Ten years, a series of rescheduling rounds and $ 1 billion of interest arrears later, Poland resumed its talks with the banks to restructure its $ 12.1 billion commercial debt ('Poland to Resume Talks with the Banks', 1993; see also Aggarwal and Allan 1992; World Economy Research Institute 1992, 128).

Figure 1.2 shows that most debtors for which DDSR deals were arranged managed to reduce net capital outflows. This is true both for 'model' debtor Mexico and for 'bad guys' Brazil and Poland. It does not apply to Venezuela, whose terms of trade deteriorated rapidly in the second half of the 1980s, due to the fall in oil prices. By contrast, Hungary exported more than 6 per cent of its income abroad in 1990. Its capital outflows thus increased in the very year that such a drain on resources was most uncalled for (see Figure 1.3). The switch to a market economy and the breakdown of the CMEA trading system entailed a severe recession; naturally, it would be desirable to be able to cope with the problems associated with the transition and not to have to deal with the debt overhang. Put differently, if Hungary

Figure 1.2   Capital flows as percentage of GNP, weighted by terms of trade

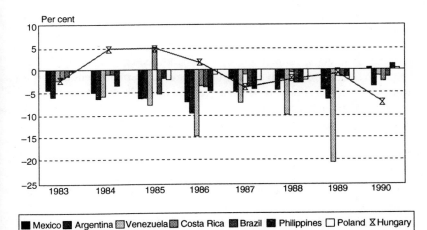

Figure 1.3   Cumulative financial flows between Hungary and all creditors, 1983–91

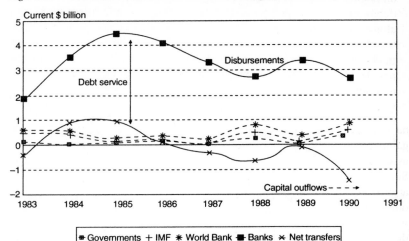

could obtain financing on similar conditions (that is, at least as much money and at least as good conditions discounted by whatever the country saves by not servicing all or parts of its liabilities) even if it had defaulted, then life would be easier now. Until 1994, Hungary has to come up with some $4 billion annually for debt service. About $1.5 of this represents interest payments. Assuming that principal repayments are rolled over (which, in turn, assumes that Hungary's creditors do not retreat from the region) interest has to be financed by a budget surplus, excess savings or FDI. As long as the latter is forthcoming at the present rate (see Chapter 4), the problem is less pressing. If it stops, further contraction would become necessary (Oblath 1992). A recession clearly helps to achieve a current-account surplus because it constrains import demand. Yet one of the lessons from the management of the debt crisis is that a 'created' (as opposed to a 'produced') trade surplus at the cost of growth is neither desirable nor, ultimately, enforceable for an unlimited period. 'Created' refers to restrictive demand management while 'produced' refers to non-recessionary restructuring. Robert Devlin has summarised this recognition as follows:

> transfers based on recessionary adjustment are perverse because payment is made at the expense of present welfare as well as the future productive capacity of the borrower. Moreover, they are especially

damaging when circumstances demand an important restructuring of the debtor economy's productive structure as opposed to a mere expansion along a path that is similar to the existing pattern of production. In contrast, with appropriate time and finance, cooperative debtors can be made to efficiently produce the trade surplus needed to pay debts. In any perspective other than a short-sighted one this is clearly a more satisfactory solution for both creditor and debtor. (1989, 245–6)

All the debtors described in this chapter who have obtained debt relief have at some point opposed the continued outflow of resources. The bargaining they engaged in was based on different political and economic assets and couched in terms that went from conciliatory to confrontational. Some had influential friends in high places (Mexico), others successfully argued for a transition-to-democracy bonus (the Philippines), and yet others moved things by their sheer weight (Brazil). In order to speculate whether Hungary could have followed alternative paths of action one must determine which of the illustrated strategies is representative beyond the specific case. Advice to debtor countries is normally limited to those that have already run up arrears and are thus practically in default (Griffiths-Jones 1988a, 1988b; Devlin 1989, Ch. 4). Performing debtors are in the minority and, presumably, do not have a problem, for if they did they would not be performing. That, in essence, is the going wisdom. Exceptions are rare (Dornbusch 1990). Hence, the available advice is not particularly helpful to Hungary. Simply slipping into default by declaring a moratorium the way Peru, Ecuador or Brazil did (or, with less fanfare but *de facto* with a similar result, as Mexico and Argentina) appears not to be a viable option. When Hungary's liquidity was threatened by the withdrawal of deposits in 1982 and in 1990, the rescue operations mounted by the IMF and the BIS were predicated upon the MNB's meeting payment schedules. The Fund argued in accordance with the rules and tried to persuade the banks not to punish a country simply because it had a 'neighbourhood problem'. Deliberately piling up arrears would probably have removed the IFI's protective cover because the Fund was always convinced that Hungary's debt service was sustainable. In fact, as long as the Hungarians propagated this view themselves, there was no reason for anybody, including Western governments, to think differently. A historical perspective on the debt crisis reveals many different ways creditors dealt with debtors, from British gunboat diplomacy *vis-à-vis* Venezuela in 1902 to the Marshall Plan as the ultimate form of enlightened concessionary financing, but there is no episode where a creditor government forced debt relief upon a debtor openly declaring that it did not need it.

If the late Németh or the early Antall governments had wanted to argue for debt relief, they could have counted on at least two assets; namely, an influential friend in high places and their reputation for being able financial managers. First, Hungary had eased the plight of East German refugees by allowing them free passage to West Germany. Whether or not this contributed to the eventual demise of East Germany, Bonn 'owed' Budapest. The West German government, in 1990, guaranteed a large loan by German banks to Hungary when all other private creditors deserted the country. Undoubtedly, this was politically motivated. It was up to the Hungarians to exploit West Germany's willingness to be helpful. They could have asked for debt relief to stabilise an emerging democracy and ensure the transition to a viable market economy. More specifically, they could have argued that the Hungarian people should not be made to pay for credit extended by imprudent bankers to a communist leadership that had wasted much of those funds. Capital outflows might have been stopped, at least for some time. Western governments have responded to such a situation, as when Turkey entered a debt crisis in the late 1970s. The 1980 adjustment package took the form of sizeable debt relief and new lending from the Fund and the Bank, as well as from bilateral sources. The latter was partly concessional. The resource inflow freed Turkey from having to run a surplus on the non-interest current account. Capital flows turned negative only after five years, thus allowing much space to steer an ambitious reform programme geared toward a more outward-oriented economic system (similar to what the Eastern European countries are trying to do today). The IFIs like to refer to Turkey as one of their babies that 'made it' because of the correct exchange rate policy. Undoubtedly, the reforms in Turkey had much to do with the country's impressive growth performance in the 1980s (Celâsun and Rodrik 1989). However, it is often forgotten that this success was facilitated by truly concessional financing more reminiscent of the post-war aid disbursements than the tough rescheduling terms typical for the (especially early) 1980s.

To be sure, the German government may have expected something in return for a more lenient treatment of outstanding Hungarian obligations. In other words, having tolerated a large number of East German refugees perhaps would not have bought the Hungarians a free lunch in Bonn. Rather, they may have faced demands to extend informal privileges to German industry, for example, in public procurement, especially telecommunications; in negotiations with foreign investors about forthcoming privatisation deals; and possibly even with respect to German manufacturing exports. This rightly would have been criticised as managed trade by Hungary's other trading partners, the GATT and the IFIs. But unfortunately such practices are pervasive anyway: bribery in lucrative public procurement contracts or select import protection in order to accommodate large foreign investors has been characteristic for the transition economies of Central and Eastern Europe. Realistically, the point is to judge whether the afforded debt relief would have been worth the price (of having to eat lunch in Bonn), and for how long.

There is no way of knowing if the French, Japanese and Swiss governments, whose banks hold most Hungarian debt, would have gone along, individually or collectively, with a German proposal. But even if they had rejected a concerted effort to organise debt relief, Bonn could have gone it alone at least for some time. About 50 per cent of Hungarian debt is owed to German banks that have built high provisions against problem debts. In addition, they sit on large hidden reserves. Banking regulations in Germany give banks indefinite tax breaks on provisions so that some form of organised and agreed-upon payment delay would have been possible without endangering the banks' health. In 1989, the discount on Hungarian debt in the secondary market was very low; hence, any unfairness perceived by the German banks *vis-à-vis* their Japanese or French competitors would have been limited to the payment schedule but not to the value of the claims. The German government may have asked, in turn, for a positive discrimination towards its exports by Hungary, relative to imports originating in the countries opposed to debt relief. This, in a sense, resembles the establishment of seniority among creditors across different sectors, namely credit and commerce.

Hungary is not a strategically important neighbour for Germany in the sense that, say, Russia is; throwing its light weight around would not have helped much. But Hungary did have a second asset: a reputation for financial management expertise. Relative to the rest of the eastern crowd, Hungarian central bankers were perceived as able managers, who knew how to administer their portfolios, by their peers in the West. This is perhaps best illustrated by János Fekete, the National Bank's long-serving Deputy Director. He visited the governor of the Bank of England in 1982 to ask for BIS assistance and was successful in defusing the first liquidity crisis. His eloquence won him respect in London, Frankfurt and New York, and he was probably the best-liked eastern banker. His contention in the late 1980s that Central Europe was *under*borrowed seems ironic in retrospect (and was certainly an opinion many officials in the MNB did not share in private), but he rarely returned empty-handed from a credit mission. He tried to hedge against exchange rate risks by diversifying the Hungarian reserve positions, but later speculated on a dollar revaluation and lost the country money. Although he became increasingly controversial in Hungary in the second half of the 1980s and was not associated with the reformers, his financial wizardry probably helped the country considerably through the first adjustment period. The point here is that the (early) kind of professionalism he represented as Hungary's foremost money manager could have been used to design credible alternative adjustment plans for the transition.

The country's reputation also depended on the perception that the personnel in the MNB were highly trained and qualified individuals. If Hungary had had the backing, in principle, by a creditor government for some kind of debt relief, it could have thrown its good reputation into designing a plan to meet restructured obligations. I have argued that there is no premium on being a nice debtor. This is borne out by the evidence comparing Hungary's treatment in the capital markets to that of other major (and naughty) debtors. It suggests that there may have been a premium for trying something different from the professed debt management strategy. The banks and the IMF would not agree with this conclusion and rather claim that 'nothing is more important for the attractiveness of a country than its debt service record' (Schulmann 1992, 9). But this argument hinges on the construction of a myth. The analysis in this chapter suggests that, without political support, debt relief would have been too costly to justify. But with such support, which perhaps needs to be provoked by sophisticated bargaining, the country could have obtained an easing of what, in effect, is an adjustment tax on its reform project. Without the latter, no doubt, the country would be better off today.

2 The Management of Industrial Policy and Trade

This chapter tries to assess the competitiveness of Hungarian industry in the 1980s. It considers explanations generally given for the dismal performance of firms, both in production and in exports. It suggests that these explanations are *de facto* not as all-encompassing as they purport to be. It then looks for additional causes that would clarify the puzzle as to why the most reform-minded CMEA country was, in many ways, not much better off than its Central European neighbours. In Chapter 3, attention is given, first, to OECD protectionism and how Hungary reacted to it. Second, I discuss ideas about development strategies held by the Hungarian policy elite.

INDUSTRY AND TRADE IN THE 1980s

Industrial Structure and Production

In 1989, more than two-thirds of Hungary's GDP was produced by agriculture and industry, and 66 per cent of the latter originated in manufacturing. Over the 1980s, the relatively high share of agriculture remained stable; the same goes for manufacturing. Industry, while contributing 59 per cent to GDP in 1980, fell to 36 per cent by 1989. This trend compares with similar developments in OECD economies but is untypical for the other countries classified as upper-middle income by the World Bank, such as South Korea and Brazil. Unlike in those NICs, the Hungarian service sector's share in GDP almost doubled. In the NICs also, the share of manufacturing in output remained relatively constant, though on average at a slightly higher level (see Table 2.1). Thus, the composition and development of Hungarian GDP in the 1980s is more similar to the composition and to trends typical for the OECD (and in manufacturing also for the NICs) than those that characterise its Central European neighbours. In both Poland and Czechoslovakia, the industry component is more important, while services account only for one-quarter to one-third of total output. This comparison somewhat conceals the dual nature of Hungarian foreign trade. As will become evident from the analysis of the commodity composition of Hungarian exports below, Hungary's trade with the CMEA resembled that of an industrial country (that is, with a high proportion of relatively sophisticated

63

Table 2.1   Percentage distribution of GDP production in 1980 and 1989

Countries	Agriculture		Industry		Manufacture*		Service, etc.†		GDP‡	
	1980	1989	1980	1989	1980	1989	1980	1989	1980	1989
Hungary	14	14	59	36	26	24§	27	50	–	29
Czechoslovakia	8	6	75	57	55	48§	14	36	–	50
Poland	15	–	64	–	44	39§	21	–	–	68
Hong Kong	1	0	–	28	22	21	–	72	20	53
South Korea	16	10	41	44	30	31	43	46	58	212
Brazil	10	9	37	43	30	27	53	48	238	319
Malaysia	24	–	37	–	21	23§	39	–	24	37
Portugal	13	9	46	37	31	27§	41	54	22	45
Spain	8	5	37	9	27	26	55	86	198	379
Austria	4	3	41	37	28	27	55	60	77	126
West Germany	2	2	–	37	32	31	–	62	819	1 189

Notes: *Manufacturing shown separately because typically the most dynamic part of industrial sector.
† Services etc. include unallocated items.
‡ GDP in $ billion. All figures shown at purchaser values except for Hong Kong and Brazil.
§ Estimate.

Figures in italics are for 1979.

Sources: UNIDO, *Industry and Development. Global Report 1991/92*; World Bank, *World Development Report 1982, 1991.*

manufactures). But in trade with OECD economies, Hungary exported products more similar to those of developing countries, including the NICs.

Through the 1970s, Hungary realised higher growth rates of per capita manufacturing value added (MVA) (4.7 per cent) than Czechoslovakia (3.8 per cent), Portugal (2.8 per cent), Poland (2.6 per cent) and Spain (0.3 per cent). In 1981, its contribution to world MVA was higher than that of Greece, Finland and Denmark (United Nations Industrial Development Organization,or UNIDO, 1985, 23/33). According to the UN's *Industrial Statistics Yearbook*, industries that became less important in the production of MVA during the 1970s included food, iron and steel and non-electrical machinery, while the share of industrial and other chemicals, electrical machinery, transport equipment and professional and scientific equipment increased.

In the 1980s, the textiles and clothing industry decreased its share in MVA along with food products and non-ferrous metals, as well as transport equipment. The share of chemicals and iron and steel increased. Other important sectors (defined as having a higher than 3 per cent share in total MVA in 1988) include wearing apparel (3.02 per cent); other non-metal, mineral products (3.03 per cent); metal products (4.02 per cent); non-electric machinery (10.26 per cent); professional and scientific equipment (5.42 per cent). As for transport equipment, this sector lost its share in MVA although it had grown during the 1970s. In turn, the iron and steel sector, losing share in the 1970s, increased its share during the 1980s. Only industrial and other chemicals increased their share over both periods. For food, sectoral output measured in constant terms relative to total manufacturing output increased significantly regardless of its loss in MVA. Of course, that is problematic (see Table 2.2).

A look at MVA from 1970 to 1988 shows that Hungarian output in the engineering branches changed by only 7 per cent, similar to Czechoslovakia. The rapid industrialisation of the East Asian NICs is reflected in average growth rates of between 37 per cent in Hong Kong and 191 per cent in South Korea. Of course, the NICs started out at a much lower level of development and have since come a long way. After the Second World War, they were underdeveloped countries, whereas the Central European economies were not. In terms of level, the share of the Hungarian machinery and transport equipment branches falls roughly in between those of West Germany and Austria and the other Central European countries. It is significantly higher than the respective shares for Portugal, Spain, Brazil and Malaysia, a second-tier NIC (see Table 2.3).

UNIDO calculates structural change as the change in the share of all branches in total MVA over a certain period (UNIDO 1991, A4). By this

Table 2.2   Branch structure of industry by gross production in constant 1986 prices

Branches	1975	1980	1989	1980/89
Mining	9.2	8.1	5.7	–2.4
Electric energy	5.1	5.7	6.2	0.5
Metallurgy	10.0	9.1	10.5	1.4
Engineering	24.0	23.5	24.8	1.3
Building material	3.2	3.5	3.1	–0.4
Chemical industry	16.3	18.6	18.5	–0.1
Light industry	14.4	13.7	12.4	–1.3
Food industry	16.8	16.7	17.8	1.1
Miscellaneous	1.0	1.1	0.8	
Total	100.0	100.0	100.0	

Source: HCSO *Statistical Yearbook 1989–1990*.

measure, compared to the other countries used here for reference purposes, Hungary has undergone one of the lowest degrees of structural change over the 15-year period to 1990. The fact that the index of change is higher for all subperiods than in the case of Taiwan, for example, suggests that structural change in Hungary has not been unidirectional (see Table 2.4).

In sum, the industrial profile of Hungary suggests an economy at a relatively advanced level of development. In terms of the sectoral division of its capital stock, the country saw happier days in the 1970s than during the 1980s. In the earlier period, engineering and other advanced industrial activities gained in importance relative to raw-material intensive or heavy industry. Developments in the 1980s partly reversed this trend. Various indicators suggest a low degree of structural change. The country has been slow at adapting to changes in the world economy in the last two decades. Its problem is not underdevelopment, but *mis*development.

Trade: Direction and Composition

Over the 1980s, Hungary's trade flows became increasingly westward-oriented. In 1979, a third of its imports originated in Western Europe while 28.5 per cent of its exports went there. By 1990, Hungary undertook more than half of its external trade with industrialised market economies, and about a third with the European members of the CMEA. On average, the Eastern European members of CMEA sold 25.2 per cent of their exports to Western Europe in 1980 and decreased their share to 19.3 per cent by 1988 (UNCTAD 1990, 81–2). Thus, Hungary's westward orientation was considerably higher in relative terms than that of the other Eastern European

Table 2.3 Distribution of manufacturing value added (%)

Countries	Food/agriculture		Textiles/clothing		Machinery/transport equipment		Chemicals		Other manufactures	
	1970	*1988*	*1970*	*1988*	*1970*	*1988*	*1970*	*1988*	*1970*	*1988*
Hungary	12	8	13	10	28	30	8	14	39	38
Czechoslovakia	9	8	12	10	34	36	6	7	39	39
Poland	20	9	19	16	24	32	8	7	28	36
Hong Kong	4	6	41	38	16	22	2	2	36	33
South Korea	26	11	17	15	11	32	11	9	36	33
Brazil	16	14	13	10	22	21	10	13	39	42
Malaysia	26	18	3	6	8	23	9	13	54	39
Portugal	18	16	19	23	13	13	10	10	39	38
Spain	13	19	15	8	16	24	11	10	45	39
Austria	17	16	12	7	19	26	6	7	45	44
West Germany	13	9	8	4	32	41	9	13	38	32

Note: Figures for Poland, South Korea and Malaysia at purchaser values.
Source: World Bank, *World Development Report 1991.*

Table 2.4   Average structural change of manufacturing value added, in degrees

Countries	1975–80	1980–85	1985–89	1975–90
Hungary	5.34	4.99	6.80	11.30
Czechoslovakia	3.32	2.96	3.12	12.31
Poland	6.03	14.02	9.27	13.50
South Korea	7.55	4.81	3.52	28.55
Taiwan	5.14	3.18	3.72	19.72
Brazil	4.04	6.03	5.20	18.48
Malaysia	5.17*	8.00	4.98	25.20
Portugal	5.30	7.02	5.18	12.00
Spain	5.46	3.43	4.94	22.64
Austria	4.18	4.99	4.29	13.15
West Germany	2.72	3.47	1.86	17.43

Notes: *Estimate. For reference to calculation of degrees, see text. Theoretical maximum value is 90.
Source: UNIDO, *Industry and Development. Global Report 1991/92.*

countries throughout the 1980s; and it followed a trend in the opposite direction from theirs. This orientation becomes especially evident when measured in volume terms. Thus, while total rouble exports to the CMEA in 1989 were only 41.2 per cent higher than in 1980 and non-rouble exports to the same group actually fell by 31.5 per cent, non-rouble transactions with all developed market economies (DMEs) grew by 72.6 per cent. Within this group, trade with the European Free Trade Association (EFTA) almost doubled, tripled with the USA and increased 9.5 times with Japan. Exports to China, too, grew by 131.9 per cent (OECD 1991, 189). Except for 1988 and 1990, Hungary has reported trade deficits with its Western trade partners since 1970.[1] Until 1981, this was characteristic for European CMEA members. Afterwards the only other countries persistently running deficits with the West were Bulgaria and, from 1987, the GDR (UNECE 1990, 143).

The increase in exports to the West corresponded with a decrease in trade with the other CMEA countries – rapidly towards the end of the 1980s – and with LDCs. Hungary's commercial relations with LDCs have been notoriously unstable. Only imports from the Middle East are really significant (Balvany 1988). By 1990 the EC had become the single most important trading partner, surpassing by itself all of Hungary's trade with CMEA. In terms of individual countries, Hungary consistently sold more than 60 per cent of its hard-currency exports to the G-5, with West Germany, the USA and Japan ranking among the first three markets. Among all developed country trade partners, individual market shares are highest for West Germany, Austria and Italy. The Japanese, USA and Common Market make up four-fifths of Hungary's trade with developed market economies.

Table 2.5 shows the commodity composition of Hungary's major export groups. By 1990, more than half of its food exports went to DMEs. This registers an increase of 20 per cent since 1979. With the LDCs' and CMEA's shares shrinking by the same amount, a proper East/South–West market shift took place during the 1980s. Almost all agricultural raw materials go into the West. The EC market has become the most voluminous, while EFTA's share has shrunk. Ores and metals are also an export item with a strong westward trend, most – if not all – of which is accounted for by the EC. In the market for fuels, EFTA lost much of its weight throughout the 1980s but still remained Hungary's biggest partner in 1990. Again, the EC absorbed progressively more imports while among the CPEs only the extra-European ones gained some. For manufactures, all eastern markets became smaller. In 1984, the CMEA imported 58.1 per cent of Hungarian manufacturing exports. The figure fell by more than one-third by 1990. All Western markets increased in importance. This is especially true for the EC whose share doubled between 1984 and 1990. In sum, the EC has become Hungary's most important market for food products, agricultural raw materials, and ores and metals. In fuels, EFTA absorbs more than half of Hungarian exports, while 40 per cent of manufactured exports go to Western Europe, and more than a third to CMEA. The East–West shift has been most pronounced in food products, yet is also very considerable in ores and metals as well as manufactures.

Table 2.6 shows the weight of different commodity groups in Hungary's exports. With the exception of an increase in ores and metals and a sharp fall in fuels, the aggregate (that is, exports to the world) commodity composition remained fairly stable over the 1980s.[2] It resembles – in trend if not in magnitude – the commodity composition to all DMEs except that here, trade in manufactures is relatively less important than in agriculture, ores and metals, and fuels. Towards the late 1980s, manufacturing trade becomes more important also with the DMEs, and especially with EFTA countries. Exports of food items decrease to the EC, while they increase for EFTA. With respect to the LDCs, manufactures make up more than four-fifths of all exports. The share of food items fell by almost half between 1984 and 1990. The commodity composition of exports to the CMEA remained fairly stable over the entire period. Noteworthy is a big increase in food products and a decrease in manufactures to centrally planned and transitional economies outside Europe in 1988–90. In sum, manufactures,

Table 2.5 Export structure (values), by destination (%)

Commodities (SITC)	Year	World	DMEs	EC	EFTA*	Other	LDCs	CPEs	CMEA	Other
All products	1984	100.0	34.7	16.2	14.9	3.6	11.4	53.9	49.6	4.3
	1988	100.0	40.5	22.6	13.1	4.8	8.9	50.6	45.5	5.1
	1990	100.0	54.1	32.2	12.0	5.5	8.3	37.6	31.9	5.7
Food	1984	100.0	36.3	25.0	8.5	2.8	11.1	52.6	50.6	2.0
(0+1+22+4)	1988	100.0	47.2	30.4	12.7	4.1	4.8	48.0	45.3	2.7
	1990	100.0	53.2	35.2	10.1	5.1	4.1	42.7	33.3	9.4
Agricultural raw	1984	100.0	76.0	41.0	31.8	3.2	5.0	19.0	7.0	12.0
materials	1988	100.0	84.9	45.3	36.0	3.6	1.9	13.1	4.3	8.8
(2–22–27–28)	1990	100.0	87.8	49.3	24.7	7.0	1.0	11.2	5.2	6.0
Ores and metals	1984	100.0	54.5	20.9	24.9	8.7	6.0	39.5	37.3	2.2
(27+28+68)	1988	100.0	71.8	27.3	33.7	10.8	3.8	24.3	23.4	.9
	1990	100.0	78.2	26.4	15.6	7.6	2.8	19.0	17.0	2.0
Fuels	1984	100.0	89.9	8.0	81.7	0.2	1.6	8.5	5.0	3.5
(3)	1988	100.0	85.0	20.3	64.3	0.4	3.7	11.2	7.9	3.3
	1990	100.0	85.2	25.2	56.8	1.0	1.9	12.9	5.1	7.8
Manufactures	1984	100.0	24.2	13.1	7.0	4.1	12.6	63.5	58.1	5.1
(5+6+68+7+8)	1988	100.0	33.0	19.0	8.9	5.1	10.4	56.5	50.4	6.1
	1990	100.0	48.1	30.4	9.6	5.8	11.1	40.7	35.9	4.8

Notes: *The column also comprises European non-EC/non-EFTA economies. Data for 1990 is likely to be somewhat inaccurate.
Sources: HCSO, Statistical Yearbook of External Trade 1984, 1988, 1990; author's calculations.

Table 2.6   Export structure (values), by commodity groups (%)

Commodities (SITC)	Year	World	DMEs	EC	EFTA*	Other	LDCs	CPEs	CMEA	Other
Food	1984	22.4	23.4	34.4	12.8	17.4	21.8	21.9	22.8	10.6
(0+1+22+4)	1988	20.4	23.7	27.4	19.7	17.0	11.1	19.3	20.3	10.7
	1990	22.7	22.4	24.9	19.2	21.0	11.3	25.8	23.7	37.5
Agricultural raw	1984	2.3	5.1	5.9	5.0	2.1	1.0	0.8	0.3	6.6
materials	1988	2.8	5.9	5.7	7.8	2.1	0.6	0.7	0.3	4.9
(2-22-27-28)	1990	2.8	4.6	4.3	5.8	3.6	0.3	0.8	0.5	3.0
Ores and metals	1984	3.3	5.3	1.3	5.6	8.2	1.8	2.5	2.5	1.7
(27+28+68)	1988	3.8	6.8	4.6	9.9	8.5	1.6	1.8	2.0	0.7
	1990	5.9	8.6	4.9	7.2	8.3	2.0	3.0	3.2	2.0
Fuels	1984	8.6	22.4	4.3	47.3	0.2	1.2	1.4	0.9	7.1
(3)	1988	3.0	6.3	2.7	14.7	0.2	1.3	0.7	0.5	2.0
	1990	3.1	4.9	2.4	14.6	0.6	0.7	1.1	0.5	4.2
Manufactures	1984	61.9	43.2	50.0	29.0	72.0	68.0	72.6	72.5	74.0
(5+6-68+7+8)	1988	68.2	55.5	57.4	46.2	72.0	80.1	76.2	76.6	81.7
	1990	62.8	55.9	59.2	50.5	66.5	84.3	68.0	70.6	53.0

Notes: *The column also comprises European non-EC/non-EFTA economies. Data for 1990 is likely to be somewhat inaccurate.
Sources: HCSO, Statistical Yearbook of External Trade 1984, 1988, 1990; author's calculations.

followed by food items, are the most important export categories from Hungary to all its foreign markets. In general, the export value of manufactures was increasing. Except for the LDCs, food remains a stable export commodity. A disaggregation of the rather broad grouping of manufactures shows that, to all countries, the share of manufacturing and equipment (SITC 7) fell from 37 per cent in 1975 to 30.2 per cent in 1989. Chemicals (SITC 5) grew from 7 per cent in 1975 to 12.4 per cent in 1989. Possibly, this reflects the decreasing contribution of the engineering branches to total MVA described in the previous section. This pattern replicates a trend already discernible in the 1970s (UNCTAD 1990, 147). The commodity composition of Hungarian exports reveals the dual nature of its trading relationships. Within the CMEA, and especially with the Soviet Union, Hungary primarily exchanged manufactures for raw materials. In trade with OECD countries, Hungary exported food, raw materials and (mostly) light manufactures against capital and consumer goods. Problems associated with this duality are discussed further below.

On the import side, the pattern looks a bit different. In 1989, manufactures accounted for 71.2 per cent of imports from all countries. Again, chemicals were the only dynamic part in this category; their share rose from 9.5 per cent in 1970 to 13.4 per cent in 1985 and 16.3 per cent in 1989. Ores and metals fell to the export level. Fuel imports peaked in 1985 at 22.1 per cent and fell to 11.8 per cent, (that is, to early 1970s levels in 1989). Food and agricultural raw materials imports are relatively much smaller than their respective exports (UNCTAD 1990, 169).

In sum, manufactures and food products make up roughly 80 per cent of Hungary's exports. Manufactures and fuels account for 80 per cent of Hungary's imports. Overall, of course, the import structure is somewhat more diversified than the composition of exports. In a recent study published by the London-based Centre for Economic Policy Research (CEPR) the authors claim that Hungary imports primarily raw materials from DMEs (Landesmann and Székely 1991, 25). The commodity breakdown in Table 2.7 shows that to be a misleading claim. In fact, manufactures make up almost 90 per cent of all Hungarian imports from DMEs.[3] Data for 1990 is sensitive, of course, to the disruptions associated with the transformation in Eastern and Central Europe (ECE). However, major changes with respect to 1989 are due to severely higher energy costs. Raw materials as such were not affected (cf. OECD 1991, 199).

In the rouble area, the engineering branch had the largest share of industrial exports. Engineering sales to CPEs consisted, roughly, of one-third transport equipment, one-quarter each of machines and machineries, and precision engineering, and one-seventh of telecommunication and

Table 2.7   Hungarian imports in 1990 (%)

Branches	CPEs*	DMEs	LDCs
By exporting countries			
Food	22.7	38.2	39.1
Agricultural raw materials	49.5	44.3	6.2
Ores and metals	53.0	33.8	13.2
Fuels	73.2	1.9	24.9
Manufactures	29.2	66.8	3.9
By commodity group			
Food	4.6	5.4	29.6
Agricultural raw materials	4.9	3.0	2.3
Ores and metals	5.4	2.4	5.0
Fuels	28.2	0.5	35.5
Manufactures	55.8	88.5	27.6

Notes: *includes transitional economies. Figures may not add to 100 due to rounding.
Source: HCSO, *Statistical Yearbook of External Trade 1990.*

vacuum technology products. More than two-thirds of chemical exports were pharmaceuticals. The share of textiles in light industry exports was higher than a third, similar to the share of the products of the canning and preserving industry in food industry exports. The distribution among the branches remained fairly stable over the 1980s.

In the non-rouble area, the dispersion between and across the branches is much higher. More (and increasingly) important in exports to the West are ferrous and aluminium metallurgy. Oil refining, plastics and synthetics each account for one-fifth of chemical exports. Pharmaceuticals only make up one-sixth of these exports. In engineering exports, machines and machineries account for one-third; transport equipment for one-sixth; electric machinery and appliances for one-seventh; telecommunication and vacuum technology products for one-sixth. More than half of light industry exports are accounted for by textiles (28.6 per cent) and leather, fur and footwear (27.1 per cent). In food industry exports, the meat industry makes up a third; poultry and egg processing almost a quarter; products of the canning and preserving industry a fifth (HCSO 1991).

Compared with the 1970s, structural adjustment slowed down in the 1980s. However, it was more pronounced in non-rouble exports than in rouble exports and production. While non-rouble machinery exports retained a constantly low share in total exports, the major part of industrial production, in general, became more export-oriented (Gács 1989). Table 2.8 illustrates the duality of Hungarian export trade for the major industrial branches. A look at the structure of Hungary's exports to the West alone makes the country seem much less of a mature economy than it actually is. However, such a comparison potentially conveys a distorted picture. Without doubt, it would have been desirable to reduce the weight of raw material-based exports (something that did not happen during the 1980s). Hungary is essentially a resource-poor country. However, that does not apply to agriculture and a few other sectors. Food processing, for example, is potentially a very profitable industry and one which fits Hungary's natural endowments rather well.

To be sure, Hungary had problems in both markets. Terms of trade deteriorated with both the East and the West. This decline was secular. Terms of trade fell by some 25 per cent from 1970 to 1989. The trend improved for the first time in 1987. Despite all these problems, Hungary remained the most open CMEA economy. From the early to the late 1980s, it doubled its exposure to international markets. It is difficult to compare this to any country outside the CMEA. Evidently, the issue was not just one of import substitution as against export promotion. The successful adjusters among the NICs, such as South Korea, began to deliver exports from the late 1970s onwards to the very markets whose exports of capital goods had helped them to build up their industries earlier. In Hungary instead, until the late 1970s, the world market was thought of mostly as a residual to the fulfilment of CMEA planning. In a sense, Hungary did gradually what the rest of CMEA was forced to do more abruptly in 1990. The only other country whose turnover with the OECD increased as rapidly is China. By this comparison, then, the trade shift from Eastern to Western markets was indeed remarkable.

Industrial Policy and Foreign Trade Liberalisation

In 1977, the Hungarian authorities formulated a new approach towards industrial policy.[4] Earlier, industrial policy had targeted sectors such as the computer industry that would, it was believed, benefit the entire economy through technological spill-overs. It was aimed almost exclusively at satisfying the CMEA markets. Neither of these objectives was able to earn the country any foreign exchange of which, towards the late 1970s, it was in increasing need (Brada and Montias 1984, 394–6). The new policy was designed to promote modern, profitable, high-value added goods of high quality throughout the economy. In the words of a government official, '... the basic source for improving equilibrium cannot be anything else but the raising of the efficiency and international competitivity of production' (Havasi 1981, 3).[5] It aimed at specialising the heavily diversified production structure. The importance of hard-currency markets was underlined by the Central Committee's decision to set aside 45 billion forints for investment projects whose output was geared towards Western markets (although this corresponded to less than 10 per cent of the total volume of productive investments in 1976–80). A catalogue of criteria was established to determine access to funds within the new programme. A novel feature was that

Table 2.8   Breakdown of industrial exports (%)

Branch (Hungarian Nomenclature)	Rouble accounts 1982	Rouble accounts 1990	Non-rouble accounts 1982	Non-rouble accounts 1990
Raw-material based	**21.9**	**19.2**	**50.2**	**50.0**
1 Metallurgy	2.9	2.6	8.5	14.4
29 Food processing	10.3	10.8	20.4	19.8
12 Oil refining	0.5	0.2	3.0	3.6
13 Organic/inorganic chemicals	1.7	0.4	2.4	2.2
14 Fertilisers/plant protection	1.4	1.4	3.0	1.9
16 Rubber	0.7	0.7	0.9	1.3
18 Other heavy industry	2.0	1.1	9.4	2.1
20 Wood processing	0.7	0.7	0.3	0.5
21 Paper	0.4	0.4	1.2	1.9
10 Metal mass products	1.3	0.9	1.2	1.9
Traditional	**11.0**	**8.1**	**9.0**	**10.5**
22 Printing	0.2	0.2	0.3	0.4
23 Textiles	4.0	3.3	3.5	3.6
24 Textile clothings	3.4	2.2	1.7	2.3
25 Leather, fur, footwear	2.8	1.9	2.9	3.4
28 Other light	0.6	0.5	0.6	0.8
Modern	**35.0**	**34.2**	**14.2**	**15.1**
15 Plastics, synthetics	0.4	0.8	1.2	3.8
5 Machines, machinery	14.7	14.4	9.0	7.9
6 Transport equipment	19.9	19.0	4.0	3.4
Progressive	**24.9**	**31.2**	**9.9**	**11.5**
7 Electric machinery	2.1	1.8	2.1	3.0
8 Telecommunications	9.0	7.9	3.0	3.5
9 Precision engineering	8.3	13.1	2.2	1.9
17 Pharmaceuticals	5.5	8.4	2.6	3.1

Sources: HCSO, *Statistical Yearbook of External Trade 1984, 1990*; author's calculations.

firms should decide for themselves on profitable investment opportunities and actually, within limits, compete for the allocation of these funds. Direct government intervention was supposed to be reduced, favouring rather indirect instruments. Also, the level of subsidies was reduced (Román and Bayer 1987). Priority sectors included engineering, agriculture and light industry. Within the former, specially targeted product groups were road vehicles, agricultural machinery, machine tools, precision engineering, vacuum technical industries and telecommunications (cf. Brada and Montias 1984, 397).

Since the introduction of the New Economic Mechanism (NEM) in 1968, the most comprehensive industrial policy designs were embodied in so-called Central Development Programmes (CDPs). In the 1980s, five of these programmes were initiated, while one was carried over from the 1970s. Three were supposed to be effective economy-wide, to promote a more efficient use of inputs and save on imports. Any firm or farm was entitled to participate in these programmes. They were called, respectively, Waste and By-product Utilization CDP; Energy Conservation CDP; and Raw Material Conservation CDP.

The two sector-specific programmes reflected a mix of import-substitution and export-orientation. The Pharmaceutical, Plant-Protective Chemicals and Intermediary Products CDP aimed at capacity expansion in order to produce goods that could compete both in the domestic market – to substitute hard-currency intermediary inputs – and in the global market. Marketing efforts were to be based, among others, on the synthesis of new products, the development of commercially viable manufacturing processes, and clinical trials of new products. Primary product groups included heart medicines, arthritic/rheumatic drugs, psychotropic and tropical disease drugs, biologically active preparations and veterinary drugs (cf. Marer 1986, 156–8).

The Electronics CDP aimed at a reduction of both the technology gap and hard-currency imports in this sector, through hard-currency and CMEA technology imports. Increased incorporation of domestic components into tradeables was supposed to lead to indirect export promotion. Hungarian electrical and transistor technologies had never graduated to integrated circuitry so that manufacturers of computers, lighting and professional equipment, telecommunication equipment, medical equipment, and instruments either needed to import components from the West – which was difficult because of the balance of payments constraint – or stop being competitive. Branches that would have benefited from an easier access to electronics components from the West included medical technology, precision instruments, telecommunications and electrical engineering (Marer 1986).[6]

Guidelines for the seventh 5-year plan (1986–90) provided the basis for industrial policy in the second half of the 1980s. The plan tried a difficult balancing act. Its major goals were to preserve the external equilibrium while reviving growth and going ahead with the reforms. The first two, in fact, were not realized. The architects of the plan considered progress at the microeconomic level the greatest challenge, based, of course, on the disappointing 1981–85 plan performance.

> The real problem is whether we can raise the cost and market-sensitivity of firms to a sufficient degree, whether we are able to concentrate investments on technological developments with quick returns, whether we can establish incentives to stimulate higher productivity and capital efficiency in various fields of the economy ... It should be clear ... that the attainment of both the foreign trade objective and the growth target decisively depend on the successful continuation of the reform process of economic control and management. (Nyers 1988, 38)

Industrial production was projected to grow by some 18 per cent; investment by more than 45 per cent. In retrospect, this was clearly unrealistic. Table 2.9 shows that investment outlays fell throughout the 1980s. Operational investments also mostly decreased but by less than investment outlays, which might indicate improved capital efficiency. In real terms, gross industrial production grew by roughly 5 per cent between 1985 and 1989: that is, at less than one-third of the projected rate.

Overall, Hungarian industry retained a bias in favour of energy- and raw material-intensive basic industries. Table 2.10 shows that until 1988, mining, electric energy, metallurgy and building material received almost half of all investments in industry. The share of engineering in total investments was actually reduced. Data on production value, sales and productivity of a number of priority activities and sectors are shown in Table 2.11. With the exception of fertilizers and plant-protectives, the data show a positive trend for all three indicators when comparing 1980 values with those for 1989. Note, however, that some or all (as in the case of pharmaceuticals and electric engineering) of these indicators turn negative when compared to 1988 values. The data need to be compared to average industrial output, sales figures and productivity to allow meaningful conclusions as to how (un)successful Hungarian industrial policy has been. According to Marer, enterprises involved in the six CDPs enjoyed an above-average growth rate relative to total industry (1986, 73). In the second half of the 1980s, the record of some key sectors turned negative. In 1989, gross production value of total industry had increased by 15 per cent over 1980. Thus, the electrical engineering branch remained below average level. The same is

Table 2.9   Investments and production 1981–89

	1981	1982	1983	1984	1985	1986	1987	1988	1989
1980 = 100									
Outlays	94.8	92.7	89.9	87.3	85.3	87.3	93.9	86.7	90.6
In operation	94.8	90.8	98.2	96.8	84.5	101.8	96.5	87.8	96.8
Gross industrial production	102.8	105.3	106.1	109.0	109.8	111.9	116.2	116.2	115.0
Net agricultural production	99.9	144.5	106.6	114.5	104.3	109.4	102.9	113.6	117.6
Previous year = 100									
Outlays	−97.7	102.3	107.6	92.3	104.5	110.3			
In operation		−87.2	120.5	94.8	91.0	101.9			
Gross industrial production					100.7	104.9	103.8	100.0	99.0
Net agricultural production					91.1		94.0	110.4	103.4

Source: HCSO, Statistical Yearbook 1989–1990.

Table 2.10   Distribution of investment in industry (%)

Branch	1981–85	1986	1987	1988	1989
1. Mining	17.5	22.1	20.1	20.3	15.8
2. Electric energy	20.6	18.1	18.9	14.5	14.6
3. Metallurgy	8.1	5.4	4.2	4.8	6.8
4. Chemical industry	15.4	17.6	18.6	20.4	18.3
5. Building material	3.7	3.2	3.0	4.1	6.8
6. Engineering	14.8	12.8	16.4	13.1	11.9
7. Light industry	7.8	8.1	6.9	6.9	8.5
8. Food industry	11.2	12.3	11.4	15.2	16.3
9. Miscellaneous	0.9	0.4	0.5	0.7	1.0
Memo:					
1+2+3	46.2	45.6	43.2	39.6	37.2
6+7+8	33.8	33.2	34.7	35.2	36.7

Source: HCSO, *Statistical Yearbook 1989–1990*.

true for sales and productivity figures where electrical engineering increased with and not above the average rate. According to this – admittedly crude – comparison, pharmaceuticals, cosmetics and household chemicals, telecommunication, and vacuum as well as precision engineering remain the only branches which actually did show favourable results. This conclusion does not say anything about causality, of course.

A few years after the formulation of the new industrial policy, reform attempts were directed at the administration of foreign trade. The fact that the two were not launched together suggests that the emphasis in the late 1970s was as yet less dramatically influenced by balance-of-payments considerations. Possibly, the deterioration of economic indicators in the early 1980s convinced the HSWP that one without the other would not suffice to restore the external balance. Until then, the few existing foreign trade companies (FTCs) operated under (informal) central control and had to conform to a large number of written and unwritten rules. Some industrial firms had already been given the right to export their own products. From the early 1980s, the institutions responsible for the conduct of foreign trade were liberalised gradually. A number of FTCs now had the general right to sell manufactures and were not confined any longer, as previously, to their 'own' suppliers' output. Hence, firms now competed on both the domestic and the foreign markets against each other. By 1987, about 100 companies enjoyed general trading rights (Naray 1989). Export concentration diminished: while in 1982 the largest five companies accounted for roughly half of all exports to the West, this share fell to one-third by 1989 (Gács 1990,

Table 2.11   Gross production value, sales, productivity of priority sectors in 1989

Sectors	GPV* as % of previous year = 100							Sales as % of:			PPE† as % of:		
	1975	1980	1985	1986	1987	1988	1989	1975	1980	1988	1975	1980	1988
Biochemistry													
Fertilizers	125	86	95	95	104	95	85	150	106	105	154	99	86
Canning industry	117	10	104	105	105	100	103	119	111	102	120	102	98
Pharmaceuticals	254	166	108	102	105	109	95	249	161	93	239	157	94
Cosmetics	228	190	106	107	106	106	102	219	185	102	225	147	101
Electronics													
Electrical engineering	133	109	101	101	103	98	95	134	108	91	154	132	99
Telecommunications/ Vacuum engineering	245	173	109	106	110	102	103	235	161	98	283	210	113
Precision engineering	249	178	106	105	105	109	110	225	159	104	277	201	108
Total	–	115	–	–	–	–	99	–	108	96	–	134	101

Notes: * GPV = Gross production value. † PPE = Production per person employed.
Source: HCSO, *Statistical Yearbook 1989–1990.*

191). In contrast to the gradual relaxation of export controls, rules governing imports were made tighter. Until the late 1970s, a system of informal control prevailed. FTCs and producers would bargain with the authorities for licences. This system was replaced by a much stricter regime in 1981 to restore the external balance. Licences were issued only on an item-by-item basis. Once Hungary had overcome its liquidity crisis, controls were loosened somewhat (see Chapter 1). Only in 1989, however, did the HSWP introduce what effectively amounted to a liberalization of most groups of commodities, initially especially engineering and food products (Gács 1990, 195).

Problems: A First Cut

Industrial policy favours certain sectors or branches of an economy in order to improve overall economic performance. To benefit from industrial policy measures, a targeted sector typically will be expected to promote specific objectives such as growth, competitiveness, input utilisation and so on. The mere existence of an industrial policy obviously does not guarantee its success, and neither can an improved aggregate growth performance unequivocally be ascribed, say, to a specific research and development (R&D) policy or trade policy assistance. *Ceteris paribus*, however, increased government efforts to increase the volume of investment in certain sectors would lead one to expect an improved performance in that particular area – and, maybe, others – provided there is a possibility of tracking an initial investment decision through its implementation phase to output results. Brada (1988, 114–16) proposes four criteria to assess industrial policies. They comprise, first, picking winners and losers; second, markets; third, allocating resources; and, fourth, generating production and exports. Hence, the first two concern the choice of objectives, the third focuses on policy implementation, and the fourth identifies necessary conditions for success at the level of the economic system as well as at the level of the firm.

An ideal industrial policy would make realistic assessments regarding which firm-competitive strengths exist to warrant promotion in order to achieve economies of scale to exploit advantages in imperfect product markets. It would also analyse (foreign) product markets to look for high income elasticities for new products and high price elasticities of market share of established products. What a government needs, in other words, is a game plan. Assisting promising sectors in a low-growth environment necessitates the contraction of losing sectors. The reallocation of resources away from losers typically encounters political opposition. Only by combining a game plan and seeing it through can industrial policy succeed. Next, managers must know how to use new technologies and incorporate them into effective production to allow economies of scale and productivity gains to come about. Finally, products must be brought to the target markets and be marketed effectively (Brada 1988, 114–16).[7] In short, things can go wrong for many reasons: because the government picks the wrong sectors; because it fails in implementing incentives; or because the targeted firms do not respond adequately to the incentives. Most authors say a combination of the above was responsible for Hungary's dismal industrial performance; the main cause, hence, was systemic. Reform, in other words, did not go far enough. Investment policy was not sufficiently market-oriented and continued to favour high-input sectors such as metallurgy and electric energy production (Bélyácz 1984). In the absence of real capital markets, firms remained dependent on the centre for investment funds, although in many areas detailed planning was increasingly slow at following quick changes in profitable export markets. As it was easier for firms to get development funds for finished products rather than for setting up facilities to produce spare parts, there was a serious lack of component manufacturing. Alternatively, make-do arrangements prevailed. In the electronics industries, for example, import controls constrained firms in need of intermediate parts to produce them themselves even though their need approached only 10–20 per cent of the lower limit of what would be an optimal serial size. This resulted in inefficiencies that prevented the electronics industry from becoming internationally competitive (Reti 1988). But neither misallocations nor cuts in investment outlays by themselves explain why certain advanced technologies have not been more diffused. The boom–bust character typical of investment cycles negatively influenced a firm's decision to adopt advanced technology such as numerically-controlled machine tools, for fear of running into financial bottlenecks later (Popper 1988). In fact, the reform did not substantially alter the Hungarian firms' risk-averseness. Without risk-taking, there can be no innovation; the absence of venture spirit was not helped by an extremely complicated system of R&D outlays (Belázs, Hare and Oakey 1990).[8]

Cooperation with Western firms did not change much of this situation. To begin with, Western firms were not generally interested in transferring the most advanced technologies to their partners in the periphery (Krasznai and Laki 1982). But even when firms managed to purchase interesting licences, weaknesses in the complementary industry referred to above forced them either to become directly involved in intermediate production – with all that that entails in terms of efficiency losses – or to accept lower quality inputs with consequences for the final competitiveness of the product in question. The inadequate stock of machinery and equipment thus directly endangered the profitability of a licence. In addition, due to bureaucratic regulations, 8–15 years could pass between a purchase decision for large investment projects and the eventual – and by then outdated – utilisation of the required technology (Gueullette 1988).

Although in the first half of the 1980s Hungary was involved in a third of all instances of industrial cooperation between the European CMEA and Western countries, its absolute technology purchases are low in comparison to other semi-developed European countries. In the mid-1980s, only Greece and Spain bought less technology abroad (Mádi 1990). In terms of export promotion, this is suboptimal because the export ratio of industrial production based on foreign licences and know-how is far above the export ratio of total industrial output. In 1987, the ratios were 36.9 per cent and roughly 20 per cent, respectively. The high ratio for licence-based production applies particularly in the light, food and chemical industries (ibid.).

Assessments of efforts at export promotion range from optimistic accounts and yet brighter expectations at the beginning of the new industrial policy (for example, Fekete 1980) to findings that 'experience has shown that export-promotion policies absorb more of the national income than they produce' (Gueullette 1988, 614). According to Greskovits (1987), hard-currency exports and export-oriented investments alike were difficult to stimulate because firms, due to the dual organisation (that is, the CMEA versus OECD orientation) of the Hungarian economy, by themselves had too little an incentive to go for it. For many firms, in fact, the CMEA market remained more profitable than the Western markets despite the 1980 price reform. This reform, the introduction of a 'competitive pricing system', linked domestic prices to those prevailing in the world market. Before firms could charge more for their manufactures, energy or raw materials in the domestic market, they needed to realise higher export prices. This reform was supposed to simulate real import competition. Due to the absence of high-quality inputs of Hungarian origin, firms were reluctant to engage in export production on the basis of export-related credits (Gueullette 1989). But Greskovits also argued that government-sponsored export promotion did make a difference. While government interventions alone could not trigger a lasting export expansion – because they were unable to substitute incentives in their entirety – even less would have happened without them.

In the given functional mechanism, the interventions ... are ... [a] necessary means to initiate outstanding achievements exhibiting a whole range of variations, from injecting credits into the economy, by pushing through investments to exacting production for export, and then the export itself. [But] *the everyday economic activity of a whole country cannot be stimulated and remunerated as a record achievement.* (1987, 222–3; emphasis in original)

At any rate, the official deregulation of foreign trade should not be taken at face value. Until the late 1980s, exporters had to put up with a series of both visible and invisible rules. Some of these were outright ridiculous, others pervasive; many were both: 'More than two decades after the 1968 reforms in Hungary, there is such a huge mass of all kinds of obligatory measures and regulations, within or outside the legal system, published or confidential, generally valid or individually applied, that in their totality would not be acceptable even in a strictly centrally planned system' (Lányi 1990, 205).

According to many observers, the introduction of a unified price system in 1980 helped exchange rate management to become a tool to boost export sales through devaluations only to a limited degree. Of course, a depreciation does improve the profitability of exports. It does not necessarily, however, significantly change relative prices and profitability of tradeables *vis-à-vis* non-tradeables and products sold in CMEA markets, as Paul Marer noted (1986, 27–9). Since price changes in the domestic market and the profitability of sales on the domestic and their CMEA markets were tied directly to prices achieved in hard currency exports, firms that sold in both markets were largely unaffected except if they depended on imports of energy, raw materials or semi-manufactures.[9] With these inputs being quoted at world market prices, their forint price rises with a depreciation. But the relative prices of tradeables may not follow to a significant degree because of cost-plus pricing outside industry's competitive sectors. In sum, depreciation increases material costs and domestic prices. The former may curb imports while the latter do not automatically do much to help boost exports (ibid.).[10] In general, the IMF seems to view Hungary's experience with competitive RER management more positively than Hungarian observers. The Hungarians' more intimate knowledge of how difficult it was to get firms to follow expenditure-switching policies may account for the difference. Also, the Hungarians were clearly worried about the inflationary effect of devaluations. The vast body of research on exchange rate management can only be hinted at here. What is important to note is the lack of a consensus and, more precisely, that a number of people question that traditional RER management could work in Hungary's institutional setting.

At a more fundamental level, the liberalisation of foreign trade practices in the 1980s did not manage to solve a series of dilemmas inherent in the dual nature of Hungary's commercial relations with, broadly, Western markets on the one hand and CMEA arrangements on the other. Theoretically, Hungary could have combined the relatively cheap and reliable supply of raw materials from the Soviet Union with its superior manufacturing endowment to develop economies of scale. Presumably, this would have enabled it to upgrade the quality of its Western exports, thus allowing continuous technology imports in order to modernise the production structure. However, the prevailing CMEA trading arrangements, based on rather narrow contingency lists, did not make for the exploitation of scale economies. One reason for narrow contingency lists was the Soviet Union's determination not to become dependent on any one supplier, especially in sensitive product groups. In this sense, the CMEA was not only inward oriented as a whole but also at the level of the individual countries.

Additionally, these lists were agreed upon by trade authorities in the countries concerned. These officials also determined the price of the products in question. If a Hungarian firm incorporated costly high-quality inputs of Western origin in its products, the return from such a sale could turn out to be negative. The pricing practice effectively provided disincentives to firm-generated technological progress: that is, for firms to raise the quality of their products (Marrese 1990, 46). Where hard-currency imports were used all the same, their single-most important effect was the disadvantageous conversion from dollar to transfer rouble which contributed to Hungary's external debt. Marrese suggests that, compared to the scope of foreign trade liberalisation, general economic reform did not go far enough. First and foremost, investment decisions aimed at intensifying exports to the Soviet Union to secure the short-term supply of fuels and other raw materials were a mistake. The same short-term orientation debilitated export prospects to Western markets because they neglected long-term efficiency considerations. In sum, progress (or its absence) in the field of economic policy clearly is related to what is happening in other fields and hence influences the general performance.

Presumably healthier foreign trade performance would have freed Hungarian policy makers from preoccupation with short-term emergencies such as repayment of loans from Western banks. This, in turn, may well have led to the introduction of a more comprehensive and internally consistent economic reform. However, for a country like Hungary, economic reform and foreign trade reform should have been implemented simultaneously in order to reinforce one another, rather than in a piecemeal, sequential manner. (Marrese 1990, 54)

Köves argues that an essentially bad policy was followed up by a bad implementation of an, in substance, better policy: 'the recognition was ... belated and that belated recognition was not followed by an adequate reaction because *the practice of economic policy systematically overestimated the potential of developing relations with the socialist countries'* (1990, 65; italics in original).

The literature reviewed so far attributed the incompatibility of government initiatives intent on promoting high-quality production and export expansion and the firms' response thereto to a system whose functioning was largely devoid of profit incentives. But export promotion through industrial restructuring was only one of Hungary's major goals during the 1980s. The other was to re-establish and preserve the external balance. To that effect, the Hungarian economy operated under a system of tight import controls, especially from 1981 onwards. The restrictions on imports and investments envisaged in the sixth 5-year plan made observers worry early that structural change, improvements in efficiency and the maintenance of achieved technological standards might be threatened (for example, see Berend 1981). Others contended that a gradual relaxation of import restrictions could go hand in hand with structural adjustment (Gács 1986). Whatever the debate, the liberalisation of the system of foreign trade in 1979 left the old trading rules essentially intact in that the external balance provided a superior rationale to guard. In Marer's words, the trade-off between modernisation and balance-of-payments equilibrium leaves only bad choices:

> it is clear that however able, well-intentioned, and cooperative are the authorities involved in CC [= convertible currency] imports license decisions, as long as they face a severe BOP [balance of payments] constraint, the licensing system as it operates now hinders Hungarian firms from becoming more competitive in the world market. A vicious circle can be seen operating: the CC BOP is in deficit because Hungarian manufactures are insufficiently competitive in part because they find it difficult to import from the West the technology and products needed because the country faces a severe BOP constraint. (Marer 1986, 45)

The strict import regime led to various degrees of import substitution throughout the economy. As illustrated in the section on trade, in the second half of the 1970s metallurgy, engineering, and the food and chemical industries had been the main sectors involved in exports to the West. Due to requirements to save on inputs, mining, electric energy production and metallurgy increased their share of overall diminishing total investment. Of course, the mining (except for aluminium) and electric energy sectors hardly exported anything at all. While the need to economise on inputs had positive effects on enterprise housekeeping it also led to higher forint costs at official exchange rates, poorer quality, longer delivery times and so on for the involved user companies. Similarly, the rationalisation of energy was necessary but led to larger-than-life investments in essentially outdated industries and actually weakened the intent to bring Hungary closer in touch with the world market. Brada (1989) also attributes the decline in efficiency in the 1980s to a large degree Hungary's severe austerity policy.[11] He argued that unless macroeconomic policy becomes less tight and stops strangling growth, the reforms alone will not significantly affect the technical efficiency of Hungarian industry (ibid, 443).

In conclusion, you name it, we have it: bad policy, bad implementation, bad responses by firms. In most studies these elements – individually or in combination – explain why Hungarian industrial policy and trade liberalisation have been unsuccessful. At the root of the failure lies the systemic inability of an economy without a functioning market mechanism to allocate investment funds, export subsidies, tax rebates and so on. In addition, Hungarian firms did not really fit their environment. According to survey results, 61 per cent of the respondents admitted that their companies had not analysed the present or future competitiveness of their rivals in the domestic and foreign markets. 'The remarkable thing here is that the enterprises in the sample have very inadequate information on their own relative competitiveness' (Bod 1989–90, 166). Over all this loomed the association with CMEA. It permitted the continuous production and export of goods that were not saleable on the world markets. In this sense, it had an anti-reform effect. Why bother with the exacting quality standards of the West if you can get by without them in the East? But increasingly, the USSR demanded hard goods for its raw materials which meant Hungarian manufactures with Western components. This was a drain on Hungary's hard-currency balance.

Is there reason to doubt this picture? The above findings would apply, in general terms, to all CPEs and transitional economies. Presumably, however, the degree to which they apply differs across countries and across industrial sectors. A large differentiation of the latter would call the generality of the finding in question, while a differentiation across countries would compel the analyst to look for additional explanations other than systemic inefficiencies. That is, if some sectors show – by whatever measure – an above-average performance, the argument of 'systemic inefficiency' would not be watertight. Either inefficiency is not as all-encompassing as it seems or select firms somehow manage to produce and export much above the level of general efficiency.[12] Also, systemic inefficiency only carries so far when looking at the different CPEs.

Czechoslovakia, at a similar level of development as Hungary, had much less of a market. According to the argument, the resulting higher degree of inefficiency should have resulted in a comparatively worse export performance. Yet, for some sectors, that is not supported by the data. For example, Czechoslovakia successfully exported electrical machinery, vehicle components and such like to the West with no less success than Hungary. The claim that some differentiation is in order is supported by a recent study that compared the balance sheets of more than 200 Hungarian firms mainly engaged in exporting with those of the rest of the corporate sector. In terms of dollar-export shares and profitability, the main exporters registered a better performance. Also, loss makers were concentrated in rouble markets. Thus, László Halpern (1992) concluded that firms were not all alike.

Among the potential 'breakthrough' sectors identified during the preparatory and implementation phase of the sixth 5-year plan, Hungary increased output in a series of product groups of the aluminium, vacuum and pharmaceutical industry. In the 'leading'-products group, production increased in a number of activities of the engineering and chemical industries. With the exception of engineering, all of these branches also increased the share sold on Western markets relative to CMEA markets in the respective product group. Table 2.12 shows these 'success stories' both in volume terms and current values. The information reported in the table is not shown to argue with the above conclusions. It draws attention to the fact that some branches and individual firms managed to be successful despite the systemic limitations to industrial policy inherent in the Hungarian economy.

For example, the company manufacturing the rubber hoses that appear in Table 2.12, Taurus Rubber Manufactures, was reported in 1983 to have acquired a 40 per cent share in the world production of these hoses which are used in the oil industry to inject water into wells or load tankers. Taurus managed to license the production of the hoses in the USA. The company renewed its ties with Western firms such as Dunlop and Semperit, known already from pre-Second World War cooperation. It also set up its own trading company to handle its exports (Colitt 1983, 16). To be sure, the international market for rubber is not an easy one. The industry is concentrated in a few countries and among a few transnational firms. Competition results from alternative suppliers (smaller companies) and substitute products (plastics). The Taurus management realised that it would not survive without innovation and an efficient marketing organisation. How the (state-owned) enterprise integrated both goals rather successfully is described in Horváth (1988, 288–93).

Table 2.12   Production and exports of select successful priority sectors

	1984 Volume and %			1984 Value and %			1990 Volume and %			1990 Value and %			1980/89
	Total	CMEA	Other	HUF*	CMEA	Other	Total	CMEA	Other	HUF*	CMEA	Other	vol†
Breakthrough													
Metallurgical aluminium (tons)	71,294	66.8	33.2	3924	62.4	37.6	122	4.1	95.6	11,815	2.1	97.9	2.3
Incandescent lamps (1000 dB)	363,423	6.9	93.4	3484	12.9	87.1	374,789	4.4	95.6	6065	3.8	96.2	10.4
Fluorescent tubes (1000 dB)	12,494	11.4	88.6	289	14.7	85.3	39,935	26.3	73.7	746	23.1	76.9	44.3
Medicaments	–	–	–	9531	91.3	8.7	–	–	–	16,475	85.0	15.0	‡
Plant protectives (tons)	28,108	78.8	11.2	4613	70.8	29.2	19,267	62.7	37.3	4508	49.4	50.6	34.2
Leading													
Rubber hose (1000 fm)	2,430	84.2	15.8	876	88.6	11.4	1957	69.9	30.1	1133	74.3	25.7	196.8

Notes: * HUF million.
† Volume change in per cent, 1980/1989.
‡ For example, increase in vitamins 4197 per cent; in human antibiotics 24 per cent.
Sources: HCSO, *Statistical Yearbook 1989, Statistical Yearbook of External Trade 1984, 1990;* author's calculations.

Hungary's largest pharmaceutical company, the Chemical Works of Gideon Richter, received technology through licensing agreements and through a joint venture with Dutch Akzo. Subsequently, it began to develop original products for introduction in the West. In the early 1980s, 75 per cent of its production went into exports, and sales figures rose 10 to 15 per cent each year (Colitt 1983, 18). In engineering, KGYV, an industrial furnace manufacturer, sold 'grasshopper' oil pumps to the USA. Medicor, the medical equipment producer, made only 10–15 per cent of its products under foreign licences and relied for the rest on its own R&D institute with a staff of some 800 engineers and technicians (Buchan 1985, 22). Even companies in crisis sectors, notably the Lenin Iron and Steel Works, succeeded in making substantial sales, including some in Western markets (Colitt 1984, 6).

In 1990, Hungary managed to increase its convertible-currency trade surplus by 50 per cent. Exports of machinery and industrial consumer goods rose, in volume terms, by 18.6 per cent and 11.4 per cent, respectively. In the first five months of 1991, sales of machinery to convertible-currency markets grew by 55.4 per cent, and industrial consumer goods by 116.2 per cent (cf. OECD 1991, 94–5). This impressive sales record cannot come out of the blue. While company management may improve pricing and marketing within a relatively short period, the quality characteristics of Hungarian exports are unlikely to have changed in a matter of months. Hence, some degree of (hidden and frustrated) competitiveness must have always existed, at least among some companies. What naturally follows is to ask what these successes were based on, and whether they could have been emulated by more Hungarian firms, and why that did not happen. This is considered in the next chapter, which concludes with some observations of how experiences with reform in the 1980s are relevant for the transformation in the 1990s.

3 International Competitiveness

COMPETITION IN GLOBAL MARKETS

Why are the Central European Countries so Bad at it?

Most studies on international competitiveness of the CPEs focus on the technological quality of Eastern European exports to the West and go into all kinds of comparisons with the NICs. Technology, of course, is only one factor affecting competitiveness. But the literature on the CMEA has largely refrained from references to, for example, cultural attitudes to explain the quality or quantity of production in Central Europe. The difference of the Eastern European worker from the committed (Confucianist and Shintoist) Japanese automobile worker or the disciplined, hardworking Korean shipbuilder surfaced only when the CPEs embarked on their transition and ran into major difficulties: the reforms in Russia are stalling, one is informed, because the orthodox Russian farmer is not up to it. Predictably, not everybody agrees. 'The idea that East Europeans need to be taught the basic facts of economic life was always absurd. Forty years of rationing, shortages and thriving black markets were an excellent course in elementary economics – better, perhaps, than a century or two of capitalism whose beneficiaries take the miracle of supply and demand for granted' ('Pioneers of capitalism', 1992). Individual attitudes clearly do influence national (and, for that matter, regional) production processes. But if it was possible, in the past, to explain technology lags without reference to the individual, one should leave the additional variable out, too, when explaining transitional difficulties today, or else check whether more parsimonious explanations in the past really did explain what they purported to.

The existing literature is often imprecise, confused and at times inconsistent due, in part, to a lack of general results. An illustrative example in this field is Poznanski (1987). He argues that the reforms undertaken in the CPEs did not improve their competitiveness relative to the West. This claim is substantiated with a couple of rather broadly tailored analyses of production and trade data. He contends, for example, that the policy changes have not helped the CPEs to reduce the technology gap. This is derived from slow productivity increases which, *in general*, undeniably exist (cf. Gomulka

1986). As was shown in the previous section, Hungarian industry managed to increase productivity above average in some select priority sectors. Productivity in the pharmaceuticals and cosmetics branches in 1989 was about 50 per cent higher than in 1980. In telecommunications, vacuum engineering and precision engineering it doubled in the same period. For total industry, the figure was 33.6 per cent. Per year, this comes to approximately 3.5 per cent and compares – not badly – with annual manufacturing productivity growth from 1980–1985 of 5.68 per cent in Japan, 2.71 per cent in West Germany and 0.5 per cent in Denmark. But such aggregate numbers are of limited use. At this level of generality, they only prove the obvious (if anything): namely, that the inefficient operation of CPEs made these countries suffer from problems that market economies faced less severely or not at all. If one wants to assess the relative competitiveness of a country such as Hungary, criteria need to be established to determine which comparisons qualify. Some that do not are listed below.

Myth No. 1: The NICs Out-Innovated Everybody Else

The NICs surpassed Western economies in relatively simple fields such as steelmaking and ship production as well as more complex technologies, such as computer peripherals and components. While it is true that, after the Second World War, the NICs were further behind the CPEs in all relevant fields of technology so that their catching-up has been impressive, it is not true that all Asian NICs, let alone those in Latin America or elsewhere, are technologically superior. Michael Porter has argued that South Korea, widely perceived to be the most innovative NIC, is still an economy whose companies are production-oriented and depend on achieving low production costs. Standardised products, often developed elsewhere, are mass-produced and compete in price-sensitive markets. On the whole, however, Korean products are usually a generation behind those of world leaders in the respective product categories (1990, 470).

The success of the Korean model is mainly based on the availability of low-cost, preferential credit, highly productive, low-wage labour, capital-intensive modern factories and foreign technology. To reiterate, although Korea has a potential for product innovation, today Korean firms mostly compete on price. According to Porter, this is true to a larger extent for the other NICs. For instance, almost all US disk drives are manufactured in Singapore, and that has been so for some time; yet no indigenous Singapore company has ever designed a disk drive on its own. Thus, while disk drives are considered complex technologies, Singapore's export of these products depends entirely on foreign-owned firms. Without the latter,

Singapore would figure much less in international trade statistics. Of Singapore's 16 most important export groups, representing about 60 per cent of its total exports in 1988/89, it had relatively strong (≥3.5 per cent) shares of world exports in nine. Except for refined petroleum products (8.06 per cent of world exports) and natural rubber (17.62 per cent of world exports), these categories were all in the area of electronics, from automatic data processing equipment via television receivers to sound recorders (UNCTAD 1992). Of course, it is generally better to host FDI than not, especially in the absence of sufficient domestic capital accumulation and/or indigenous technology. Yet if the host country does not manage to upgrade its indigenous production/innovation facilities, it remains vulnerable to trade diversion. It is for this reason that the North American Free Trade Agreement (NAFTA) causes worries in Singapore. US companies, it is feared, might relocate their production facilities to Mexico. Klodt argues that future Eastern European specialisation might be based on technological cooperation with Western companies in 'mobile Schumpeter industries' such as industrial chemicals (Klodt 1991; see also 1990). Thus, one should distinguish meaningfully between the four East Asian NICs, which in many respects are very different from each other. That Singapore has attracted more FDI than Hungary is a trivial finding. It does not support the conclusion that the NICs, in all industrial sectors, disposed of a higher level of technological development than Hungary or any other CMEA economies.

Myth No. 2: The NICs Out-Competed the CPEs in 'Potential' Markets

Poznanski also argues that given the steady decline of CMEA market share in Western imports of manufactures the NICs have managed to take away potential markets for CPE manufactures. What is a potential market? If he means all those in which the NICs have made inroads the statement is both superfluous and difficult to interpret. Are clothing, toys, sporting goods, watches and clocks – which made up 47.54 per cent of Hong Kong's exports in the mid-1980s and gave it a share of 45.32 per cent in world exports in these product groups – a potential market for any or all CMEA countries? Making this argument is a bit like saying that Argentina, an NIC, won the world soccer championship in 1982. The participating CPE teams, in contrast, fared rather badly. Thus, an NIC has deprived, say, Poland of its *potential* victory. At a more serious level, this discussion reveals a narrow view of international competitiveness. Competing effectively in world markets, one is made to believe, somehow depends on the manufacture of the goods normally associated with the output of Asian NICs. Yet there is no compelling logic why Hungary – or any other middle-income country – would need to emulate the undisputably successful conquest of OECD markets by the NICs in the very same product groups. For example, Swiss exporters make a lot of money selling chocolate to the rest of the world. Why not try to market a carefully designed brand of Hungarian salami? What counts a lot, in brief, is to produce for and find markets with high income elasticities. That is not the same as saying Central Europeans need to engage in the production of microchips. Or, to stay with sports, Hungary may never compete in a meaningful international soccer contest, but that did not stop its kayak team from winning a gold medal in the Olympic games in Barcelona.

Instead, one should look at product substitution from different suppliers in actual markets to try to determine whether it was against the CPEs that the NICs built their export success. Inotai (1986) did this for CMEA machinery exports (Standard International Trade Classification, or SITC, 7, 87, 88) to the OECD, 1973–84. He showed that the CMEA did not follow worldwide market trends in telecommunications and so on but instead remained with the most backward sectors, such as traditional machinery, whose demand contracted. In fact, in these branches the CMEA even lost market shares against non-NIC LDCs.

Conclusions based on simple comparisons of volume are problematic for a variety of reasons. One is that decreasing market shares may be due to upgrading in an economy that moves to higher-value-added production. The increase in the number of supplier countries of certain products is another. For example, the fact that Eastern Europe in the 1970s was outmatched most in miscellaneous manufactures such as garments and footwear applies to Italy as well, which is still the world's number one exporter of footwear.[1]

Treating the CMEA countries en bloc is a problem which becomes apparent in Poznanski's standard conclusion: reforms, he says, have not gone far enough, except in Hungary. It is up to the reader to guess what this means. Is Hungary the only competitive CMEA member? Does it therefore hold its own in the struggle for market shares against the NICs? Such a conclusion would question much of the conventional analysis reviewed in Chapter 2. Furthermore, that the introduction of reforms will enable an economic system to defend itself better against the potential loss of shares in export markets is not a *sequitur* but an assumption. It could well be that a partial relaxation of central planning weakens the state's ability to influence economic outcomes without a strengthening of efficiency generated by market forces. In other words, perhaps the relationship between reform and competitiveness is not linear: more reforms do not necessarily lead to higher productivity or translate into export success. It is often implicitly assumed that the total control over resource allocation by the state accounts for the dismal performance of the planned economies. Inasmuch as state control was considerably relaxed in Hungary, one might then intuitively expect a different outcome for Hungary. But intuition does not substitute for evidence, and it follows nowhere from the analysis that Hungary is somehow 'doing better' than the rest of the CMEA, and why and in which sectors.

Myth No. 3: Technological Backwardness Does not Delay Catching Up

Nonetheless, Poznanski reiterates his conclusion in a later article. There, he sets out to prove that the technological backwardness of Eastern Europe is due to systemic factors (1988). While in this work he actually does look at single commodities making up a one-third of all CMEA exports to the EC, Eastern Europe and the NICs are again treated in the aggregate. Hence, countries as diverse as Hong Kong, Mexico and Romania are compared. The NICs are used to lend credence to the following line of reasoning: if it is shown that the NICs managed to reduce their technological lag with the West, one may safely refute the idea that technological backwardness possibly works against latecomers trying to catch up. In other words, everybody could be happy and developed; if some countries are not, they have only themselves to blame. To nobody's surprise, the article concludes just that. The flaw in this essentially deterministic reasoning is readily apparent to anybody who has ever sat through an undergraduate class in social science methodology. The only thing the NICs disprove is the inevitability of dependency. Given that dependency theories have been out of fashion for some time, this could be termed the least interesting result in development literature. To see whether or not, and in which conditions, backwardness impedes bridging the technology gap, how some countries managed to overcome technological backwardness, and what other factors are critical ingredients for catching up, suggests the need to trace the development paths and experiences of former colonies after the Second World War. This is not to suggest an agenda for research: my point here is simply about avoiding methodological flaws in setting up an argument. The experience of the NICs and also second-tier NICs such as Malaysia suggests that some countries can indeed overcome backwardness, but there are a number of other critical factors that can help or impede competitiveness.

Inconclusive Evidence: The Impact of Import Restrictions

In Hungarian government circles, the severe import restrictions since 1981 were often seen as a major factor in withholding essential inputs to Hungarian industry without which exports could not remain competitive.

But Inotai cautioned that NICs and second-tier NICs have managed to boost exports while cutting back certain imports (1988). Import constraints may hit less developed countries harder than more advanced ones; but second-tier NICs such as Malaysia or Thailand are, on the whole, certainly less developed than Hungary. According to Inotai, the maintenance of an outdated and non-competitive production structure in Hungary led to non-competitive import demands (that is, only the second-rate technology that firms could handle), thus compounding rather than alleviating the problem. For example, it would be important to keep acquiring advanced Western investment goods even under a system of controlled imports of consumption goods in order to modernise production but, in engineering, Inotai shows that the small CMEA countries imported at best at the level of Morocco and Tunisia, and less than half of that of Portugal. By contrast, Mexico, Pakistan and Brazil managed to increase their capital goods imports under even harder circumstances.

After the 1980 price reform Hungarian products should not have been too expensive to compete because domestic prices were tied to world market prices. But at times they were. The problem consisted of the slowness of the bureaucracy continuously to convey (at times highly and frequently fluctuating) world market prices to the producer. In addition, firm managers resisted falling prices. As the actual pricing decisions were made by managers, stockpiles of unsold goods often resulted. Import restrictions caused the utilisation of CMEA intermediate inputs which made delivery times more unreliable and lowered quality. Accustomed to relatively unsophisticated markets, many companies then turned out products that were not price-competitive (Kovács 1984).

In a study of information technologies, Geipel, Jarmoszko and Goodman suggest that the performance of Hungarian firms in this field was hampered by problems elsewhere (1991). For example, promising microcomputer and software industries lost ground after the investment scale-backs following increased debt service payments in the early 1980s. When after 1985 the electronics sector once again received more investment, COCOM rules forced Hungarian manufacturers to undertake uneconomic investments to develop technology freely available in the West. Despite this suboptimal arrangement Hungarian companies, such as the Institute for Co-ordination of Computer Techniques, earned $18–20 million through software exports to the West from 1979–1983; and the successful microfloppy disk manufacturer, Budapest Radio Engineering, was actually competing against world leaders in hardware technology like Sony, Maxell and Seagate (Sealy 1983, 18–19).

As in other branches, the government's inconclusive ideas about industrial policy did not help. 'A problem common to all of Eastern Europe's computerization efforts was the absence of strategies to replace older industries with the manufacture of more advanced technologies, or to promote aggressively the automation of outdated industrial processes by using IT [information technologies]' (Geipel, Jarmoszko and Goodman 1991, 415). In addition, there was a size problem in that CMEA's integrated computer development programme favoured large enterprises such as, for example, the East German Robotron. Smaller producers – often important innovators in other countries with a successful record in information technologies – found it difficult to get capital for investment or vital components for products. These problems notwithstanding, Hungary has been having some success, especially for IBM-PC software in the West European market. Breakthroughs often relied on technical ingenuity rather than state-of-the-art endowments. Graphisoft, a company that created a programme for computer-aided design used by architects, started out with two borrowed Apple computers and a few thousand dollars. By 1991, the firm had captured 50 per cent market share in Western Europe and 10 per cent in the USA for this particular kind of software (Maass 1992). Hungarian programmers were being leased throughout Europe to compensate for a general lack of IT personnel. Sometimes they were part of swap deals (for example, with Siemens) to finance the purchase of expensive equipment such as hardware. Prospects may improve further due to licensing agreements concluded in the early 1990s, such as that with US-based Dataproducts, and following legal changes which bring Hungarian copyright laws in line with international norms.

What to Do? Listen to the Experts

Unfailingly, with the victim stranded, the saviours are not far away. Both before and after 1989 experts (and others who regard themselves as such) have published countless pieces of advice intent on helping Central Europeans to get into navigable waters. Not surprisingly, given the intricate subject matter, a large number of these analyses suffer from serious shortcomings. What is less intelligible is that some of these shortcomings could have been avoided by more careful research. Often, perhaps, studies of various quality were rushed into publication so that they could join in the fashionable chorus of well-meaning Western transformationalists.

One such example is Tovias's essay on EC–Hungarian relations (1991). He finds that Hungary enjoys comparative advantages in the production of fresh and frozen meat, while having become less apt at making brooms and raising live animals for food. Tovias concludes this from revealed comparative advantage (RCA) indices as pioneered by Bela Balassa and others.

RCAs measure the contribution of a particular industry to a country's exports relative to this industry's share in world (usually, manufacturing) exports.[2] The Balassa index is only appropriate in an environment whose industrial output is not heavily distorted through subsidies. Jeffrey Sachs's famous example of Polish orchid production is illustrative. Nobody who has ever been to Poland would believe for a moment that the country has a comparative advantage in tropical flowers but, with heavily subsidised energy prices, it becomes profitable for individual farmers to grow these flowers although this is otherwise a drag on the entire economy. Nonetheless, Poland has an RCA in orchids because the Balassa index is not sensitive to domestic resource costs (DRCs). Tovias is aware of these limits because he writes: 'Insofar as some of Hungary's exports are heavily subsidized, the indices for these sectors will be *less significant or useful*' (Tovias 1991, 292; emphasis added). Nevertheless, he goes ahead and uses them anyway. The list of products that the calculation of the index gives rise to is quite entertaining. Thus, we learn that Hungary has a comparative disadvantage in pepper and pimento which – these being crucial ingredients to Hungary's foremost national recipe – presumably suggests that the road from communism to capitalism is as gruesome as the passage from (homemade) goulash to (imported) frozen pizza.

Thus, when tariffs and non-tariff barriers (NTBs) abound in certain product categories, the Balassa index will often be misleading. Competitive or potentially competitive products may appear to be comparatively disadvantageous for a country precisely because of their competitiveness which provokes protectionist responses from the importing country.[3] Tovias claims to control for that by looking into average tariffs and NTBs applied by the EC on imports from Hungary. Among other things he finds that rates applied on agricultural products are higher than average rates, and that one-quarter of all Hungarian exports are affected by at least one NTB. Since Tovias's RCA index revealed that the country has comparative advantages and disadvantages within the same sectors – food and agriculture – his discussion of commercial factors remains inconclusive. Do tariffs and NTBs exert a negative effect on (selected) exports or not? Clearly, there could be other factors depressing exports. In fact, Hungary may be confronted with QRs but not even fill the respective quotas. This argument is often used – instrumentally – to reject larger quotas within the Multi-fibre Arrangement (MFA) which regulates textile and apparel imports from developing countries into the OECD. The mere existence of trade barriers is not sufficient to conclude that Hungary's export volume would be higher in the absence of these barriers.

Hughes and Hare calculate DRCs for a series of industries (1991). DRCs are the ratio of value-added at world and domestic prices to the domestic value of final output. They find fruit and vegetable products, oils and fats, and cereal products are negative value-added. Tovias claims that Hungary has a comparative advantage in fruit and vegetable juices, pig and poultry fat as well as sunflower seed oil and unmilled cereals (1991). This is the opposite of what Hughes and Hare find! Competitive sectors from the latter study include, for example, meat, fish and dairy products, but also manufactured products, machinery, electrical equipment, transport equipment and instruments. Thus, on that basis Hughes and Hare consider Hungary's comparative advantages to lie with light industrial sectors, chemicals (including pharmaceuticals), and precision engineering.

That studies differ in their findings is understandable. The truth is apt to be more complex than such generalised analyses. One of their major shortcomings is that they ignore the individual enterprise as unit of analysis. However, to the degree that these studies inform decision-making today – either at the national level in Budapest or in the context of assistance programmes administered by the EC Commission or the IFIs – they may cause the government to favour specialisation in the wrong kinds of things. Tovias's approach – looking at past exports to derive present-day competitiveness – has been successfully ignored by latecomer countries. Applied to Japan, the advice would have been to stick with toys and forget the manufacture of cars, televisions, steel and chips. Luckily, Japanese policy-makers would not have any of this advice. Also, these studies implicitly take prices as given. As alluded to in the introduction, a relatively new but considerable body of literature on high-growth economies in Asia suggests that their competitiveness is best understood in a dynamic context where it has more to do with deliberately 'wrong' prices and not only with comparative advantages. One particularly illustrative example would be Alice Amsden's discussion of the role of government in the development of the South Korean steel industry (1989, Ch. 12). In other words, competitiveness and comparative advantages are not necessarily the same thing.

Hungary's Shares in Select Product Markets

Hungary's share in total OECD imports in dollar terms was 0.203 per cent in 1989. This represents a loss of 8 per cent since 1979. Table 3.1 shows how that compares with data for a few select other countries. The pattern of market share loss is typical for Central Europe; Czechoslovakia's fell by 22.5 per cent, and Poland's by 38 per cent over the same period. The two Asian NICs reported here more than doubled their share, while second-tier NIC Malaysia's share decreased by 6 per cent. EC newcomer Portugal also

Table 3.1   Shares in OECD import market (%)

Countries	1979	1982	1985	1988	1989
Hungary	0.221	0.187	0.191	0.200	0.203
Czechoslovakia	0.240	0.217	0.192	0.187	0.186
Poland	0.440	0.269	0.282	0.276	0.273
Taiwan	1.041	1.321	1.926	2.353	2.256
South Korea	0.959	1.071	1.431	2.211	2.069
Malaysia	0.739	0.590	0.700	0.643	0.695
Portugal	0.277	0.292	0.381	0.507	0.545
Austria	0.972	0.919	0.945	1.238	1.192
West Germany	10.974	10.186	10.407	12.782	12.211

Source: OECD, *Series C. Trade by Commodities* 1989; author's calculations.

almost doubled its share, Austria's increased by 22.6 per cent; and West Germany's by 11.2 per cent.

Disaggregating Hungary's 8 per cent loss by commodities reveals that the decrease is due to losses in beverages and tobacco (–59.2 per cent);[4] chemicals and related (–10 per cent); machinery and transport equipment (–36.7 per cent); and miscellaneous manufactures (–40.9 per cent). Again, a similar trend is discernible for Czechoslovakia and Poland. All NICs, Portugal and Austria, on the other hand, increased their share in SITC groups 5, 7 and 8. To determine against whom Hungary lost shares in OECD imports it is thus not sufficient to undertake comparisons at the level of one-digit SITC groupings. Competition takes place in markets for actual products, not in their statistical aggregation.

Hungary has meaningful (here taken to mean equal to or close to 1 per cent) shares in world exports of pharmaceuticals (SITC 541); live animals for food (SITC 001); footwear (SITC 851); plumbing, sanitary and lighting equipment (SITC 821); and manufactured fertilisers (SITC 561). These commodity groups made up 10.38 per cent of Hungarian exports in 1982; by 1990 their share had fallen to 9.41 per cent. In 1982, the country captured 11.48 per cent of world exports in the markets for these products, in 1988 a mere 6.28 per cent. The share of exports in dollar terms that went to hard currency markets varied from one-quarter in the case of footwear to 60 per cent in the case of fertilisers. On average, Westward-orientation in all of these categories increased, most pronouncedly in footwear, followed by 821, 001, 541 and 562. This reflects the general trend of Westward-orientation of Hungarian food products and manufactures. Taken together, Hungary lost roughly 50 per cent of its market shares in these groups between 1982 and 1988 (see Table 3.2).[5]

Table 3.2 Hungarian exports to the world market

	1982				1986				1988				1990			
	As % of:			% to:	As % of:		% to:		As % of:		% to:		As % of:		% to:	
SITC	TotX	WX	CPEs	Other	TotX	WX	CPEs	Other	TotX	WX	CPEs	Other	TotX	WX	CPEs	Other
541	3.82	2.28	62.4	37.6	4.22	2.00	62.0	38.0	4.32	1.50	56.5	43.5	4.48	–	54.5	45.5
001	3.36	5.79	56.2	43.8	1.93	3.18	35.9	64.1	1.82	2.58	37.8	62.2	1.80	–	35.5	64.5
851	1.62	1.22	75.6	24.4	1.71	0.97	68.6	31.4	1.65	0.72	57.6	42.4	1.09	–	36.2	63.8
561	1.41	1.75	39.8	60.2	1.05	1.04	28.9	71.1	0.94	0.81	31.3	68.7	0.91	–	29.4	70.6
821	0.17	0.44	53.0	47.0	0.38	0.80	42.8	57.2	0.44	0.67	25.1	74.9	1.13	–	20.2	79.8

Notes: The SITC commodity codes refer to pharmaceuticals (541), live animals for food (001), footwear (851), manufactured fertilisers (561), plumbing, sanitary and lighting equipment (821).
TotX = total Hungarian exports.
WX = world exports.
CPEs = centrally planned and transitional economies.
Other = DMEs and LDCs.

Sources: HCSO, *Statistical Yearbook of External Trade*, various volumes; IMF, *International Financial Statistics*, various volumes; UNCTAD, *Trade and Development Report*, various volumes; UN, *International Trade Statistics Yearbook 1992*; author's calculation.

In pharmaceuticals, Hungary lost market shares alongside the NICs, among which Hong Kong is the biggest contender, and the few LDCs that are marginally in the market (see Table 3.3). The DMEs consolidated their dominant position which was already very strong in the early 1980s. For all countries outside the core group of industrialised market economies, the market for pharmaceuticals is a difficult one. The pharmaceutical industry is a highly profitable, research-intensive business characterised by intense competition from increasingly fewer, globally active companies. Two-thirds of total sales take place in the developed countries; penetrating markets requires a highly developed marketing network. While some NICs such as Brazil, India, South Korea and Taiwan have launched ambitious programmes for indigenous production, their success depends critically on whether they will master the advanced levels of scientific knowledge and production techniques necessary for the development of new drugs. Next to sales of technically less advanced indigenous medicines, the manufacture of new products under licensing agreements or joint ventures with transnational firms may be a viable strategy to get involved in global sourcing (cf. UNIDO 1991, 200–12). Hungary, for example, has cooperated with UK-based ICI and Wellcome, both among the world top 20 pharmaceutical companies in terms of R&D. However, the cooperation was in plant-protectives. At any rate, a Hungarian market loss in this area is not surprising. Hungary traditionally was CMEA's primary supplier of pharmaceuticals.[6] With this market largely gone, pharmaceuticals exports cannot be expected to recover world market shares, unless there is a major involvement of foreign technology.[7] In part, the consolidation is due to investment patterns by multinational firms in Western Europe, especially in new EC members. Ireland and Spain doubled their market share in 1982–9 to 4.64 per cent. Their gain corresponds with the loss experienced by the NICs, Hungary and the LDCs.

The NIC with the highest share in the market for live animals, Turkey, has been losing its position even more rapidly than Hungary (see Table 3.4). Only two NICs, Mexico and Malaysia, managed to increase their share. Among the LDCs it is of all countries the Sudan which increased its share in OECD imports. In light of the starvation in that country this is simply a sad fact and does not have much to do with competitiveness. The market consolidated for the DMEs, particularly the rich ones among them. The ten biggest DME exporters raised their market share by 4.6 per cent in 1982–9. In 1989 and 1990, beef and pork output in Western Europe, where markets are largely saturated, declined. Hungary increased its deliveries of live animals for food and remained strong through 1990 especially in live pigs. Its beef and veal exports, however, declined in volume terms from the mid-1980s to 1989. More precisely, the fall in exports to the USSR was

Table 3.3   World market shares in pharmaceuticals (SITC 541) (%)

Countries	1982	1984	1986	1988	1989
Hungary	2.28	2.15	2.00	1.50	1.9*
Yugoslavia	1.73	1.11	0.99	0.59	–
Singapore	1.14	0.83	0.66	0.60	0.49
Hong Kong	1.10	1.07	1.14	1.40	1.90
Brazil	0.41	–	0.34	0.32	0.57
Mexico	–	0.40	–	–	0.50
South Korea	–	–	–	0.36	–
Memo:					
NIC	4.38	3.41	3.13	3.27	3.46
LDCs	0.79	0.93	0.83	0.82	0.33
DMEs	91.01	91.52	92.97	93.12	92.82
Total	98.46	98.01	98.93	98.71	98.51

Note: *Estimate based on Hungarian trade statistics, converted at IMF-quoted
exchange rates. (Figures may not add to 100 due to rounding.)
Sources: HCSO, *Statistical Yearbook of External Trade 1990*; UN, *International
Trade Statistics Yearbook*, various volumes.

Table 3.4   World market shares in live animals for food (SITC 001) (%)

Countries	1982	1984	1986	1988	1989
Hungary	5.79	4.83	3.18	2.58	3.46*
Turkey	7.48	5.53	–	3.82	3.88
Yugoslavia	2.43	2.01	1.56	2.58	1.87
Mexico	2.29	2.61	3.51	2.64	3.27
Malaysia	–	0.36	0.74	1.56	2.19
Thailand	–	–	0.19	–	–
Memo:					
NIC	12.20	10.51	6.00	10.60	11.21
LDCs	7.44	7.59	1.59	2.94	2.02
DMEs	76.93	78.20	90.34	84.23	81.93
Total	102.36	101.13	101.11	100.35	98.62

Note: *Estimate based on Hungarian trade statistics, converted at IMF-quoted
exchange rates. (Figures may not add to 100 due to rounding.)
Sources: HCSO, *Statistical Yearbook of External Trade 1990*; UN, *International
Trade Statistics Yearbook*, various volumes.

compensated only in part by increased exports to Western Europe. The strongest increase in 1989 was in exports of live cattle and calves where Hungary performed significantly better than the average for north-western, southern and eastern Europe (see UNECE 1991b). By contrast, footwear is evidently a market where the NICs succeeded against the DMEs as well as Eastern Europe (see Table 3.5). In 1982, the DMEs still had a share of world exports more than twice as high as the NICs. By 1989, they had pulled more or less equal. Big winners are South Korea, Hong Kong, Malaysia and also Brazil. The NICs' gain more or less reflects the DMEs' and Hungary's losses. Interestingly, Hong Kong, Korea and Taiwan have begun moving the production of simpler styles offshore to China, Thailand and Indonesia. Thus, competition from Asia is now present in low-cost products as well as at the higher end of the market, in leather and sport shoes, for instance (see UNIDO 1989, 294–9).

Increasing dispersion among supplier countries is a significant characteristic of the market for fertilisers (see Table 3.6). While in 1982 only 22 countries accounted for 94.06 per cent of world exports of manufactured fertilisers, by 1989 this share was down to 89.57 per cent. Relatively,

Table 3.5   World market shares in footwear (SITC 851) (%)

Countries	1982	1984	1986	1988	1989
Hungary	1.22	1.12	0.97	0.72	0.6*
South Korea	13.98	12.87	14.84	21.75	5.71
Yugoslavia	6.57	5.49	4.51	1.99	1.26
Brazil	5.19	11.83	8.23	7.25	8.05
Hong Kong	2.09	2.26	2.23	3.76	6.47
Thailand	0.60	0.80	0.87	1.44	1.08
Malaysia	0.54	–	–	–	19.73
Mexico	–	–	0.38	0.46	0.36
Indonesia	–	–	–	0.41	–
Memo:					
NIC	28.97	33.25	31.06	37.06	42.66
LDCs	1.24	0.86	0.46	0.95	1.70
DMEs	65.38	62.65	65.92	59.0	48.89
Total	96.81	97.88	98.41	97.73	93.92

Note: *Estimate based on Hungarian trade statistics, converted at IMF-quoted exchange rates. (Figures may not add to 100 due to rounding.)
Sources: HCSO, *Statistical Yearbook of External Trade 1990*; UN, *International Trade Statistics Yearbook*, various volumes.

Table 3.6 World market shares in manufactured fertilisers (STTC 562) (%)

Countries	1982	1984	1986	1988	1989
Hungary	1.75	1.34	1.04	0.81	0.98*
Yugoslavia	1.37	1.10	1.35	1.20	1.14
Israel	2.08	2.22	2.16	2.34	2.09
South Korea	3.12	3.17	2.34	1.06	–
Turkey	0.69	–	–	2.24	0.71
Indonesia	–	–	0.69	1.29	0.85
Singapore	1.70	0.99	–	–	–
Memo:					
NICs	8.96	7.48	6.54	8.13	4.79
LDCs	4.23	6.17	5.67	1.30	3.32
DMEs	80.87	79.70	80.78	77.03	74.69
Total	95.81	94.69	94.03	87.27	83.78

Note: *Estimate based on Hungarian trade statistics, converted at IMF-quoted
exchange rates. (Figures may not add to 100 due to rounding.)
Sources: HCSO, *Statistical Yearbook of External Trade 1990*; UN, *International
Trade Statistics Yearbook*, various volumes.

Hungary lost more of its market share than did all DMEs; but less than all
NICs and all LDCs. And, compared to the NICs, its market share was absolutely lower only than Israel's and Yugoslavia's. Rather surprisingly, Hungary
imported more fertilisers than it exported (see UNIDO 1991, 229–55).

In the market for plumbing, heating, and lighting equipment, Hungary
and the NICs increased their market share by 68.2 per cent and 63.3 per
cent, respectively, while the DMEs lost a share of 5.2 per cent (see
Table 3.7). The biggest winner was South Korea which tripled its market
share. The only NIC that competed with the DMEs in terms of level of
market share is Hong Kong, which has become the world's fourth biggest
exporter of these goods.

In sum, out of five markets in which Hungary had meaningful shares in
world exports, it lost market positions in four during the 1980s. But the
NICs also lost in three out of these five markets. In the three markets where
both lost (that is, SITC 541, 001 and 562), Hungary lost relatively less in
two, SITC 541 and 562. In terms of absolute market shares, it competed
with the most successful NIC, Hong Kong, in 541, was second behind
Turkey in 001, and third behind Yugoslavia and South Korea in 562. In the
sector where both Hungary and the NICs won, the relative increase in
market share is very similar. In terms of absolute market shares, while

Table 3.7 World market shares in plumbing, heating and lighting equipment (STTC 812) (%)

Countries	1982	1984	1986	1988	1989
Hungary	0.44	0.58	0.80	0.67	0.74*
Hong Kong	4.85	5.94	4.96	5.75	8.48
South Korea	–	–	0.75	1.81	1.89
Mexico	0.98	1.43	0.78	0.91	1.14
Brazil	–	–	0.93	–	0.51
Yugoslavia	1.33	1.18	0.83	0.68	0.46
Turkey	–	–	–	0.48	–
Singapore	0.48	0.57	–	–	–
Memo:					
NIC	7.64	9.12	8.25	9.63	12.48
LDCs	0.65	0.61	–	–	–
DMEs	89.03	87.21	88.96	86.77	84.38
Total	97.76	97.52	98.01	97.07	97.60

Note: *Estimate based on Hungarian trade statistics, converted at IMF-quoted exchange rates. (Figures may not add to 100 due to rounding.)
Sources: HCSO, *Statistical Yearbook of External Trade 1990*; UN, *International Trade Statistics Yearbook*, various volumes.

behind Hong Kong and South Korea by a wide margin, Hungary competes at a similar level with countries like Brazil and Mexico.

Taken together, this means that the 'competition-from-the-NICs' argument needs to be used very much more carefully. Of the five product groups in which Hungary has some share of world trade, this applies only to one, namely footwear.

A Constant-Market-Share Analysis of Hungarian Export Performance 1982–7

The loss of a country's share in world exports may be due to one or more of three factors:[8] (1) the country exports goods for which demand grows relatively more slowly than average demand: (2) the country directs its exports to importing countries that grow relatively more slowly than, on average, the rest of the world; (3) the country's export enterprises are, for a variety of reasons, not competitive. Roughly speaking, (1) and (2) represent demand effects, while (3) refers to supply factors of the country in question. This relationship may be expressed as an identity.

Change in exports ≡ increase (decrease) in world demand + increase (decrease) in competitiveness

The reader is referred to the appendix of this chapter for a more formal presentation of this method. In this identity, the competitiveness term is obtained as a residual. In other words, everything that is not explained by structural demand factors must be due to the changing competitiveness of a country or, more precisely, its firms. While this is intuitively convincing, the residual is difficult to interpret. Competitiveness means many things to many people; it depends on the pricing of products, their quality, marketing, export financing, delivery conditions and so on, all of which may vary considerably within a national manufacturing sector. It is important to note that it surely does not depend only – for a variety of interesting products not even mainly – on (relative) prices. For example, a small country with rapidly growing demand in its export markets may not have the supply capacity to keep up with demand. Its market share might then diminish. In comparison, a large country delivering to more stagnant markets would hold its market share more easily. However, nothing suggests that the bigger country would necessarily be more competitive (Leamer and Stern 1970; Richardson 1971).

However, most studies implicitly concentrate on prices as the sole determinant of competitiveness, but only because value data are more easily obtainable than information on other supply elements of competitiveness. An example would be the analysis of South European manufactures exports to the OECD in the 1970s (UNECE 1982, 503–61). A much less detailed application of the constant-market-share (CMS) analysis to Hungarian exports is found in Hoen and Wagener (1989). The article suffers from the highly aggregated trade data used. As stated before, Hungary's overall share in OECD imports amounts to some 0.2 per cent. Hence, in many commodity groups, Hungarian exporters do not compete at all with other exporters. In other words, while one may conclude – as Hoen and Wagener do – that Hungary improved its export performance due to its competitiveness in machinery and consumer goods between 1980 and 1984, the usefulness of such a finding is not clear. In these two rather large commodity groups, Hungary reached a 1 per cent share of its total exports to the OECD in very few subgroups: vehicle parts and accessories, furniture, select garments and apparel, and footwear. Disaggregating yet further, 75 per cent of Hungary's position in electric household appliances was made up of refrigerators. Thus, it may make sense to say that they have been successful in exporting, say, refrigerators and coats and jackets for women. They are certainly *not* competitive in machinery and consumer goods in general.

The simplification that goes along with using value data is apt to confuse results rather seriously. For example, if a country manages to lower its export prices *vis-à-vis* its competitors – surely a sign of increased competitiveness – and the elasticity of substitution between its products and those of its competitors is less than one, then its export shares possibly would appear to have fallen, in obvious contradiction of their being more competitive.

Data

In the analyses that follow value data has been checked against quantity data. The reason for not using quantity data altogether is that they are less complete and not always comparable across countries because of different units of measurement. Shoes, measured in pairs, are difficult to compare to fertilisers, measured in tons, for example. (Contrary to commonly held beliefs, however, apples and oranges do not pose such a problem.) If the change over time in the commodity value data exhibited the same sign as the respective quantity data – if, in other words, the elasticity of substitution is sufficiently high – the commodity was included. If an increase in value shares corresponded with a decrease in quantity shares the commodity was also included because the implied increased unit value suggests an increase in quality, technological improvement or some other form of product upgrade. Technically, this could also be due to a higher rate of increase of export price inflation. But since Hungary is a price-follower in all its markets and, additionally, the analyses below are based on a high level of commodity disaggregation (where high elasticities of substitution prevail), that is less likely. If, as discussed before, value shares fell while quantity shares rose, the commodity was not included. This need not be reason for concern because it only applied to two out of 25 commodity groups in the first time period and to four out of 30 in the second. In sum, export gains can result from selling more of something or commanding a higher price for it.

The data used are from the microfiche edition of the OECD commodity trade statistics. Availability of data constrained the choices of a proper base year. Either 1980 or 1981 might have been more appropriate than 1982, but the commodity tables begin only in 1982. Due to the revision of the classification,[9] data until 1987 and from 1989 are not comparable at the 3-digit level of disaggregation. The reference group against which Hungarian performance is measured consists of three groups of NICs: (1) Asian (Singapore, South Korea, Taiwan, Hong Kong), (2) Latin American (Mexico, Brazil), (3) South-East European and Mediterranean (Yugoslavia, Turkey, Israel). Commodity groups at the 3-digit SITC level were included in the dataset if they fulfilled certain elasticity criteria referred to above and represented at least 1 per cent of Hungary's exports to the OECD. A finer disaggregation of the data was found not to be useful. The reporting practice of the OECD includes countries only above a critical minimum value. The considerably different export commodity composition between Hungary and the NICs at the level of individual products would distort results because more often than not data would not be reported for the respective other country or country group. The commodities included represent between 51 and 58 per cent of all Hungarian exports to the OECD. More importantly, they reflect the structure of total Hungarian exports to developed market economies, with manufactures providing the single biggest item, followed by food products (see Table 2.6 in Chapter 2).

Results

Table 3.8 gives the results of the analysis. The tables illustrating the computations (A3.1 and A3.2) are included in the appendix to this chapter. In both periods, Hungary's exports grew by less than they would have if its market share had remained constant. The relative loss was higher from 1982 to 1984 than in the later period. During the first period, the composition and/or orientation of Hungary's exports exerted a negative effect. From 1984 to 1987, the pattern became positive. In both periods, there are strong negative residuals. In sum, compared to the NICs, Hungary lost shares in the OECD markets. For 1982–4, these losses were due to an inconvenient fit between the structure of Hungarian exports and its respective commodity and regional markets as well as a loss of competitiveness. For 1984–7, only the competitiveness effect is negative. Hence, it would appear that the analysis resurrects what was previously called a myth: that the NICs, at Hungary's expense, increased their share in OECD markets. While this is true, it is not particularly interesting. The rivalry of states for market shares increases with the number of potential exporters. Shares fall unless overall market demand increases. More interesting would be to understand the details: that is, where and why in the huge OECD market Hungary lost market shares.

Table A3.3 shows structural and competition effects disaggregated to individual product and country markets. From 1982 to 1984, Hungary registered a strongly negative effect in its product and country pattern from exports to the EC. This appears to be due to the fact that the US and major Asian economies managed to get out of the recession of the early 1980s much faster than the EC which, of the three groups mentioned, is Hungary's largest export market. In the second half of the 1980s, the EC contributed strongly to the overall positive pattern of Hungary's export

Table 3.8   Decomposition of Hungary's export performance with the OECD

Period	Change	OECD demand growth	Commodity effect*		Regional effect*		Interaction Effect*		Competition Effect*	
1982–84	258447	208.7 539409.0	134.7	348136.0	–89.2	–230443.0	–25.2	–65036.0	–129.1	–333619.0
1984–87	521644	149.7 781028.0	12.7	66049.0	44.1	230321.0	1.5	7840.0	–108.0	–563594.0

Note: * First figure in these columns shows the percentage; second figure shows $000.

trade, in line with Hungary's stronger export performance. This suggests the pitfalls of a narrow geographical concentration of export markets, which is natural for small economies. When demand on the major market enters into decline or simply grows less dynamically than other markets, the exporting country is affected disproportionately. In terms of competitiveness, about 60 per cent of Hungary's dismal performance in both periods was accounted for by its standing on EC markets. It fared relatively better on the US market, followed by all other OECD members grouped together (R-OECD). It is noteworthy that Hungary lost competitiveness in all three regional markets over the entire period. In terms of commodities, Hungary's export product mix exerted a negative effect in about two-thirds of all subgroups in the first period. In the second period, however, in two-thirds of all subgroups the commodity composition registers a positive effect; there is a considerable bundling of positive effects through the manufacturing sector. This suggests that, in the first period, Hungarian exports (with the exception of ores and metals) went to the 'wrong' market. During the second period, with the demand constraint in its major market relaxed, Hungarian exports of food, agricultural raw materials, ores and metals, and fuels were somehow not the 'right products' to supply to the EC. Manufactures, instead, were the 'right products' going to the 'right market': that is, high-growth products were sent to high-growth markets.

In the food sector, Hungary gained competitiveness in one out of six subgroups during 1982–4 and in five out of eight during 1984–7. In agricultural raw materials, it once lost and once gained in the subgroup that makes up this sector. In ores and metals, it lost in all subgroups during both periods. In fuels, it lost in one of two sectors in 1982–84 and in one of one in 1984–7. In manufactures, it lost in 10 of 14 subgroups in the first period and in 14 of 17 in the second. In short, not surprisingly, there are relatively more subgroups in which the country lost rather than gained competitiveness in the five years under consideration.

Table 3.9 summarizes these results. By and large, the same number of subsectors exerted a negative effect on Hungary's (geographical and commodity) export mix and on its competitiveness in both periods. However, there is a curious discrepancy regarding manufactures in 1984–7. How does one explain that in an area where the 'right products' were sent to the 'right market' the country exhibited an above-average loss of competitiveness? Whatever the reason, it is far from obvious that this is because the NICs pushed Hungary out of EC markets.

In theory, if two countries are the only suppliers of specific goods to an external market and send all their exports there, and one of them loses market shares over time, one might suspect with good reason that an actual

Table 3.9   Losing/total product groups, in totals

Commodity groups	Structural		Competition	
	1982/84	1984/87	1982/84	1984/87
Food	4/6	5/8	5/6	3/8
Agricultural raw materials	1/1	1/1	1/1	0/1
Orea and metals	0/2	2/3	2/2	3/3
Fuels	1/2	1/1	1/2	1/1
Manufactures	10/14	1/17	10/14	14/17
Total	$16/25 \approx {}^2/_3$	$11/30 \approx {}^1/_3$	$19/25 \approx {}^3/_4$	$21/30 \approx {}^2/_3$

substitution is taking place. One country, in sum, turns out to be more competitive than the other. The critical element here is the absence of additional exporters. Alternatively, consider two countries which export, in the presence of other suppliers, to two markets but which concentrate their sales on one (that is, the same one) of the two. Assuming that the secondary market exhibits a higher than average growth rate with faster rising import demand which the two countries cannot match with their exports – because, for example, their exporters are not too familiar with that market – fiercer competition may ensue in the primary market to get rid of surplus capacity. In practice, neither of these two situations resembles the respective positions of Hungary and the NICs in the EC market.

As becomes clear from Table A3.4, neither Hungary nor the NICs are dominant suppliers in any of the commodity groups in which Hungary lost competitiveness. Only in select food products and textiles and apparel do the NICs reach a market share of above 10 per cent. Not surprisingly, intra-EC trade accounts for most imports of member states of the Community. The only exception is apparel (SITC 848) in 1987. This means that actual substitution may have taken place also between EC and Hungarian products. Note that intra-EC (as a share of total EC) imports in food, agriculture, raw materials, fuels and a number of manufactures rose.

Tables A3.5 and A3.6 illustrate the weighted averages of market concentration of the NICs and Hungary. Only in the food sector are the ratios equally high. This opens the possibility that actual substitution (for example, against Brazilian meat) has taken place. For manufacturing, this is rather doubtful. In Hungary's problematic commodity groups, the NICs earn 60 to 70 per cent of their export revenue from sales to the OECD, yet they sell only one-quarter of these exports to the EC. For Hungary, in contrast, around 40 per cent of its exports to the OECD result from sales of these problematic product groups, but some 70 per cent of these goods go to the EC market. For select chemicals, such as hydrocarbons, and for women's garments, this figure is still higher. Again, this suggests that Hungary's difficulties may result more from peculiarities it encountered in the Community market rather than from effective product substitution through the NICs.

To be sure, the argument is not that Hungary was as competitive as the NICs in the EC market: it was not. And it may be that some goods produced in the NICs drove Hungarian exports out of the market, but there is absolutely no way to prove this. In the light of the evidence illustrated below, it appears that other variables should also be considered, and that greater caution should be used in the analysis of aggregate data.

The Political Economy of Protectionism

Hungary's commercial relations with the EC have never been easy. Most other exporters into the EC probably would say the same. The difference, as I try to show in this section, lies with the relatively more disadvantageous treatment Hungary received compared to both other CMEA members and other non-EC competitors. Of course, problems are seldom exclusively the result of external factors. As will become evident in the next section, Hungarian policy-makers, while complaining about what they perceived as unfair trade practices, did little outside negotiation rooms to remedy the situation. And worse yet: 'It seems that our sensitivity to discrimination is related to the fact that efforts at boosting exports occur mostly in those areas where the obstacles are greatest' (Köves 1985, 218).

Hungary joined the GATT in 1973. Officially, it should since then have enjoyed most favoured nation (MFN) status with the OECD countries. As usual, it is necessary to read the fine print on the contract. Typically, the OECD countries had set discriminatory QRs to protect their domestic industries, but most contracting parties to the GATT gradually removed these QRs: not so the EC. Until 1982, successive rounds of talks between the Community and Hungary had been fruitless (Nyerges 1986). Indeed, the USA, Japan and Canada started taking sides and deplored the EC for not doing away with its restrictions (Van den Bossche 1989, 149; Haus 1992). Inotai suggests that trade political obstacles affected 25–30 per cent of Hungary's exports to the USA, 10–22 per cent to EFTA's Austria, Switzerland and Sweden, and more than 50 per cent of those to the EC. That is more than for any other CMEA country (1987, 28). He argues that there was an inverse relationship between Hungarian reform and EC trade liberalisation.

on the one hand the Hungarian economy has developed a relatively most intensive division of labour with the EC, ... and the closest relationship between the direction and the rapidity of the reform and the external environment has been most manifest in the case of Hungary, on the other hand, it is just toward Hungary that the EC applies most export-restricting means or explicitly discriminative trade political instruments. (Inotai 1987, 29)

In the meantime, the two sides had begun to negotiate bilateral trade agreements to regulate access to the Community market in sensitive sectors. The first agreement, in 1980, provided for export restraint and quotas in sheep and goat meat. Later agreements controlled quotas for calves for fattening (1988), textiles (1987–91) and steel (1987–8). The latter two were based on VERs. Some new ground was broken with the 1988 Trade and Cooperation Agreement (Matejka 1988; Senior Nello 1990; Tovias and Laird 1991, 16–32). Taken together, the Community's treatment of Hungary was relatively worse than that enjoyed by most competitors of the CMEA. In addition, it is important to point out that MFN, in the EC's tariff hierarchy, is the second least favoured status. Only countries that are not GATT members face still higher tariffs. This means that Hungary is treated like the USA or Japan, while several comparable economies enjoy preferences under the Lomé Convention, or the general system of preferences (GSP) and so on.

Big-bloc Protectionism and Small Countries

Being small-volume exporters was no insurance at all to the CMEA when, from the mid-1970s, the new protectionism replaced tariffs that had been lowered in successive rounds of trade liberalisation. Possibly, the CMEA economies were a ready target for (price- or quantity-distorting) NTBs because they did not represent a significant import market for the OECD and, hence, lacked any bargaining power to negotiate the imposition of lower import controls by the OECD members. Often, of course, they were suspected of subsidising exports. That may well have been the case. The problem – as shown below – was that it was next to impossible to ascertain the existence of export subsidies. However, the EC Commission had an institutional bias in favour of NTBs; exporters were hardly ever given the benefit of the doubt.

Olechowski and Yeats estimated that, in 1976, 21 per cent of Eastern Europe's and the Soviet Union's exports to a large majority of OECD countries were affected by quotas and licensing arrangements (1982, 234). This compared with 5.6 per cent for the LDCs and 6.2 per cent for the DMEs. Exports to the USA and EFTA (between 1 and 4 per cent) and Canada and Japan (11–18 per cent) were less subject to NTBs than those into the Community (27.3 per cent). Other NTBs affecting some share of CMEA imports into the EC included minimum prices (6.6 per cent), variable levies (4.5 per cent), and specific measures against state-trading countries (8.9 per cent). Taken together, the Community applied restrictions on 31 per cent of imports from developed countries, 34.5 per cent of imports from LDCs, and 61 per cent of CMEA imports.

Olechowski and Yeats computed coverage, uncertainty and frequency indices for individual CMEA countries. The uncertainty index measures the ratio of the number of traded four-digit CCCNs (Common Customs Classification Nomenclature) with at least one component tariff line subject to NTBs and the total number of traded NTBs in a given product group. If there are substitutes to the restricted product in the product group, they could become subject to similar restrictions. A frequency index measures the share of tariff lines in a particular product group covered by NTBs (Laird and Yeats 1990, Ch. 2). Their estimates reveal that Hungary was especially vulnerable to import control measures. Almost all of its exports were subject to some form of NTB. Quotas and licensing ruled 34 per cent of its exports to the Western countries in question, 18 per cent were affected by minimum prices, and 13 per cent by variable levies. The EC, again, topped the list: all three indices were higher by a wide margin than those computed for the other OECD economies. Restrictions were lowest on Hungarian exports to the USA, Canada and Norway, and still below average in Austria, Switzerland and even in Japan (Olechowski and Yeats 1982, 237). In general, NTBs affected mostly agricultural products. Restrictions also applied, on average, to 58 per cent of foodstuff exports, 26 per cent of textile exports and 19 per cent of footwear exports. The percentage of manufacturing exports restricted by the OECD countries was much lower (between 2 and 9 per cent). Again, the sectoral restrictions applied much more to exports to the EC than to any other market included in the study. The only exception are exports of food products to Japan. Of particular significance is that EC restrictions were much more pervasive in the manufacturing sector (SITC groups 6–9) where the other OECD economies restricted a lower share of CMEA's exports or, indeed, none at all (ibid, 242). In sum, NTBs affected CMEA countries more than any other group of exporters, although Eastern Europe's share in western markets was rather low. Hungary's exports, within the CMEA, were the most restricted. This was the result of particularly tough EC import policies, which covered not only the traditionally sensitive sectors but also manufactures. One might argue that the EC was more protectionist than North America because imports from the CMEA as a share of its total imports were much more significant than for the USA and Canada; but that would fail to explain the relatively more liberal attitude of the EFTA countries whose import shares from the CMEA countries were close to that of the Community.

Messerlin (1992) estimates the average levels of protection against Hungarian agricultural exports to the EC in the second half of the 1980s, expressed as *ad valorem* equivalents, at 101.5 per cent, or double their price. These are estimates arrived at by calculating the difference between domestic and world market prices due to price support measures and so on. Annual increases of the level of protection amounted to 23.2 per cent, which is considerably higher than the ratios for the (presumably less competitive) then non-reforming CMEA countries, namely Romania, Bulgaria and the USSR. About one-half of Hungarian exports of textiles and apparel fall under the MFA. One-third of MFA-defined categories is found in Hungarian exports to the EC. Messerlin argues that seemingly low utilisation ratios of quotas are due to the way the quotas are granted; large ones, such as in textiles, contain an incentive to capitalise on a potentially monopolistic market while relatively higher transaction costs are responsible for not entirely filled small ones (ibid, 6). In iron and steel, roughly 85 per cent of Hungarian exports are subject to NTBs, mostly in the form of minimum prices incorporated in the national quotas.

The existence of NTBs and their actual impact on trade levels are two different things. In fact, one cannot infer depressed export levels from more or less comprehensive restrictions on trade. Their applications simply suggest that managed trade may have contributed to Hungary's dismal export performance. Alternatively, if they did not, one might wonder why they were instituted in the first place. Given the importance of the EC as Hungary's major export market, it is worth investigating the relationship between EC protectionism and Hungarian export performance. One of the main instruments the EC uses to guide imports into its market are anti-dumping measures.[10] Between 1980 and 1988, the Commission concluded 264 investigations of dumping. It thus claimed 50 per cent of all anti-dumping cases in the world (five times more than the USA). In two-thirds of these cases, the Commission accepted price undertakings by the exporter in question; for the rest it imposed duties. More than one-third of all cases were against Eastern Europe, which compares to one-quarter for the Far East and one-fifth for Western Europe. Not to worry, says the Commission, 'by far the vast majority of imports into the Community are not affected by anti-dumping actions in any way whatsoever' (Commission of the European Communities 1990, 26). It may escape one's imagination why such considerable activity is invested to regulate a minute (if that is the opposite of 'vast') import flow. Somewhat ironically, the Commission also 'hoped that the figures will decline further following the economic reforms which are currently under way in certain of these countries' (ibid, 24). More reforms presumably translates into higher competitiveness: not exactly a guarantee for being spared accusations of dumping. At any rate, the Commission helped its conclusion along by a rather arbitrary use of statistics. It argues that despite its frantic anti-dumping activities, Eastern Europe's exports grew by 19 per cent in value terms from 1980 to 1988 (ibid, annex Q). This growth is definitely below average; all other countries' change in EC imports was 36 per cent. Yet that is not the interesting question:[11] much more significant is what kind of products were subject to anti-dumping investigations and, subsequent to the determination of injury, how their exports developed.

From 1980 to 1991, the Commission initiated anti-dumping investigations against 19 products (or product groups) in Hungary's exports. In five cases, no injury or dumping was found. Ten investigations were concluded by price undertakings on the part of the Hungarian exporter; duties were imposed on only two products. During the same period, seven anti-dumping rulings expired after an average duration of roughly six years. Several of these cases underwent reviews, and previously imposed measures were renewed or reinstated. Altogether, Hungarian exports covered by anti-dumping rulings were somewhere in the area of 4 per cent of total exports.

Table 3.10 shows that in five out of nine cases export values and volumes decreased in one or more years following the institution of an anti-dumping ruling. In two cases an increase of the sales price (which is what an undertaking is) led to a decrease of unit sales. In the two remaining cases – namely polyvinylchloride and hardboard – the anti-dumping ruling appears to have had no effect on either export volume or value. In contrast, when the restriction on exports of light bulbs expired, volume sales increased by 30 per cent. Both light bulbs and refrigerators belong to the commodity groups that are included in the data set used for the CMS analysis above. In this sense it is instructive to see that investigations were also launched against other CMEA countries, but not against the NICs. In fact, only rarely did anti-dumping rulings affect both Hungary and the NICs. It was the case for Brazil (hardboard, copper sulphate) and Yugoslavia (likewise, plus electric motors). For the purposes of this discussion it is not important to determine whether the CMEA countries dumped more than the NICs or whether they dumped at all; the argument is whether Hungary and the NICs were

Table 3.10   Anti-dumping and exports in select product groups 1982–87, value and volume indices

Product (SITC)	Data type	1982	1983	1984	1985	1986	1987
Artificial corundum (522.57)	Value	181	–	67	103	100	108
	Volume	281	–	95	140	100	87
Copper sulphate (523.19)	Value	115	123	100	102	141	139
	Volume	83	93	100	95	91	80
Polyvinylchloride resins (583.4)	Value	100	120	117	142	174	*247*
	Volume	100	108	101	138	137	*151*
Hardboard (641.61)	Value	100	319	251	–	267	*417*
	Volume	100	315	264	–	204	*278*
Flat glass (664.3)	Value	58	70	60	49	100	87
	Volume	62	87	78	61	100	70
Electric motors (716.2)	Value	100	65	78	78	122	157
	Volume	100	70	91	99	107	116
Refrigerators (775.21)	Value	100	100	96	80	85	126
	Volume	100	101	100	79	64	80
Electric light bulbs (778.2)	Value	100	87	83	79	*132*	143
	Volume	100	83	86	87	*117*	109
Sanitary fixtures (812.2)	Value	64	100	91	–	–	121
	Volume	54	100	96	–	–	93

Note: Index is 100 in the year anti-dumping ruling is imposed. For electric motors and light bulbs first undertaking in 1980, renewed in 1982. Figures in italics denote expiry of ruling.

Source: Official Journal, various issues; OECD *Series C, Trade by Commodities* [microfiche]; author's calculations.

treated with an even hand, so to speak, and not whether they earned it. At any rate, the latter is impossible to determine. Since the EC – for obvious reasons – did not want to rely on the distorted domestic prices of CMEA exporters to determine the existence of dumping, it used estimated surrogate producers' costs and prices. This effectively precluded a CMEA firm from *ever* being more efficient than their EC competitors: 'it is structurally impossible for the NME [non-market economy] producer to have a comparative advantage greater than that of the surrogate' (Vermulst 1987, 491).

Piontek maintains that the increasing number of anti-dumping charges against exporters into the EC had nothing to do with changed pricing policy on the part of the exporter (1987, 73). Of course, that applies to the NICs as well. However, the NICs, being in some cases sizeable importers of EC goods, probably were in a better bargaining position in anti-dumping cases than the CMEA, CMEA exporters being an easier target for Community producers than the NICs because the way CPEs were dealt with in the investigations[12] undertaken by the Commission suggests why they lost shares in the OECD and, especially, EC markets *vis-à-vis* the NICs: 'With these highly contingent and lawyer-intensive protectionist instruments inevitably also comes discrimination among trading partners. As in previous such periods, the weakest were hit the hardest' (Helleiner 1991, 7).[13]

Problems: A Second Cut

So far, the discussion has focused on the external environment and how, in particular, EC protectionism helps to explain why Hungary lost disproportionate shares in the OECD markets relative to some NIC competitors. This is an important point to make, especially in the light of studies which conclude that Central European exporters of manufactures are not really competitive at all, and hence should phase out production. Instead, it is argued, they might stay with rather simple, low or medium-value-added goods. This advice – if followed on a large scale – contains the risk of regressive development, namely a specialisation on simple processing industries (cf. Hrnc̆ír̆ 1993).

Underlining the adverse environment provided by Hungary's major export market is only part of the story. Policy is theoretically no less flexible than the environment to which it reacts. In other words, the mere existence of protectionism cannot by itself explain a good or bad export performance. Indeed, the latter also depends to a considerable degree on the export policy of the country in question. In particular, two aspects appear crucial.

- Is there systematic intelligence gathering and evaluation about (actual and potential) commercial policies in the main export markets?
- Does the government design programmes in terms of market and/or product diversification and/or upgrading to help its industry adjust to protectionism?

In the case of Hungary, a short answer to the two questions is, no.[14] For example, the Ministry of International Economic Relations does not keep a comprehensive record of NTBs against Hungarian exports. This may be less of a problem for big companies who can afford to find out for themselves, but it is definitely a hindrance for smaller or medium-size businesses which may want to venture into international markets. Academic writings on protectionism normally abhor its welfare-reducing consequences. The consensus against protectionism is almost unanimous. Only a few disagree (for example, Strange 1985). The fact is that managed trade has grown in importance. It is based on a coalition of concerned industry and the state. Regardless of whether or not the distributional welfare effects resulting from protectionism are desirable, targeted countries should not leave adjustment to their firms alone. If they do, their exporting industry competes on an uneven playing field because it competes against industry *and* the state in the foreign market. While it is generally known that VERs and OMAs (orderly market arrangements) now regulate trade in sectors that make up some 50 per cent of world trade, each country is affected to differing degrees by the various measures. The incidence of NTBs depends on fairly obvious factors such as a country's export composition and orientation but, as usual, the devil lies in the detail. Exactly where the nexus between surplus capacity in the importing countries and product specialisation in the exporting country is dynamically most inconvenient demands a comprehensive analysis of the protectionist behaviour (or the lack thereof) against one's own exporters and against those of one's competitors; an assessment of developments in the relevant markets (growth, changes in tastes and so on); and up-to-date knowledge of home producers' ability to substitute discriminated products against similar ones, diversify production, upgrade output and the so on. Consider Table 3.10. One way to escape anti-dumping rulings is to try to move into different markets. That happened in only two of the nine products included in the table. In artificial corundum, Hungary managed to increase exports to Japan.[15] Likewise, it increased sales of electric light bulbs to the USA, thus diminishing the relative importance of the problematic (that is, the EC) market.

To reiterate: attributing Hungary's dismal export performance partly to Western protectionism which affected the CMEA differently from the

NICs does not explain the lack of a systematic reaction from Hungary to counteract adverse developments in its trade environment. Undoubtedly, some of the NICs designed policy responses that helped their producers and exporters to adjust to developed-country protectionism (Hughes and Newbery 1986; Yoffie 1989). This is true even for *laissez-faire* Hong Kong. In 1977, though ultimately without accepting its recommendations, the administration established an advisory commission for diversification in order to react to the damage OECD protectionism inflicted on its textile and apparel industries (Haggard 1990, 152). By 1987, Hong Kong's textile exports to non-OECD countries were twice as high as to the OECD. It appears that Hong Kong's adjustment to protectionism is mostly due to the structure of its manufacturing sector; many small enterprises with a high degree of flexibility managed to switch production and markets (Li 1991).

The USA is the world's largest importer of textiles and apparel and, in the mid-1980s, bought more than half of its supplies from just five Asian producers: South Korea, Japan, Hong Kong, China and Taiwan. It ran sizeable and growing deficits with all of them. This was despite the attempt to protect domestic industries through MFA. The increased willingness of the Reagan administration to employ all sorts of protectionist devices, along with similar tendencies in the EC and a higher degree of self-sufficiency in LDCs, left the East Asian exporters no choice but to adjust their industrial capacities to stagnant markets. Not all succeeded in doing this.

In Japan, the government tried to stimulate new products and technology, to modernise production capacity and to move into high-value-added products. These policies, first enacted in 1974 and extended several times through the 1980s, had only a limited effect. In fact, now Japan emulates the US policy *vis-à-vis* East Asian exporters by withdrawing GSP status and negotiating bilateral OMAs (Chung-In Moon 1989, 198). In its strategic aims, the Korean Textile Industry Modernisation Act of 1979 resembled Japan's Temporary Law for the Structural Re-organisation of the Textile Industry of 1974, except maybe in its explicit emphasis on strengthening market information. Due to lower labour costs, Korean textiles were relatively more competitive than Japan's; consequently, concentration lay on upgrading and not on abandoning the industry. Means to this end were long-term, low-interest loans (with lower rates for credits used to develop technology rather than modernise plants); public investments to assist small-scale firms, and tax incentives (ibid, 201). In comparison, Korean adjustment was more successful than the Japanese. It appears, however, that rising domestic labour costs and productivity improvements of the textile industry in some of the importing countries will threaten Korean competitiveness in the 1990s, both from low-cost producers such as Malaysia and China and/or from high-value added producers, (for example, Germany). What is important about Korea is that the government recognised the limits to industrial expansion early enough to institute policies that would help its firms through adjustment.

In Taiwan, too, the government was aware of its eroding comparative advantage in the sector. Given the importance of the industry in the economy it was not prepared to steer producers away from textiles and apparel. On the contrary, in 1980 it announced a plan whose name speaks for itself. Through the Ten Year Textile Industry Revitalisation Plan, the government promoted vertical integration, technological innovation, R&D and modernization of equipment. Moon argues that small and medium-size enterprises (SMEs), which are mostly family-based operations and account for 98 per cent of Taiwanese businesses, have resisted vertical integration, and that upgrading and innovation has been lacking (ibid, 203). It is not clear whether his latter observation applies to the larger Taiwanese firms as well, but the government certainly is aware that low productivity and mainly low-value-added output of the small and medium-size firms are the major reasons for the problems that Taiwanese exporters are facing in international marketing, labour recruitment and financing. In fact, in 1990 the government drafted an Omnibus Industry and Business Assistance Programme. This programme provided for joint R&D between universities and industry to be put at the disposal of interested SMEs, improvement of vocational and training and cheap credits to purchase automation equipment, as well as marketing assistance. Vertical integration is not a prerequisite for access to these funds; the programme is targeted specifically to assist SMEs (cf. Ku 1990). The intended result may come about indirectly with the introduction of capital markets which allow SMEs to raise formerly untapped equity capital.

The Malaysian Development Authority (MDA), issued a report in 1985, detailing the problems the textile industry faced. International trade restrictions, especially from the USA, were only one; yet in contrast to most others (for example, low productivity, no indigenous technological base, too few trained personnel) protectionism was a problem which domestic reforms were unlikely to remedy by themselves. Consequently, the Fifth Malaysia Plan (1986–90) promoted upgrading, rationalisation, modernisation and diversification (for example, into quota-free pure silk, handloomed cottage industry fabrics and so on). The latter are produced in government-owned firms which will be privatised if they prove successful. Interestingly, both Malaysian industry and the government regard public intervention as suboptimal, but OECD protectionism 'virtually requires that the state exercise a heavy hand in industry decision making' (Douglas 1989, 437).

Whether adjustment to protectionism in the East Asian NICs worked according to plan is less important than whether it worked better than elsewhere. Undoubtedly, it did. Could Hungary also have done better? In the textiles and apparel sectors, probably not. Since the diversification of exports away from the Community was not an option because of the pervasiveness of protectionism against textile imports into the OECD in general, only upgrading remained. That, for reasons suggested elsewhere, was difficult in the short run in an economic system such as Hungary's, but it might be an option for the future. There are indeed examples of import-led innovation in the textile industry (Marin 1986). Hungarian garment producers have a good track record in commissioned labour. In the early 1990s, this sector attracted a higher than average share of foreign capital, offering to Western investors primarily professional knowledge and precise work. The Styl Company, for example, has been delivering commissioned work to Western fashion designers such as Bäumler, Maitland and Escada (Csejtei 1992).

In 1989, the production value of the textile industry represented 4.2 per cent of total industrial production value and the sector employed 6.5 per cent of the industrial workforce (HCSO 1991). Hence, in terms of employment (if not in output) it was one of Hungary's more important industrial sectors. Phasing-out, in effect, would have been difficult in a system accustomed to full employment. Yet that does not mean that the NICs' positive adjustment does not carry any lessons for Hungary. In the NICs, firms were helped to cope with the problem of adjustment; in Hungary, strange as that may sound, they were left alone. The country should have tried, among its Western export markets, to diminish the dependency on the EC. Obviously, a large-scale shift in the direction of exports is easier said than done, but in Hungary it was not even tried.

As pointed out above, import discrimination varies across the OECD economies. For some sectors, it is generally high, although not all products or product groups within any one sector are affected equally strongly. Opportunities to diversify existed, for example, with respect to the US market. After the granting of MFN status in 1978, Hungarian products became more price-competitive and, consequently, sold better. Interestingly, bilateral trade statistics with the USA make Hungary seem much more of a developed country than in its commercial exchanges with the EC. More precisely, in the mid-1980s machinery and consumer products made up 50 per cent of exports to the USA, which was more than twice the figure for the EC (cf. Lőrincze 1988). Advanced firm-to-firm cooperation existed for the development and manufacturing of engines and other vehicle parts and in the pharmaceutical and chemical industry. Exports in other sectors were also above-average high-value added. This is true for the food industry where most exports were highly processed and marketed under proper brand names to satisfy the sophisticated US market. That sophisticated demand is an essential ingredient for the development of first-rate quality is a prominent argument of Michael Porter's (1990). 'It is not an exaggeration to say that American sales educated our meat industry' (Lórincze 1988, 230). According to a Hungarian official, impediments to a further expansion of Hungarian products in the US market were due to low brand-recognition outside the East Coast and the Mid-west; technical standards and requirements; different practices in marketing and after-sales services; and, lastly, market information (ibid, 231–4). Surprisingly, in the view of the same official, it was up to Hungarian companies to deal with these problems. Government help would be provided *ex post*: 'As the market share of our export increases, we will have to influence the market with targeted promotional campaigns' (ibid, 234). It remains obscure why firms accustomed to a sellers' market and quite often in monopolistic positions, should be expected to judge appropriately the demands of a highly sophisticated and competitive environment. According to the survey by Bod (1989–90) referred to in Chapter 2, Hungarian managers often had no clue where their competitive edge was, or even whether they had one. That means somebody should have helped them to obtain the necessary information *before* they ventured abroad. Once firms have established a position in a market they probably need less assistance than they do initially to lower the costs of entry.

In Taiwan, the China External Trade Development Council (CETRA) engages in research of foreign markets to provide Taiwanese businesses with information they would find hard to come by otherwise. In turn, the government has high-quality information about its home producers because exporters' associations are required to catalogue and file their members' production interests and capabilities. How the two – *potential* buyers and *potential* sellers – are made to meet resembles an arranged wedding in the best tradition and is worthy of a lengthy quotation. Wade describes the activities of one of CETRA's overseas offices of which, in 1983, it had 42:

> The New York office, in addition to the usual functions of processing trade enquiries and organizing participation in trade shows, also carries out market research. For any sector it begins by studying the size and origin of U.S. imports by individual items. It then makes a first cut on which items Taiwan-made products could compete with. It studies their

price and quality. When a particular item is identified as promising, the New York office asks firms in Taiwan to send samples and price lists. Representatives of the office then visit importers and wholesalers with the samples. If the buyers are interested, the office telexes back to the manufacturers. If the buyers are not interested, the office finds out why and sends the buyers' reason back to the manufacturers also ... [CETRA's] ... effectiveness is related to, among other things, the large amount of information available to the government on the production range of specific firms (Wade 1990, 146–7).

The Textiles Section of the Malaysian Ministry of Trade and Industry also helps (mostly with information) their manufacturers to plan an adequate export strategy (Douglas 1989, 427–8). What remains to be explained is why the Hungarians did not engage in similar sorts of exercises.

IDEAS AND DEVELOPMENT STRATEGIES

So far in this chapter it has been argued, in short, that some firms and some sectors do not fit the generally bleak picture of Hungarian industrial development during the 1980s. Furthermore, it is suggested that EC protectionism may be more responsible for Hungary's dismal export performance than is commonly acknowledged. The third element discussed was policy: how reforms were designed inappropriately or inconsistently or, mainly, did not manage to elicit the desired outcomes due to the fundamentally unresponsive nature of the economic system. In this section, an additional determinant of Hungary's economic performance in the 1980s is discussed, namely (ill-informed) ideas about feasible development strategies held by policy-makers, academics and other involved elites.

Development strategies may be distinguished by four components (cf. Haggard 1990, 27–8). They feature a certain *orientation* (for example, export promotion or import substitution). They make use of specific *instruments* (for example, tax allowances). They engage economic *actors* (for example, private firms versus state-owned enterprises). They *integrate* (or not) given goals and choices so as to achieve coherence and consistency. Insofar as development strategies are identifiable with government policy, they are subject to both external and domestic constraints.[16] To relate to either, policy elites avail themselves of ideas, broadly conceived as 'more or less coherent frameworks of policy-relevant knowledge ... These ideas originate among professional economists and policy analysts and are transmitted internationally through international organisations, bilateral aid missions, and the training of professional economists and domestically through universities, research centers, and think tanks' (ibid., 46–7).

Notions about how to reduce the weight of the public sector in national income, establish fiscal balance, manage export-inducing exchange rates and so on are global 'truths' in the sense that non-believers are denied access to adjustment and assistance programmes administered by international organisations. There is considerable latitude and even disagreement across international organisations with respect to the 'idea' of structural adjustment. UNCTAD, for example, regularly criticises the World Bank for favouring liberalisation over development, conceived of as some form of sustainable (including, indigenous) industrialisation. But among the principal agencies administering adjustment programmes – the World Bank and the IMF (plus their main shareholders) – much the same ideas prevail.

Ideas are clearly not only home-made. To the extent that they are, however, ideas help to explain why countries pick certain development strategies and not others. Haggard (1990) suggests that the more autonomous elites are from social or international constraints,the more important ideas become in determining policy choice. Perhaps, but the opposite could be true as well. For example, the decision to honour or default on one's international loans – surely an international constraint – clearly may be influenced by other than just material variables. In what follows it is argued that Hungarian policy elites had rather clear ideas where to go (orientation), but they were less clear about how to do it (instruments and actors). They were, loosely put, long on strategy and short on tactics.

Orientation

Towards the late 1970s the Hungarian leadership recognised that the growth-cum-debt strategy had reached the limits of sustainability. Increased energy prices and higher international interest rates had begun to worsen the balance of payments and to turn further borrowing into an impractical option. In addition, the political climate between East and West was deteriorating and, Hungary being a raw-material and capital importer, it seemed advisable to curtail as much as possible any potential repercussions on the country from the international commodity and financial markets. In practice, this meant that a specific type of development strategy, relying on relatively cheap foreign resources and large inputs of raw materials into the production process, had to stop.

Theoretically, redefining Hungary's relationship with the world markets left two options. Either the country accepted that international changes of relative prices forced it to undergo structural adjustment, or it followed an inward path, trying in effect to disengage from the global markets and shut out disturbances generated there. In party lingo, the latter was often referred to euphemistically as 'strengthening CMEA cooperation', meaning that integration between the CPEs would substitute for East–West trade and capital flows. There is no reason why disengagement should not have been possible for the CMEA as a whole (assuming, of course, more effective integration mechanisms than those which had theretofore been practised). This is not to say that such an option would have been especially attractive. In fact, pursuing CMEA integration instead of, rather than together with, structural adjustment would have relegated the CMEA area to a status of eternal underdevelopment and led to social regression. Note, however, that this may also result from extreme adjustment strategies, such as Ceaus‡escu's debt-reduction programme at the cost of degenerating the social and economic fabric of the Rumanian society.

However, disengagement was not an option for Hungary as an individual Central European economy. Two elements – a large internal market or the availability of resources in demand on the world market – would have enabled Hungary to deepen import substitution, but it disposed of neither. In fact, while turning inward was the issue of debate for some time, it never had much influence and hence is not treated here.[17]

Until the late 1970s, a large part of the Hungarian leadership felt that the country's problems primarily originated in the capitalist world: that is, OPEC and OECD economies. Of course, while rising oil prices, growing inflation and erratic exchange rate fluctuations throughout the industrial world made life more difficult for the Hungarian planners, 'it [is not] possible to explain development difficulties and economic tensions *exclusively* ... by external ... factors' (Köves 1985, 75; emphasis in original). Analysts knew that the country might have weathered the crisis better had it not been for the relative neglect of services; too little investment in infrastructure (transport, distribution, storage, sales, flow of information) which was at half the rate of the OECD average; and primarily, a wrong choice of industrialisation targets. Investments in the energy sector and the raw-material branches were generally too high, to the detriment of a rather low share of manufacturing in total industrial output (Kádár 1980).

They also knew that the level of product concentration in foreign trade was very low, revealing an inadequate export specialisation. For example, in 1982 more than half of Hong Kong's exports took place in three product groups (at the 3-digit SITC level). Even a non-export oriented country like India concentrated 50 per cent of its exports in nine product groups. Instead, the 15 product groups in which Hungary achieved the highest shares of world exports accounted for only a good third of its total exports (UNCTAD 1985). The low level of product concentration applied especially to engineering products although in these markets a critical value of sales must be reached to recover the high proportion of development costs (Kádár 1984b, 241). Exports reflected a higher-than-average capital intensity while the labour-intensity was not much higher than the national average. Such a structure was not favourable for a country essentially short of capital and with comparative advantages in wage levels and professional skills (ibid, 244). Seemingly paradoxically, the low degree of export specialisation went hand in hand with a level of concentration of firms that was among the highest in the world. The absence of SMEs indirectly burdened the trade balance in that it led to a faster-than-average growth in imports of components and parts (Kádár 1980, 286).

Observers were aware of the advent of new competitors from southern Europe and South-East Asia in precisely those industrial branches – textile and apparel, metallurgy, household machinery – in which Hungary had specialised during the 1960s. This opened the uncomfortable possibility of 'double structural outflanking': on the one hand, through expanding supplies of low-labour cost developing countries, and on the other from relatively higher-quality products from the NICs:

> in the long run it will not be possible to maintain Hungary's competitiveness against the developing countries that rely on rich natural resources, cheap labour, imported Western technology and market organisation, and enjoy also the benefits of preferential tariffs and trade policies. The cost of keeping former market positions would be to put up with lower prices and declining export gains (or even losses) … it is justified to consider Hungary's present exports to the OECD countries as being 'structurally non-competitive'. (Kádár 1984b, 248)

Instruments

Hence, you open up. But how? According to Kádár, the way out of this was by stimulating high-quality goods so as to capitalise on superiority in R&D, and by resisting trade barriers. He illustrated that the more industrialised countries were characterised by policies of structural transformation – and hence, intent on widening the international industrial division of labour – the likelier they were to import Hungarian finished products (Kádár 1984b, 249). Selecting markets is a prerequisite to export success; in this case, sales efforts should have concentrated on the USA, Japan, Germany, the Netherlands, Sweden, Spain and Turkey because

Hungarian exports to these countries displayed an unusually high proportion of chemicals and machinery relative to other industrial products.[18] Given that a growing share of world trade in manufactures was done through multinationals and their subsidiaries, Kádár believed that closer firm-to-firm cooperation was required to actually reach Western markets, market the products and guarantee quality control as well as give aftersales service. Of special importance were capital imports for the acquisition of modern technologies and management skills, notably in the vehicle and pharmaceutical industries (1983a, 121–3). How to do that? Krasznai and Laki judged the prospects for cooperation with Western firms rather bleak (1982), although they maintained that Hungary possessed comparative advantages in the qualification and cost of the workforce, a developed infrastructure and so on. While the attractiveness of the latter is for foreign firms to judge, both static and dynamic comparisons of R&D inputs and intermediate outputs reveal a Hungarian performance superior to that of the other CMEA countries. Hungary was the only country to register an improvement in its patenting activity in the USA and West Germany (Hanson and Pavitt 1987, 59). Bodó-Vértes (1984) illustrates successful cooperation during the 1970s between Hungarian and West German firms in the machine-tool industry.

In a situation where the CMEA economies had no plans to increase imports and, hence, sales possibilities, Western firms' interest was bound to be minimal. In addition, the depressed CMEA area competed for cooperation with rapidly expanding markets elsewhere, (for example, in the Middle East or Asia). Also, since the first oil crisis Western firms had tried to insure themselves against risk and capital fluctuations by preferring lasting capital investments over more traditional market and contractual relations. Sure enough, in the authors' words, 'countries successful in raising the development level of the economy and in catching up with developed industrial countries could be found exclusively among those following an economic policy characterized by the dual criterion of the increase of exports and the import of foreign capital' (Krasznai and Laki 1982, 154). A schematic presentation of the argument goes like this: opening up makes it necessary to upgrade the economy. Upgrading, in turn, requires the participation of TNCs (transnational corporations). The first part of the statement is almost tautological. Evidence for the second is more ambiguous: in what way are TNCs a prerequisite for development? TNCs are critical for technology, capital and market access (Stopford and Strange 1991), but this is a too general assertion to inform policy-makers. Even if there is a more precise answer to that question, a programmatic challenge remains. FDI in Hungary was insignificant and, for a variety of reasons, likely to remain so.

This was realistically assessed by Hungarian analysts: 'why should foreign capital come with open arms to Hungary when it can make investments elsewhere under more favourable conditions?' (quoted in Rejtö 1983, 333). The more favourable conditions the author refers to include underutilisation of domestic capacities in TNC host countries, more advantageous tariffs and legal regulations and so on. The question remained rhetorical until the late 1980s. Only then did legal changes create conditions that attracted a strongly increased inflow of foreign capital. So while the part of the Hungarian economic elite not directly involved in the administration unequivocally underlined the importance of setting up long-term relationships with foreign capital, Hungarian policy-makers never overcame the taboo against majority foreign ownership. Without the latter, joint ventures remained a rare phenomenon in Hungarian business relations with Western firms, so the question then was how to make do without FDI. Let us consider these two problems – the role of TNCs, and upgrading the economy in their absence – in turn.

Krasznai and Laki's description of the impact of FDI is imprecise. Historically, FDI has not been the main channel of technology transfer in Western Europe or Japan. US FDI became really important in Western Europe only after the Second World War; in Japan, foreign technology came more in the form of patents. German innovative leadership in the chemical industry, for example, was related to exceptionally extensive R&D activities, giving rise to clusters of radical and incremental innovations (Freeman 1988, 69). Japan also assimilated and diffused foreign technology despite its significant exclusion of FDI. Today, developed countries acquire much of their technology through reverse engineering. For developing countries such as South Korea, technology imports were mainly embodied in capital goods (Hanson and Pavitt 1987, 50). Very little is known, in general as well as at the level of select industries, about the concomitants of total factor productivity (TFP) growth, much less about its determinants. Whether foreign participation in ownership improves TFP at the country or industry level is just one of the many open questions. More likely than not, research on different instruments available for the acquisition of technology will have to go a long way from descriptions of recent trade and industrialisation experiences before advancing theoretically convincing explanations (Helleiner 1992). Simply copying Western 'models', as attempted in Hungary, may be inadequate (Greskovits 1988).

Taiwan's electronic industry in the 1980s provides an example of how a country managed to move upmarket by itself rather than being 'lifted' by spin-offs from the activities of TNCs. In the early 1980s, subsidiaries of TNCs mainly operated labour-intensive production in Taiwan and ran high-value added production elsewhere. Robert Wade describes the process (1990, 103–10). The government realised the significance of indigenous public research and training capacities. The institutions entrusted with the fulfilment of the 1980–89 Information Industry Development Plan first decided on a strategy: the designers were wary of bumping into competition from the cash-rich and big Korean conglomerates that advanced into memory chips. Instead, they promoted lower-volume but custom-tailored chips which would help them to realise high differentiation in any type of electronics-dependent consumer product. The government contracted Chinese-American firms to assist in the design. Next, they initiated commercialisation by setting up a laboratory and production facility and underwrote the cooperation between indigenous producers and a TNC. This was done to set up a plant for the end-products. The product itself, however, had been developed before. Eventually, they provided fiscal investment incentives and concessional credit to integrate the public research laboratories with private firms. All told, the transfer and assimilation of advanced technologies were helped along by a public R&D organisation. This organisation, the Electronics Research and Service Organization, with, in 1987, a staff of 1700 and a budget of $100 million, thus provided an interface between domestic producers and the rest of the world.

The more a country depends on cheap labour to attract TNCs, the less influence it has on the relationship with the foreign firm. Relocation then depends on only one variable, namely wage levels. Even if globalisation does not mean that TNCs can shift production costlessly and overnight, low wages alone are less likely to keep a site attractive to a TNC. It may cost the host country dearly when a TNC moves out. In the 1980s, Taiwan has managed to graduate from mere assembly operations to higher-value added production (in which, to be sure, its skilled labour is still relatively cheap). Thus, it raised its attractiveness to the TNCs and preserved an industrial sector not dependent solely on intermediate processing. To return to schematic arguments: the government – through its extensive activities in R&D promotion and implementation, including the purchase of licences – managed to upgrade without depending on the TNCs. The latter (for example, McDonnell Douglas in aircraft production) joined the party once that had happened, which was the other way round from how the Hungarians saw this process working. Taiwan's successful attempt to escape dependence on TNCs while continuing to cooperate with foreign capital may not be representative for developing countries – comparisons with other countries would be necessary to assert that – but it suffices to show that the import of foreign capital may be most fruitful if complemented by indigenous efforts to upgrade the economy.

The question policy-makers should pursue, it seems, is how small, resource-poor economies can adapt the structure of R&D, design/production and trade to new technological developments. To relate this to priority industrial development in Hungary, as outlined in the sixth and seventh 5-year plans: what have been the conditions of success, for example, of the drugs, enzymes and fine chemicals industries – all highly R&D and capital intensive – in small countries such as Switzerland and Denmark? Small size may be a serious obstacle to adaptation. In absolute terms, small countries have fewer resources to finance their R&D expenditure. Hence, it is more difficult for them to join world leaders in technologically advanced sectors unless their firms are globally integrated (as, for example, Swiss-Swedish ABB or Finnish Nokia), which is something that CMEA typically were not. Typically, they settle for more traditional sectors of industry; but even there they may run into trouble if larger countries increase the technological sophistication of the less technologically advanced sectors, limiting small-country firms' ability to pursue an edge in innovation, or if NICs enter markets in which they have cost advantages (Walsh 1988). Kádár actually studied the industrial development of Scandinavia, the Netherlands and Switzerland. He argued that small-country development happened around select, related branches whose evolution is mutually reinforcing. Applied to Hungary, this would have meant that:

> a strategic centre of gravity ought to have been formed from the food-processing economy and should have meant the priority of a comprehensive system encompassing agriculture, the processing of agricultural products, the production of machinery for agriculture and food-processing, the production of fertilizers and plant-protective agents, veterinary technologies, infrastructure for food production and bioindustrial activities. (1985, 250)

This resembles what Porter calls 'clusters' in successful industrial economies (1990). But possibly Kádár thought of graduation rather than integration. His prescription would then echo 'stage'-theories of growth. Hungary, in other words, would feature labour-intensive agriculture and, over time, develop capital- and skill-intensive bioindustry. Not always, however, is the traditionally important sector (here, agriculture) significant to spin off more sophisticated manufacturing activity. In Korea, for example, the early growth sector – cotton spinning and weaving – was of no importance for the take-off of cement production, shipbuilding and steel production. In Amsden's words, the South Korean case attests to the existence of non-linear diversification (1989, Ch. 10). This point is important because some of the more successful Hungarian exporters produce goods outside the range of Kádár's 'comprehensive system'.

Kádár, thus, managed to outline *ex-post* development plans for the Hungary of the 1960s and 1970s. Arguably, an idea of how success stories came about in the past is an essential prerequisite for designing concepts appropriate for contemporary development, but the latter never materialised. Kádár, as well as most others, failed to substantiate proposals about how to reconcile conflicting targets in the present. For example, in discussing the requirements for production policy, Kádár lists the protection of the external equilibrium among the priorities, alongside the improvement of the income-generating capacity through value-increasing development (1984b). Evidently, there was a trade-off involved. Either Hungary continued to restrict imports to generate a current account surplus, or it modernised its production structure to increase exports.[19] Wallace and Clarke aptly summarised that the Hungarians were up against more than a simple decision dilemma: 'Unfortunately, but inevitably the difficulty to be overcome makes for difficulty in overcoming it. The CMEA economies ... need ... extra investment and improved technology, in order to trade successfully with the West in general; but to satisfy this need, they first have to trade successfully with the West' (1986, x). But the latter was inconceivable without liberalising the tight import regime. A gradual liberalization of imports was only feasible if domestic demand was constrained elsewhere. With investments at record lows already, household consumption would have had to be reduced, but that was a politically unacceptable option. Since 1956, keeping the population happy had been one of the key elements of Hungarian politics. The fact that in periods of structural adjustments populations – especially low-income groups in low-income countries – typically suffer was conspicuously absent from the Hungarian discussion. Márton Tardos (1981) was one of the few to argue against import restrictions and in favour of a (relative) deceleration of domestic demand. Apparently, the material and energy-intensive branches represented an easier target; there was a consensus in principle if not in practice to reduce outlays to the natural-resource intensive sectors and to disinvest, in general, from unprofitable activities. However, this academic consensus never translated into much policy action.

In a curious display of programmatic paralysis, the people in the think tanks never changed their discourse regardless of the deteriorating economic situation. The only practical proposal generated by the academic elite, namely to cut back allocations to unprofitable high-input sectors, was never implemented. Instead, investment patterns were based on what one observer later bluntly denounced as '"Stalinist" structural priorities' (Csaba 1989, 17). What remained were helpless statements and half-baked ideas.[20] In what was perhaps an implicit recognition of their ineffectiveness, articles discussing development concepts often reiterated the 'outstanding importance of capturing technological trends', without bothering to explain just how to do that, given the limits to indigenous innovation and joint venture operations. At times, language papered over real difficulties and acquired a tint of ridiculousness. 'Taking into consideration the limited availability of intellectual capacities and development resources, Hungarian industry will probably be able to reach, or at least approach, peak-level technology only in exceptional cases' (Varga 1984, 99). When nothing else helped, these essays ended with the familiar call, in highly general terms, for reform.

Systemic and Financial Constraints on Ideas

Ultimately, industrial policies are made by politicians and enterprise strategies by managers. Neither are made by academic experts. Thus, the discrepancy between the recommendations advanced in the economic literature on the one hand and the everyday reality of the Hungarian economy does not come as a surprise. However, the fact that the economy kept getting worse without provoking an alarming echo in a large body of that literature can be understood only in reference to the political context of the early and mid-1980s. First and foremost, the Soviet Union as a qualifying (or disqualifying) factor in the implementation of any reform was on the reformers' as much as the conservatives' minds in the Hungarian party, at the very least until Gorbachev came to power. The Soviet Union controlled the boundaries, so to say, of permissible political and economic fantasy in Central Europe. While it became increasingly clear that something had to happen to drastically alter the essentials of the economic structure of the country – when, alas, the systemic question posed itself – proposals of this sort were definitely outside those boundaries until 1985. The term 'socialist market economy' was not yet accepted terminology, and neither were the reformers, despite growing social discontent, in a position to challenge these boundaries by themselves. Some reformers clearly did not even think that political liberalisation was feasible or, for that matter, desirable. Kádár insisted that political centralisation, the 'capacity of will transmission' from a national state to society, was a necessary condition for structural adjustment in underdeveloped or crisis-ridden countries, unable to rely on incentives (1984a). If political and economic liberalisation go together, he argued, the preservation of power might be in question. In the end, in fact, the conservative establishment staged its own demise (cf. Wallace 1989; see also Köves and Marer 1991, 18). That said, there were a few rare exceptions. At the beginning of the period of structural adjustment, László Antal, then an analyst at the Ministry of Finance's research institute, emphasised that good economic policy was impossible in the context of a bad economic mechanism (1979).[21] His call for change basically came down to saying that the entire system needed an economic and political overhaul.

It took a series of worsening economic indicators from 1984 onwards (notably, among others, falling capital productivity, deterioration of the export composition, exploding subsidies, rising inflation, and numerous cases of enterprise insolvency) and government intransigence (embarking on an unrealistic growth campaign) plus the passage of a couple of years to provoke the drafting of a document, in the autumn of 1986, that picked up the debate again (Antal *et al.* 1987). In a sense, *Change and Reform* argued that only through a radical change in the system of economic management, namely the creation of a functioning market and competition or, in the words of the authors, 'the establishment of the inner motivation "*to operate profitably at any price*"' (ibid, 195; emphasis in original) would there be a chance to attain 'increased profitability ... and ... structural changes that help adjustment to the world economy' (ibid, 188). Costs for this should be borne by loss-making enterprises and consumption. Although some of the authors associated with the government subsequently got fired because of co-authoring what amounted to a political manifesto, many of its recommendations regarding financial management, questions of ownership and even – though with some delay – political participation found their way into the stabilisation programme issued by the party in the autumn of 1987 (cf. Csaba 1989).

The other main reason explaining the discrepancy between economic analysis and economic reality, and also between party programmes and central management practice, lies with the handling of the 1982 liquidity crisis. That is, to ensure that the country would stay afloat, government agencies resorted to a command-style intervention in the enterprises. Interference could be operational ('It would be appreciated if you did so and so') or come *ad hoc* in terms of individual fiscal or financial policy measures. This obviously contrasted with the more loosely regulated pre-crisis approach and inevitably confused both managers and other economic actors (Csaba 1989). But the wisdom of the emergency measures was not questioned even by the most genuine reformers inside and outside the party. For instance, Rezsö Nyers and Márton Tardos argued in 1979 against a temporary reduction of consumption and investment. That would, they believed, solve only one of the problems facing the country, namely the external imbalance, without pushing the system to become more efficient.

This resembled the proposal later elaborated by the authors of *Change and Reform*, in that they favoured a programme generally focused on reduced state intervention. But five years later – the liquidity crisis was mostly over by 1984 – although acknowledging that the option of accelerating economic changes, including market-guided capital mobility (that is, investment), still existed and was superior to short-term control measures, they cautioned that:

> as long as maintenance of the country's solvency and of normal living conditions of the population cause acute tensions and threaten with a social crisis, no adequate solution can be found for the long-term strategic questions, but only the security of supply can be maintained. The strategy of catching up with the leading countries will only be possible if the threat of economic instability can be satisfactorily eliminated. (1984, 9)

Options other than contraction existed in theory and were pursued in practice. Turkey, for example, also ran into substantial balance of payments problems in the late 1970s. In response to debt servicing difficulties, the 1980 reforms were followed by a rapid growth of exports of goods and services. The reforms included a devaluation, provision of export incentives, liberalisation of imports (Turkey had traditionally been a thoroughly inward-oriented economy), price liberalisation and interest rate reform. Some World Bank economists claim that 'Turkish medicine' could have cured the Hungarian ills, too (that is, the excess of vertical dependencies and the lack of innovative activities by firms), and that such reforms, along with technological change, would have facilitated structural adjustment (Balassa 1988).

The availability of such an option obviously depends on how seriously liquidity constraints are perceived. For example, it must have been clear to the Turkish leadership that the West, in the year of the Soviet invasion of Afghanistan and the seizure of the US embassy in Tehran, was not going to let a NATO member state slip into default on its international loans. On balance, Hungarians viewed the financial crises as more severe than outside commentators. Obviously, their stakes were higher. When already a member of government and hence in a position to influence economic policy and foreign economic diplomacy, Kádár still categorically stated that:'unless we alleviate external balance tensions on our own, and continuously improve our foreign trade performance, no political action can improve our image abroad and aid us in obtaining the external resources necessary to introduce comprehensive modernization and sustain our debt-servicing activities' (1990–91, 16).[22] With that, the discussion comes full circle.

FIRMS AND INSTITUTIONS

The material presented in this chapter lends support to the argument that not all problems faced in the 1980s were homemade. This contrasts strongly with the ideas which have effectively governed the transition programmes in the former CPEs. As discussed in the introduction, international assistance programmes and structural adjustment packages administered in Central Europe since 1989 blamed all of Eastern Europe's problems on the distorted constitution and inefficient operation of its economic system. Get rid of your system by way of, first, stabilisation and, second, liberalisation; that, the Hungarians and all other representatives of the new breed of *homo economicus convertens* were told, will solve your problem. The prescribed treatment will only produce the expected effect if the diagnosis is correct. If it is not, the treatment will remain, at best, unsatisfactory or, worse, it may harm the patient.

My argument is that the diagnosis was largely correct but incomplete. A relatively small but decisive part of Hungary's problems was due to exogenous factors, namely the protectionist trade policies of the EC. If Hungary's export problem is – wrongly – perceived only as a result of bad economic planning, there is no need to spend much time thinking about an adequate international distribution of adjustment and its costs. *They* adjust, *we* watch. Second, it has been shown that the Hungarian state, in comparison to upwardly mobile industrialising countries in East Asia, facing much the same problems, had neither the institutional means nor the right ideas about how to respond to these challenges. One may doubt whether most of the advice guiding the fairly successful stabilisations that took place since 1990 in Eastern Europe will also help the region to overcome its transformation hang-over. Stabilisation is different from restructuring; the IMF's and the World Bank's worldwide record in, as well as many Western governments' experience with, the latter are impressive only for their lack of success. In what follows we will try to draw a few lessons from this analysis for development strategies in contemporary Central Europe.

Firms

For many firms, 'selling as usual' became increasingly difficult following the events of 1989. Inputs were disrupted, markets vanished, and access to credits tightened. All of this worsened their competitiveness. Clearly, many bankruptcies are necessary to phase out production that is unsustainable. The case for this is well established and need not be repeated here. But consider the following. Many Hungarian firms producing machinery and engineering goods which sold successfully in OECD markets in the 1980s were affected, at least in part, by the same set of problems. A crude version of the neoclassical argument for efficient resource allocation would have it that all subsidies are bad and must be cut. Consequently, if the success of these firms in the past was based on distorted prices, they are not *really* competitive. Taken to its extreme, this reasoning can lead to regressive specialisation; since a country cannot prosper on pig farming alone, Hungary would lose any prospect of catching up. The theoretical battle among neoclassical true believers and more interventionist-minded economists about how to deal with economies of scale and learning, imperfect capital markets, externalities, market disruptions (clearly of relevance in Central Europe) and differential growth potentials will not be decided any time soon. But soon Central European policy-makers must decide how to retain a relatively integrated industrial base in their economies. And, for the time being, the firms referred to above may be the single-best indicator around which sectors they might organise this.

For firms to enter a market they must be able to handle the required technology and dispose of sufficient investment funds. A number of Hungarian firms have proved in the past that they can fulfil the first condition. By 1993, they had problems with the latter. The knowledge and skills constraint, in other words, was less binding than the investment constraint. The paradox of development, in Carlota Perez's words, is that:

> previous capital is needed to produce new capital, previous knowledge is needed to absorb new knowledge, skills must be available to acquire new skills and a certain level of development is required to create the externalities that make development possible. This is why the rich get richer and the gap remains and widens for those left behind. All development policies have in one way or another been geared to breaking away from this vicious circle. (1988, 89)

In the short term, the choice is between helping a potentially viable industry along or, possibly, losing it. This must not be taken to mean that traditional industrial policy is the only viable development strategy. In the long term, much will depend on education, vocational training, R&D, the import of investment goods, cooperation with TNCs and so on. But these things take time to exert an impact. How well the helping-along works depends on investing much educated effort in deciding which sectors or firms to target. What the East Asian countries (except Hong Kong) referred to throughout this chapter have in common is that their choice has been, more often than not, to assist their priority industries. Second, also more often than not, they have picked the right sectors and firms. An incomplete theoretical understanding of this (as well as frequent cases of industrial policy failures) cannot deny that countries such as Singapore belong to the few role models around (cf. Ray 1992, 52).

Institutions

Hungary's problem with GATT was twofold. The country had far too high expectations about the benefits of membership. When those expectations were not fulfilled the country lacked a strategy to somehow make do without more immediate tariff concessions. What was missing was, say, an Agency for National Business Development. Modelled on similar institutions in East Asia, it could have pondered which industries and markets to diversify, and through which policies to achieve this. 'It should think of itself as a strategic oligopolist, scrutinising the actions of rival governments and taking account of these actions and reactions in framing its policies for investment, trade and technology' (Wade 1990, 372). This has nothing to do with old-style central planning *per se*, although one should acknowledge the risk that it deteriorates into that. The argument simply acknowledges the many non-economic (informational, institutional and even political) problems enterprises outside the most developed OECD countries have in bringing a product to a market and gaining some share in it, even if their product is potentially competitive.

Today, the Hungarians seemingly have forgotten their doubtful honeymoon with GATT. International trade arrangements usually are not drawn up for the benefit of small (that is, weak) and relatively underdeveloped economies.[23] The Hungarians entertain high expectations regarding the Europe Agreements with the EC and, again, do not command sufficient human resources to think about flexible responses should things go badly.[24] For example, for reasons that are understandable politically but which perhaps do not make much economic sense, Hungary (as well as Poland and the former Czechoslovakia) prioritised the Europe Agreement before thinking about the option of liberalising trade within Central Europe. Since intra-industry specialisation is rather high in trade with these two countries, one might wonder whether eastern trade initiatives should not have been developed in line with those in the western direction (cf. Bakos 1992a).

A new institution in a country that is busy trying to reduce the excess weight of government may seem a funny proposal. Indeed, setting up a nononsense agency that manages to attract the highly talented civil servants required for its successful operation would not be easy. Perhaps the Hungarian government should send young graduates to places like Taiwan or South Korea to learn more about the operations of business and the relationship between business and government in those countries. Alternatively, it might set up a 'growth centre' at one of the universities in the country and invite Asian scholars to visit. In short, it should try to tap an important resource – ideas – that has produced more practical evidence about how latecomers can 'make it' than much Western scholarship.

APPENDIX: THE CONSTANT CMS ANALYSIS

The identity goes as follows:

$$\Delta m = m' \Delta M$$

$$+\left\{\sum_i \sum_j m'_{ij} \Delta M_{ij} - \sum_j m'_j \Delta M_j \right\} + \left\{\sum_i \sum_j m'_{ij} \Delta M_{ij} - \sum_j m'_j \Delta M_i \right\}$$

$$+\left\{\left[\sum_i m'_j \Delta M_i - m' \Delta M\right] - \left[\sum_i \sum_j M'_{ij} \Delta M_{ij} - \sum_j m'_j \Delta M_j\right]\right\} \quad (3.1)$$

$$+\sum_i \sum_j M_{ij}^{t-1} \Delta m_{ij}$$

where

m = OECD imports from Hungary
M = OECD imports from the NICs
i = imports of good i
j = imports into country j (here: US, EC, Rest-OECD)

The first term on the right-hand side of the identity represents the growth of Hungary's exports to the OECD associated with the general increase of exports of the reference group (here: NICs). The second and third term reflect the demand for particular commodities and in specific countries, respectively. They will be positive (negative) if the commodity composition and regional orientation of the exports by the country in question are relatively more (less) concentrated on high-growth markets than the exports of the reference group. The last term represents the residual (that is, whatever is not accounted for by structural demand effects in the changes of Hungary's export shares in the OECD market).

The identity could be written without the fourth term on the right-hand side. Consider, for example:

$$\Delta m = m' \Delta M - \left\{\sum_i m'_i \Delta M_i - m' \Delta M\right\} + \left\{\sum_i \sum_j m'_{ij} - \sum_i m'_i \Delta M_i \right\}$$

$$+\sum_i \sum_j M_{ij}^{t-1} \Delta M_{ij} \quad (3.2)$$

While no case of exceptional beauty either, this formulation is at least a little shorter and reveals – except for the value of the commodity pattern effect – the same results. So why not use it instead? One weakness of all CMS formulae is that one may compute (contrary to the above formula) first the market distribution effect and then the commodity composition effect. This will not change the sum of the demand effects but will give different values for the commodity and market distribution of a country's exports. Richardson reports that these variations, including of sign, may be rather substantial (1971, 233). The fourth term in equation (3.1) does not resolve this problem, but it introduces symmetry in the formulation of commodity and regional effects and offers the following simple interpretation help: if positive, it enforces the structural effects; if negative, then the country in question has a problem with its commodity composition or market orientation, or both. Hoen and Wagener, accordingly, call this term 'structural interaction effect' (1989, 66).

Table A3.1   CMS analysis of changes in Hungarian exports to OECD *vis-à-vis* NICs, 1982–84 ($ thousands)

Area	NICs' export 1982 (1)	NICs' export 1984 (2)	Hungary's export 1982 (3)	Hungary's export 1984 (4)	ΔM (2)÷(1)−1 (5)	$S_j m^t_j \Delta M_j$ (5)×(3)	$S_j m^t_j \Delta M$ 0.44×(3)	$S_i S_j m^t_{ij} \Delta M_{ij}$ (6)
Regions								
USA	8 679 691	15 653 311	99 946	174 754	0.80	79 957	43 976	138 680
EC	6 540 533	7 176 366	823 773	789 822	0.10	82 377	362 460	169 258
R-OECD	5 908 811	7 516 605	302 209	519 799	0.27	81 596	132 972	284 128
Total	21 129 035	30 346 282	1 225 928	1 484 375	0.44	243 930	539 408	592 066
Commodities *SITC*	(1)	(2)	(3)	(4)	(5)	$S_i m^t_i \Delta M_i$ (5)×(3)	$S_i m^t_i \Delta M$	$S_i S_j m^t_{ij} \Delta M_{ij}$ (6)
001	212 200	159 986	71 249	53 051	−0.25	−17 812	31 350	−24 653
011	367 390	511 833	198 513	215 184	0.39	77 420	87 346	33 374
014	319 006	341 330	57 152	60 551	0.07	4 001	25 147	5 055
081	1 226 525	1 474 482	26 930	17 673	0.20	5 386	11 849	19 671
112	150 937	148 526	31 683	20 865	−0.02	−634	13 940	−5 424
288	89 712	169 561	22 188	25 543	0.89	19 747	9 763	28 418
291	177 113	194 984	47 256	55 032	0.10	4 726	20 793	−3 042
334	3 627 401	4 965 561	74 664	248 196	0.37	27 626	32 852	5 099
335	178 181	321 345	35 642	43 362	0.80	28 514	15 682	18 770
423	32 759	47 634	28 359	37 025	0.45	12 761	12 478	110 811
511	139 391	539 023	81 959	61 910	2.87	235 222	36 062	98 104

Table A3.1   (cont.)

Area	NICs' export 1982 (1)	NICs' export 1984 (2)	Hungary's export 1982 (3)	Hungary's export 1984 (4)	ΔM (2)÷(1)-1 (5)	$S_j m_j^t \Delta M_j$ (5)×(3)	$S_j m_j^t \Delta M_j$ 0.44×(3)	$S_i S_j^t m_{ij}^t \Delta M_{ij}$ (6)
515	105 262	324 816	24 438	30 368	2.09	51 075	10 753	57 205
562	153 976	188 397	38 472	42 472	0.22	8 464	16 928	22 420
583	305 245	529 175	22 202	33 359	0.73	16 207	9 769	7 543
658	419 975	605 734	25 695	26 628	0.44	11 290	11 306	4 885
672	389 131	540 245	33 746	37 678	0.39	13 161	14 848	-2 100
674	668 066	1 114 389	26 544	29 824	0.67	17 784	11 679	-1 117
684	100 119	445 238	46 122	83 323	3.45	159 121	20 294	137 132
778	932 271	1 506 033	57 409	55 189	0.61	35 019	25 260	19 709
784	560 480	1 071 255	26 311	61 464	0.91	23 943	11 577	28 661
821	945 655	1 463 443	34 794	35 088	0.55	19 137	15 309	1 975
842	2 046 228	2 480 034	56 318	52 042	0.21	11 827	24 780	8 215
843	3 062 104	4 001 896	93 773	88 816	0.31	29 070	41 260	4 773
848	1 525 568	2 203 275	28 810	26 920	0.44	12 676	12 676	4 886
851	3 394 340	4 998 087	35 699	42 812	0.47	16 778	15 708	11 696
Total	21 129 035	30 346 282	1 225 928	1 484 375	0.44	822 509	539 409	592 066

Note: (6) was computed from the growth rates of the cross classification of NICs' exports by regions and by commodities and then multiplied by the respective cross classification of Hungarian exports in 1982.

Source: OECD, *Series C. Trade by Commodities* [microfiche]. Author's calculations.

Table A3.2 CMS analysis of changes in Hungarian exports to OECD *vis-à-vis* NICs, 1984–87 ($ thousands)

Area	NICs' export 1982 (1)	NICs' export 1984 (2)	Hungary's export 1982 (3)	Hungary's export 1984 (4)	ΔM (2)÷(1)-1 (5)	$S_j m_j^t \Delta M_j$ (5)×(3) (6)	$S_j m_j^t \Delta M_j$ 0.44×(3) (6)	$S_i S_j m_{ij}^t \Delta M_{ij}$ (6)
Regions								
USA	18 023 588	25 239 607	183 127	203 373	0.40	73 251	104 382	71 674
EC	8 346 385	15 368 307	845 593	1 253 479	0.84	710 298	481 988	739 984
R-OECD	7 115 421	12 036 713	341 507	435 019	0.69	235 640	194 659	273 580
Total	33 485 394	52 644 627	1 370 227	1 891 871	0.57	1 019 189	781 029	1 085 238
Commodities SITC	(1)	(2)	(3)	(4)	(5)	$S_i m_i^t \Delta M_i$	$S_i m_i^t \Delta M_i$	$S_i S_j m_{ij}^t \Delta M_{ij}$ (6)
011	511 833	1 177 017	215 184	278 694	1.30	279 739	122 655	183 682
014	341 330	358 281	60 551	83 019	0.05	3 027	34 514	994
044	66 741	21 245	19 494	28 946	-0.68	-13 256	11 112	-14 628
054	896 401	1 090 713	34 427	61 539	0.22	7 574	19 623	12 353
058	1 732 644	1 931 089	27 612	66 987	0.11	3 037	15 739	10 486
081	1 474 482	1 351 001	17 673	27 845	-0.08	-1 414	10 074	-3 148
112	148 526	361 209	20 865	23 146	1.43	29 837	11 893	17 973
222	431 785	692 829	21 297	21 509	0.60	12 778	12 139	22 595
287	322 247	243 139	27 429	10 223	-0.24	-6 583	15 634	-14 940
288	169 561	249 839	25 543	31 259	0.47	12 005	14 559	12 631
291	194 984	279 571	55 032	79 792	0.43	23 664	31 368	29 746
335	321 345	352 520	43 362	41 451	0.10	4 336	24 716	-15
511	539 023	351 024	61 910	80 366	-0.35	-21 668	35 289	199

Table A3.2 (cont.)

Area	NICs' export		Hungary's export		ΔM $(2)\div(1)-1$	$S_j m^t_j \Delta M_j$	$S_j m^t_j \Delta M_j$	$S_i S_j m^t_{ij} \Delta M_{ij}$
	1982 (1)	1984 (2)	1982 (3)	1984 (4)	(5)	(5) × (3)	0.44 × (3)	(6)
562	188 397	319 281	42 472	45 628	0.69	29 306	24 209	46 374
583	529 175	795 256	33 359	66 436	0.50	16 679	19 015	35 505
658	605 734	1 066 684	26 628	40 042	0.76	20 237	15 178	20 089
672	540 245	1 064 174	37 678	65 733	0.97	36 548	21 476	82 478
673	364 316	487 151	50 446	36 007	0.34	17 152	28 754	49 082
674	1 114 389	1 314 423	29 824	53 897	0.18	5 368	17 000	26 002
684	445 238	909 058	83 323	88 683	1.04	86 656	47 494	119 547
775	1 200 476	2 376 033	29 400	42 500	0.98	28 812	16 758	59 750
778	1 506 033	2 634 788	55 189	82 928	0.75	41 392	31 458	55 005
784	1 071 255	2 018 127	61 464	54 730	0.88	54 088	35 034	49 334
791	6 471	7 128	5 900	2 886	0.10	590	3 363	18 429
821	1 463 443	2 964 666	35 088	68 976	1.03	36 141	20 000	36 735
842	2 480 034	3 907 346	52 042	98 274	0.57	29 664	29 664	36 228
843	4 001 896	5 965 091	88 816	143 885	0.49	43 520	50 625	70 170
845	3 616 028	6 506 144	38 487	61 695	0.80	30 790	21 938	45 610
848	2 203 275	3 632 963	26 920	40 573	0.65	17 498	15 344	30 230
851	4 998 087	8 216 837	42 812	64 222	0.64	27 400	24 403	46 742
Total	33 485 394	52 644 627	1 370 227	1 891 871	0.58	854 917	781 028	1 085 238

Note: (6) was computed from the growth rates of the cross classification of NICs' exports by regions and by commodities and then multiplied by the respective cross classification of Hungarian exports in 1982.

Source: OECD, *Series C. Trade by Commodities* [microfiche]. Author's calculations.

Table A3.3　Structural and competition effects disaggregated to individual markets (%)

	1982/84 Structural effects	1982/84 Competition effects	1984/87 Structural effects	1984/87 Competition effects
Regions				
USA	179.8	19.1	−10.7	9.1
EC	−366.9	60.9	84.8	58.9
R-OECD	287.1	19.9	25.9	31.9
$ Total	52 657 = 100 %	−333 619.0	304 210.0	−563 594.0
Commodities				
001	−106.3	−1.9	−	−
011	−102.5	5.0	20.1	21.3
014	−38.2	0.5	−11.0	−3.8
044	−	−	−8.5	−4.3
054	−	−	−2.4	−2.6
058	−	−	−1.7	−5.1
081	14.8	8.7	−4.3	−2.4
112	−36.8	1.6	2.0	2.8
222	−	−	3.4	4.0
287	−	−	−10.0	0.4
288	35.4	7.5	−0.6	1.2
291	−45.3	−3.2	−0.5	0.9
334	−52.7	−50.5	−	−
335	5.9	3.3	−8.1	0.3
423	186.7	30.6	−	−
511	117.8	35.4	−11.5	−3.2
515	88.2	15.4	−	−
562	10.4	5.5	7.3	7.7
583	−4.2	−1.1	5.4	0.4
658	−12.2	1.2	1.6	1.2
672	−32.2	−1.8	20.0	9.7
673	−	−	6.7	11.3
674	−24.3	−1.3	3.0	0.3
684	221.9	29.9	23.7	20.3
775	−	−	14.1	8.3
778	−10.5	6.6	7.7	4.8
784	32.4	−1.9	4.7	9.9
791	−	−	4.9	3.8
821	−25.3	0.5	5.5	0.5
842	−31.4	3.7	2.2	−1.8
843	−69.3	2.9	6.4	2.7
845	−	−	7.8	4.0
848	−14.8	2.0	4.9	2.9
851	−7.6	1.4	7.3	4.5
$ Total	52 658 = 100 %	−333 619.0	304 210.0	−563 594

Source:　Author's calculations.

Table A3.4   Shares in total EC imports of Hungary's problematic product groups: NICs, Hungary, intra-EC (%)

	1982			1984			1987		
SITC	*NICs*	*Hungary*	*EC*	*NICs*	*Hungary*	*EC*	*NICs*	*Hungary*	*EC*
Food									
001	2.5	1.9	74.8	3.1	2.4	76.1	2.9	1.8	79.2
014	16.1	2.5	68.9	19.0	2.3	68.1	*12.6*	*2.0*	*72.4*
081	17.7	0.3	34.1	20.8	0.2	35.0	*16.5*	*0.3*	*40.0*
112	1.0	0.6	80.0	0.9	0.4	81.5	0.8	0.2	92.8
222	–	–	–	5.6	0.4	15.7	10.7	0.2	35.2
423	2.3	0.6	63.5	1.1	0.0	72.4	–	–	–
Agricultural raw materials									
291	*7.5*	*4.8*	*35.0*	7.0	5.2	38.0	7.0	5.6	42.9
Ores and metals									
287	–	–	–	3.8	0.0	15.4	3.8	0.0	14.5
288	0.9	0.8	54.9	2.0	0.6	55.4	2.8	0.9	13.4
684	1.2	0.5	61.6	2.6	0.6	58.9	3.5	0.4	65.1
Fuels									
335	2.7	1.1	44.8	3.2	1.3	47.6	2.4	1.1	59.2
Manufactures									
511	1.3	1.5	75.3	2.8	1.1	76.3	*2.4*	*1.1*	*77.3*
515	1.9	0.5	59.0	8.0	0.6	53.1	–	–	–
562	2.6	1.2	63.2	4.0	1.3	61.8	6.2	0.9	59.9
583	*0.8*	*0.1*	*81.0*	1.1	0.1	80.7	1.4	0.2	82.6
658	11.2	1.4	62.7	13.3	1.1	40.6	14.4	0.8	55.0
672	*2.9*	*0.7*	*70.2*	1.1	0.4	81.6	4.3	0.4	83.3
673	–	–	–	1.7	1.1	68.3	1.9	0.5	76.3
674	*1.8*	*0.3*	*74.5*	1.2	0.3	75.7	1.8	0.4	77.6
775	–	–	–	5.4	0.7	67.2	8.1	0.5	70.7
778	4.6	0.6	57.6	4.3	0.5	55.3	5.3	0.4	61.2
791	–	–	–	0.1	1.4	73.0	0.3	0.3	61.0
821	3.5	0.6	72.8	3.7	0.6	70.8	3.6	0.6	75.5
842	23.6	1.2	46.0	26.1	1.0	42.7	*24.8*	*1.2*	*44.7*
843	23.4	2.1	49.6	24.0	1.8	49.4	22.4	1.4	51.7
845	–	–	–	21.2	0.8	57.7	21.2	0.6	61.0
848	29.8	1.1	42.3	33.4	1.0	38.3	37.5	0.8	36.0
851	12.5	0.5	66.7	14.5	0.8	62.3	17.1	0.6	69.7

Notes: Figures in italics indicate product groups where Hungary did not lose competitiveness. EC = intra-EC.

Sources: OECD, *Series C. Trade by Commodities* [microfiche]; author's calculations.

Table A3.5 Problem cases 1982–84: relative weight of export share to EC market, Hungary and NICs, in 1982.

SITC	Hungary Export share to EC	Relative weight	NICs Export share to EC	Relative weight
Food				
011	81.8	16.2	59.1	1.7
014	52.7	4.7	61.5	1.5
081	72.9	2.2	95.7	5.8
112	69.3	2.6	22.4	0.7
423	21.3	2.3	76.3	0.1
[	70.1		78.7	
Ores & metals				
288	66.1	1.8	28.3	0.4
684	45.8	3.8	54.0	0.5
[	52.3		42.6	
Fuels				
335	68.4	2.9	35.1	0.8
[	68.4		35.1	
Manufactures				
511	80.4	6.7	41.9	0.7
515	54.7	2.0	46.9	0.5
562	74.5	3.1	39.0	0.7
658	54.5	2.1	19.9	1.4
778	50.8	4.7	24.3	4.4
821	74.4	2.8	17.1	4.5
842	76.1	4.6	40.1	9.7
843	93.4	7.6	32.0	14.5
848	67.4	2.3	33.2	7.2
851	59.1	2.9	12.7	16.1
ϕ	72.9		26.6	

Sources: OECD, *Series C. Trade by Commodities* [microfiche]; author's calculations.

Table A3.6   Problem cases 1984–87: Relative weight of export share to EC market, Hungary and NICs, in 1987 (%).

SITC	Hungary Export share to EC	Relative weight	NICs Export share to EC	Relative weight
Food				
011	76.8	14.7	28.7	2.2
112	61.5	1.2	13.6	0.7
222	58.8	1.1	83.8	1.3
[	74.6		43.2	
Agricultural raw mats				
291	80.2	4.2	28.9	0.5
[	80.2		28.9	
Ores & metals				
287	7.2	0.5	58.2	0.5
288	70.4	1.6	28.7	0.5
684	41.5	4.7	32.2	1.7
[	45.8		36.4	
Fuels				
335	64.5	2.2	16.2	0.7
[	64.5		16.2	
Manufactures				
562	75.8	2.4	70.1	0.6
583	61.9	3.5	28.6	1.5
658	50.9	2.1	32.2	2.0
672	35.3	3.5	21.0	2.0
673	69.9	1.9	21.9	0.9
674	68.6	2.8	11.8	2.5
775	84.9	2.2	24.3	4.5
778	51.8	4.4	21.5	5.0
791	62.5	0.1	24.5	0.0
821	73.5	3.6	11.0	5.6
843	82.9	7.6	31.5	11.3
845	81.1	3.3	28.7	12.4
848	67.3	2.1	34.4	6.9
851	74.7	3.4	17.2	15.6
[	65.9		24.5	

Sources: OECD, *Series C. Trade by Commodities* [microfiche]; author's calculations.

4 The Management of Foreign Direct Investment: A Preliminary Assessment

FDI has become one of the most important sources of capital in the 1980s. Estimates hold total FDI flows in 1990 at around $225 billion. FDI is concentrated within a 'triad' consisting of the USA, Western Europe and Japan. In these countries, it is partly driven by an accelerating pace of technological innovations which shorten the life-span of capital stock. About 15 per cent of FDI goes into the developing countries and, although their share in total FDI flows has been falling, it has come to account for three-quarters of all long-term capital inflows to LDCs from private sources. One reason for the growing concentration of FDI in developed countries has to do with the creation or preparation of integrated markets: the European Economic Area (EEA) in and around the EC, NAFTA with the USA as its core and increasingly also within the Association of South East Asian Nations countries. The EC's drive towards a higher degree of integration reduced transaction costs and provided new incentives to invest for both European and non-European investors. This translates into disincentives for production in 'outsider'-type-countries whose relatively lower labour costs may be offset by the expected profitability of doing business within the area of integration (Katseli 1992). Even in the absence of such regional blocs, the comparative advantage of low labour costs clearly carries only so far. When relative wages grow in the host country, 'in a multi-country world and in the presence of footloose factors, ... footloose activities will tend to contract in the original countries and be transplanted to more profitable locations' (ibid, 27–8). On average, FDI grew $2\frac{1}{2}$ times more than merchandise trade and 3 times more than world output in the second half of the 1980s. According to the UN Transnational Corporations and Management Division (UNTCMD), foreign affiliates of TNCs produce almost twice as much as is traded on the world market for goods and services, and this figure does not even account for the increasing volume of intra-firm trade.

Of course, FDI and TNCs are not synonymous. At times small investors set up joint ventures to facilitate retail or to produce something in a foreign market without engaging in a global network of development, production, marketing and distribution that is generally taken to be the hallmark of a

TNC. Alternatively, a TNC may prefer to license the manufacturing of a product to a partner firm in a foreign country without actually acquiring equity; hence, the resulting transaction would not qualify as foreign investment. Instead, such transactions have come to be called new forms of investment (NFI: Oman 1986). This distinction is important in individual cases but the general picture is thus: transnational firms (whose numbers are growing) have come to control an increasing share of world output. This trend is unlikely to reverse in the foreseeable future, for at least two reasons. First, the international capital market is one of the most highly integrated, truly global markets. This is so by design and by default: by design, because an unprecedented wave of liberalisations in the 1980s has abolished most controls on capital in the majority of developed and developing countries; by default, because once freed they are difficult to re-regulate, in contrast to international trade. If policy-makers in one country introduced restrictions on capital movements they would most certainly cease to attract new foreign capital and also be up against an increasingly sophisticated technology allowing domestic capital to move abroad (illegally, if necessary). Second, while chief executive officers (CEOs) of TNCs were once the best-hated bad guys, second only to bankers, for many Third World governments, development economists, the very same UN Center on Transnational Corporations (the predecessor of UNTCMD) and pressure groups in LDCs and OECD countries alike, they are now viewed in a more benign light. Indeed, as the subtitle of the UNTCMD's annual report on FDI suggests, they have come to be regarded as *engines for growth* (UNTCMD 1992).[1] How governments deal with them, thus, is a decisive determinant for the development of their economies. TNCs are thought to contribute to growth because they help the country to acquire and use advanced technology, raise productivity and engage in international trade. Inasmuch as they undertake their investment in cash, they also ease the foreign exchange constraint on indebted countries. TNCs are similar to other foreign investors with respect to the provision of capital, technology and know-how. At the same time, they are different in that they determine the what, where and how of much international production. In other words, if a producer of cable casings decides not to invest in a host country, that country may still end up manufacturing excellent cable casings. If car manufacturers decide to not invest in that same country (presuming there is no such indigenous industry), it is unlikely ever to develop its own automobile industry. In other words, TNCs are key in some industries and not in others; and this varies across countries.

Today, rather than thinking about how best to protect their national markets against TNCs, governments in developing countries, so to speak, cannot get enough of them. Many countries have liberalised institutional restrictions on FDI in the hope of attracting as much foreign capital as possible. The heavy demand is not matched with sufficient supply. In 1990, 20 LDCs received some $23 billion in FDI (World Bank 1991), accounting for about 93 per cent of all investment flows to LDCs. Hungary, while a new player in this game, was among the top ten[2]: in 1991, it attracted foreign capital flows to the tune of $1.7 billion. This sum needs to be seen in perspective. Estimates of future capital flows to Eastern Europe differ widely and wildly. 'Needs-based' scenarios which assess the capital that would need to be invested in order for Eastern Europe to achieve Western capital-labour ratios around the turn of the century range from more than $420 billion per year (Collins and Rodrik 1991, 76–80) to a cumulative $2.5 trillion until 2002 to attain average EC standards of living (Boote 1992; see also Rácz 1993).

The control over a growing volume of world production by globally active firms under the conditions of capital scarcity means that host countries compete against each other in their quest for wealth. Put differently, governments today must guarantee a legal framework, create a reliable infrastructure and provide skilled labour to attract foreign capital. Ultimately, this has always been the case. But while it was possible into the 1980s for national economies to integrate themselves into the world market without relying on equity investments from abroad, this has now changed according to some observers (for example, Stopford and Strange 1991, 1–2). Without foreign capital, small countries especially risk being excluded from high-growth sectors that require extensive R&D, modern plants, sophisticated quality control and extensive marketing networks. Globalisation opens many opportunities; but it also entails formidable risks, notably for societal groups and sectors that neither are nor will become competitive on a global scale. Therefore, governments must reconcile their programme of integration into the world economy with demands placed upon them by domestic interest groups. Clearly, the latter may be in flat contradiction of the global agenda (ibid, 33).

The new popularity of FDI in general and TNCs in particular means that foreign firms expect to be courted before they make an investment decision. The courting often comes in the form of incentives (tax breaks, tax holidays, cash contributions and so on). How well or badly an incentive works depends on the specific case: that is, the objectives of governments *vis-à-vis* the objectives of foreign firms. Of particular importance is whether the foreign investor wants to sell to the domestic market or produce for export. In the former case, its interest may be in protection or in price controls; in the latter it would typically be competitive exchange rates or export subsidies.

Incentives, in turn, unless given on an industry-wide basis, may put local producers at a cost disadvantage relative to the foreign firm. Sometimes governments are unable to ignore the protest this gives rise to; and, hence, they must find some form of compensation for indigenous manufacturers or, ideally, integrate them with the foreign venture as, say, suppliers of components. Incentives are therefore a tricky matter for decision-makers. The OECD cautions against incentives for foreign investors in Eastern Europe. According to Robert Cornell, OECD's deputy secretary general, investments either pay or they do not pay, but neither depends on the availability of incentives. The latter, thus, are simply a waste of money and should be done away with ('Opportunity East', 1992, 2).

These and more questions confront countries seeking foreign equity participation. In contrast to most, the former CMEA member states had virtually no experience with the management of FDI. Until the late 1980s, they did not want sizeable foreign capital in forms other than credit; and, given the then prevailing legal conditions, they would not have attracted much FDI even if they had welcomed it. To be sure, joint ventures did exist under the old regimes, yet their scope was necessarily limited. Foreign firms were unable to penetrate regional markets because joint ventures were not granted trading rights. Therefore, to export to other CMEA markets, they needed the foreign trade organisations. Exports possibly never materialised that way because the host country was more interested in keeping the hard goods to itself (Marer 1987). In addition, more than in other parts of the world, change in policy-makers' or firms' preferences due to altered external circumstances may have led to conflicts of interest and endangered the initial agreement between joint venture partners (cf. Gabrisch and Stankovsky 1989, 52). The transfer of technology was limited to the acquisition of capital goods and production agreements on the basis of licences.[3] Not much has been written about this because the combination of official secrecy in the East and corporate secrecy in the West made it difficult to research (Holliday 1984).[4]

The Hungarian government liberalised FDI regulations in 1988. The new code went into effect on 1 January 1989. Since then, the country has managed to attract about one-quarter of all FDI flowing into the area, including the former Soviet Union. Hence, two to three years of data are available to attempt a cautious appraisal of how successfully the new Hungarian government has been dealing with the challenges outlined above. In what follows, first an overview of the presence of foreign capital in Hungary is given. Second, an attempt is made to determine whether the incentive programme of the government has led to the desired results. Third, there is an illustration of how host-country policies conducive to attract foreign capital have conflicted with transition policies designed in conjunction with the IFIs.

FDI IN HUNGARY

Development of Foreign Equity

The number of joint ventures in Hungary rose rather rapidly around 1986. Before the new law came into effect, the country hosted some 270 joint ventures. Relative to the early 1980s, the average size of joint ventures increased as well as the average ratio of foreign participation. More than 80 per cent of partner firms came from Europe, about 6 per cent from the USA. Two-thirds of all committed foreign capital originated in five countries, namely South Korea, West Germany, Austria, Switzerland and the Netherlands. Manufacturing and financial services each attracted one-third of all FDI; in manufacturing, the chemicals and engineering branches alone attracted more than 40 per cent of the capital committed to this sector (*East-West Joint Ventures News* 1989). By early 1990, joint ventures or wholly-owned subsidiaries of foreign firms accounted for some 3–4 per cent of the value of total economic activity in Hungary. European capital still dominated and contributed more than half of total FDI. However, US capital was second only to Austrian capital and considerably more voluminous than the German involvement. More than 60 per cent of FDI inflows were committed to manufacturing which thus became the most important recipient of FDI and, at 72 per cent, also accounted for the largest share of total capitalisation (*East-West Joint Ventures News* 1990).[5] These trends stabilised during 1991 and 1992. In late 1992, more than 12 000 joint ventures and wholly-owned foreign companies, not all of which were already operational, accounted for an FDI stock of $3.2 billion (*East-West Joint Ventures News* 1992). Almost two-thirds of the invested capital was of European origin, more than 10 per cent from the USA, and some 7 per cent from LDCs. Japan did not yet appear in the figures. That was bound to change as soon as Suzuki's sizeable commitment to setting up a plant to assemble passenger cars finds its way into the statistics.

Incentive Packages and Export Results

To a potential foreign investor, incentives intended to influence a location decision can come in different forms, from tariff protection to tax holidays to cash grants. They may or may not improve the prospects for the return on the investor's equity; if they do, they are effective. Also, incentives may make a critical difference in an investor's location decision; to the extent that an investment is made which in the absence of an incentive would not have materialised, the incentive is efficient. In turn, ineffective or inefficient incentives are those that act as the wrong kind of determinant to an investment decision (for example, fiscal measures while the investor is really rather interested in buying into a market protected against other foreign competitors through tariff barriers) or those that are being given although the investor would have made a location decision anyway. In the latter case, the government would waste money, which is apparently suboptimal behaviour: *apparently* suboptimal because, as Stephen Guisinger suggests, 'incentives may be effective in an asymmetrically perverse way: an increase in incentives may produce no net gain in competitive situations, but unilateral withdrawal may be highly detrimental to a country's inflow of foreign capital' (1986, 166). Hence, since the bidding for FDI is highly competitive, 'wasting money' may be a requisite not to forgo desired capital inflows. Another important element is the timing and duration of incentive schemes (cf. Stopford and Strange 1991, 147).

Clearly, analyses of the efficiency of incentive schemes designed to attract FDI remain ultimately unsatisfactory as long as they are not carried out at the firm level. Surveys could explore whether or not firms would have made certain location decisions regardless of incentives. Evaluation of this kind of information would reveal, to firms and foremost to governments, which negotiated arrangements are reasonable and which are not. In fact, Stopford and Strange suggest that this is the direction future research should take (1991, 231). Tentative analyses of the effectiveness of incentive schemes are feasible even without elaborate survey results. Evidence, of course, comes indirect and circumstantial rather than in the form of 'hard' data, but even survey results may be softer than they imply. Managers are unlikely to admit that an investment scheme they have taken benefit from was unimportant for the investment decision. Yet, with a considerable degree of caution in interpreting the material at hand, preliminary findings may be drawn. In what follows, an attempt is made to judge if the foreign capital invested in what had been designated priority sectors by Hungarian authorities has made an above average contribution to the growth of Hungarian exports into the EC. To that end, the incentive package is described first. Next, export growth of products manufactured in sectors that benefitted from foreign capital is compared to overall export growth.

Hungary's Foreign Investment Act came into force on 1 January 1989. It was superseded by a December 1990 amendment which came into force on

1 January 1991. In essence, the 1990 version is currently still valid (Ministry of Finance 1991). The incentive package was essentially based on fiscal measures. In the original version of the law, three types of incentive scheme were offered to foreign investors. First, joint ventures and wholly-owned foreign firms with a capitalisation of more than HUF 25 million and a minimum foreign share of 30 per cent, active mainly in manufacturing or the operation of hotels built by the company, were entitled to a 60 per cent tax allowance during the first five years. From the sixth year, the allowance was reduced to 40 per cent. Second, if these firms were active in sectors whose development the government deemed particularly important, the initial tax allowance was 100 per cent, followed by a 60 per cent allowance after five years. Third, for companies operating with a lower share of foreign capital, (that is, 20 per cent or a minimum of HUF 5 million), the allowance was 20 per cent.

This last provision was abolished in the 1990 amendment. In addition, Hungary raised the stakes. In order to qualify for the tax reductions, the minimum amount of foreign capital required was doubled, to HUF 50 million. Also, incentives were now phased out after ten years which means that foreign capital will then be treated just like domestic firms. However, this does not apply to joint ventures which registered before the amendment was enacted. In making the decision to limit the duration of tax allowances, the Hungarian government may have benefited from international experiences with foreign-owned companies. Since investment projects build up human capital over time, these 'sunk costs' may constitute an effective exit barrier even after tax concessions run out (cf. Stopford and Strange 1991, 147). In late 1991, the tax code provided for a further tightening. It stipulated that, in order to benefit from further tax concessions, joint ventures needed to be set up before 1 January 1994, after which they will no longer be granted reductions (*east-west* 1992, 25).

On the other hand, administrative entry barriers to FDI were considerably lowered in that foreign investors no longer needed approval by a whole handful of concerned ministries. In addition, government procurement was opened to foreign bidders. The new version of the law reflected a narrowing of the incentive package. The proliferation of the relatively lowly-capitalised joint ventures in wholesale and retail made it unnecessary to continue to attract capital flowing into this part of the service sector. Also, Hungarian entrepreneurs protested against what they saw as a discriminatory practice against domestic capital, since the tax concessions granted to joint ventures obviously put them at a cost disadvantage. The incentive scheme also became more industry-oriented which reflects the development priorities of the Hungarian government; the desired foreign participation in the privatisation of industrial assets requires relatively larger amounts of capital.

The industrial breakdown described above showed that manufacturing did in fact attract the largest volume of foreign capital inflows. But the incentive package had another objective: to help the country to build up an internationally competitive export base. Did that work? UNECE, referring to information from the HCSO, says yes.[6] More precisely, it is argued that the percentage of export sales by joint ventures is higher than the sales/exports ratio of other companies. Furthermore, it is also higher than their share in total value added; hence, firms incorporating foreign capital are more export-oriented than the average firm (*East-West Joint Ventures News* 1992). For obvious reasons, this information is extremely important for an evaluation of the effectiveness of foreign investment management by the Hungarian authorities. The analysis reported by UNECE implies that the Hungarians should continue to offer incentives to foreign investors. At least, they do not argue that bright export results would have come about without the granted incentives. That makes UNECE incentive- and industry-friendly. Since it is traditionally less anti-interventionist than the IMF and the World Bank, that is not surprising. The real problem is how convincing the argument is. There are three caveats. First, since the Economic Commission for Europe does not have data on firms, it cannot undertake an independent verification of HCSO's claim. Second, it would be desirable to track trade flows related to joint ventures with as little lag as possible to be able to react flexibly should the hoped-for export stimulus from foreign capital not work. Ideally, this would entail also a related analysis of import flows. It is often charged that TNCs import more than local manufacturers which, of course, has consequences for the balance of payments. Third, the UN analysis does not distinguish between firms which qualified for Hungary's incentive package and those that did not.

Below an attempt is made to remedy some of these shortcomings. Table 4.1 presents the areas designated as specially important by the Hungarian authorities. A more detailed version of this list is available in Ministry of Finance (1991). Since firm data are not available, a substitute is needed. The principal source on foreign equity participation in the Hungarian economy is *Joint Ventures in Hungary with Foreign Participation*, compiled by the Hungarian Chamber of Commerce. However, this publication reports firms' activities the same way they are registered with the authorities. Often, this is rather general. For example, a joint venture may be listed as 'designing technology', or as being engaged in 'production of machines'. Thus, it is impossible to trace these firms' output in commodity statistics. A less comprehensive but more detailed source on major deals involving

Table 4.1   Activities of 'special importance'

Electronics
(a)   Production of active, passive and electro-mechanic components
(b)   Production of computer peripherals
(c)   Productions of electronically operated telecommunication main and subexchanges
(d)   Production and application of robot technology
(e)   Production of computer assisted designing-, constructrion systems (CAD)
(f)   Production of electronic equipment and concomitant services – carried out by the producer – including the production of prime necessity electronic articles
Vehicles and Components
Machine tools
Machines and equipment for the agriculture, food-processing industry and forestry
From among *machine-building* elements the production of
(a)   cast, forged or press-forged component, or high-pressure prefabricated elements
(b)   components or parts for general use (such as hihg-quality fittings, valves, hydraulic and pneumatic elements, etc.)
(c)   up-to-date binding elements
(d)   industrial tools (dies) and apparatuses
(e)   up-to-date materials and basic materials (technical ceramics, etc.)
From among *packing techniques* the production of
(a)   materials and means for packaging
(b)   packaging machines
From among *pharmaceutical articles, plant-protecting agents and intermediates* the production of
(a)   new medicines (also for veterinary hygiene)
(b)   composite plant-protecting agents of a new type
(c)   key intermediates for pharmaceutical and plant-protecting agents
Development of domestic protein stock
Food-processing products
such as
        semi-manufactures and by-products of meat and bacon-processing; meat and bacon products; cheese; canned fruit; canned vegetables; conserves of animal origin; brewery products; mineral waters, soda waters and soft drinks
Activities listed above in the framework of industrial commission work
Production of propagating or breeding materials
such as
        articles produced from cereals, leguminous plants, oil-seed as well as the production of seed-potatoes, grains of rough fodder or propagating materials of fodders rich in juice, as well as other kinds of propagating materials
Agricultural production
such as
        culture of wheat and maize
Tourism
(a)   Establishment and operation of facilities serving medicinal and thermal tourism if operated by the (legal or natural) person having established them
(b)   Reconstruction of ancient castles (manor houses) and their utilization for purposes of tourism
(c)   Establishment and operation of hotels (or their network) if operated by the (legal or natural) person having established them, including hotel and other catering services
Services of public telecommunication

Source: Ministry of Finance (1991).

foreign companies is *Business Eastern Europe* which is a trade and finance weekly targeted at Western managers. While it does not report all agreements between Western and Eastern firms, it generally covers the major incidents of joint ventures, greenfield operations, licence or cooperation agreements and so on, especially as far as TNCs are concerned. Information is given by sectors, detailing the equity participation of the foreign investor and/or the total capitalisation of the project. Most importantly, the entries of the firms' output are sufficiently specific so as to identify the products in question in commodity statistics.

Now, if some product, *a*, is found among Hungary's exports there is no watertight way of knowing whether it was manufactured by joint venture *A* or domestic firm *B*. Is it heroic to assume that is manufactured by *A*? Less than it may seem. The concentration of Hungarian industry (see Chapter 2) entails that often there is no more than one manufacturer of a certain product. This is true for tractors, for example, and not true for pickled vegetables (both products are included in the dataset). Second, foreign investors sometimes start manufacturing a new product. For example, following Audi's decision to set up a car engine plant in Hungary, another German company set up a joint venture to manufacture component cables for these cars. With this, they are in a monopoly position because nobody else in Hungary makes these specific items. Thus, the more pickled vegetables the dataset contains the more imprecise the results are going to be.[7] Of course, this can be controlled for. It is important to keep in mind that the analysis is done to reveal a tendency (is foreign capital more outward-oriented?) rather than a parameter (by how much?). In order to avoid Hungarian data sources, I used EUROSTAT's database on EC external trade. The EC's combined nomenclature goes down to eight digits; that makes it possible to identify very specific products in EC imports from Hungary. Most information on firms was sufficiently specific to determine their output at the 6- and 8-digit level of the combined nomenclature. When output was classified in too general terms (for example, 'generators') but still represented a clearly identifiable class of products, a 4-digit entry was accepted. When the latter condition was missing (for example, 'medicaments'), the firm was not included. It would clearly be desirable to use OECD data rather than EC data to include exports to the USA and Japan. However, EURO-STAT is much faster at publishing trade statistics and hence allowed to include data for 1991. For the OECD data, availability ended in 1990 at the time of writing. It is possible that the use of OECD data would not make much of a difference. An important trend in worldwide FDI in the 1980s was the development of regional networks by TNCs. In this context, Central and Eastern Europe 'belong' to Western Europe. Where non-European firms invest in Central and Eastern Europe, they do so partly to pre-empt trade diversification following the creation of EEA and related moves resulting from the completion of the EC's internal market. Most of their exported output, therefore, is likely to go to Western Europe (cf. Katseli 1992). It would thus not be 'lost' in EUROSTAT statistics. Regional networks characterise not only TNCs with their homebase in triad countries but also more recent FDI exporters. For example, South Korean trade with Hungary was valued at more than $100 million in 1991, compared to negligible levels in the mid-1980s. However, big Korean companies such as Daewoo, Samsung and Hyundai simultaneously invested in Hungary to take advantage of its pending trade liberalisation with the EC in 1992.

No fewer than 62 projects were identified in industrial and agricultural activities designated as having special importance by the Hungarians. Of the 35 projects started in 1989, 20 qualified for tax concessions. The other 15 were NFI (cooperation agreements and so on) or committed sums too low to be eligible for tax exemptions. In 1990, 14 of the 27 projects received tax concessions. Most of the projects qualifying for tax concessions were highly enough capitalised and incorporated a sufficient share of foreign capital to qualify for a 5-year tax holiday (about 16 in 1989 and 11 in 1990). The small number of projects that qualified for tax reductions but not for tax holidays made it infeasible to analyse possible differences in export performance between these two classes of foreign investor. Eight projects did not export their output; five of them were NFI deals. Data on joint ventures whose operation was stated to begin in 1992 were excluded, as were firms with the explicit intention of producing only for the local market. Evidently, this biases the results. Statements can only be made about firms incorporating foreign capital that export, not about firms incorporating foreign capital in general. To include the latter, one would need to measure the ratio of each firm's share in total exports and output and thus arrive at a weighted average of the share of firms incorporating foreign capital in Hungarian exports. But that is easier said than done because, due to the large number of substitutes traded in consumer goods markets, output for local sales is more difficult to identify with a certain firm. Therefore, while it would undoubtedly be desirable to construct such a measure, it would increase the margin for error (again, as long as firm statistics are not available). Firms that only market, service and so on, without producing tangible output, were not included. A complete list of the foreign and domestic firms involved in the deals plus information about capitalisation, for instance, is found in the appendix to this chapter. The results of this exercise are depicted in Figure 4.1. The reported growth rates are in value terms; if volume terms are used the rates would change in magnitude but almost never in sign. Only for precision instruments

Figure 4.1   Export growth by sector (previous year = 100)

(a) All businesses

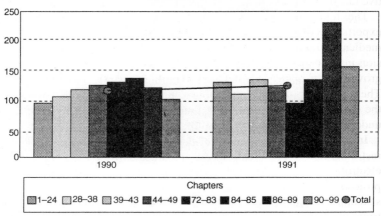

Notes: 1–24 Agriculture; 28–38 Chemicals; 39–43 Plastics; 44–49 Wood, paper,
cork; 72–83 Metals; 84–85 Machinery; 86–89 Transport equipment;
90–99 Precision instruments.
Source: EUROSTAT; author's calculations.

(b) Businesses involved with foreign capital

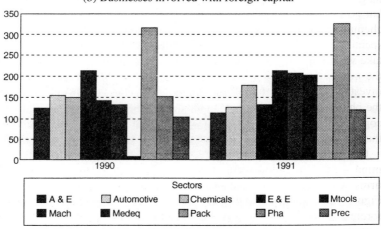

Notes: A & E = Agriculture and equipment; E & E = Electric equipment and
electronics; Mtools = Machine tools; Mach = Machinery; Medeq =
Medical equipment; Pack = Packaging; Pha = Pharmaceuticals; Prec =
Precision instruments.
Source: *Business Eastern Europe*; author's calculations.

(all exports) in 1989/90 and the automotive sector (only joint ventures and related exports) in 1990/91 is a negative growth rate accompanied by a positive rate of volume growth.

The figure illustrates that, for the most part, FDI- and NFI-related exports grew more than all exports taken together. This does not apply to medical equipment in 1989/90 and to agriculture and equipment and precision instruments in 1990/91. For electrical equipment and electronics, the growth rate is higher only in the first period and almost equal in the second. These comparisons are done on a cross-sectoral basis since hardly any of the categories used by *Business Eastern Europe* can be neatly subsumed under the aggregate chapter headings used by EUROSTAT.

In 1989/90, differences for machine tools, machinery and precision instruments are rather small (the same is true for electrical machinery and electronics in 1990/91); in all other sectors the growth rates of FDI-related projects are higher by two to eight times. However, the trends are not consistent over time. In some sectors, differences in growth rates narrow (electrical machinery and electronics), whereas in others they widen (machine tools, machinery). This could support an argument in favour of phasing out incentive packages, at least as far as export stimulation is concerned. An interesting case is the chemical industry: while FDI-related projects do indeed sport high rates of export growth in both periods, the chemical industry is not one of 'special importance', and hence enjoys tax reductions but no tax holidays. This seems to contradict statements on behalf of the chemical industry listing tax holidays as an essential requirement for prospective investment deals in ECE (Schriber 1992). Of course, TNCs will take what they can get; successful FDI management requires determining the minimum point at which a given calculated return pays for a foreign investor without additional incentives. Since the chemical and especially the pharmaceutical industry may indeed be Hungary's internationally most competitive industries, the expectation of safe returns probably rendered the issue of tax holidays much less important.

On the whole, then – although bearing the qualification made above in mind – foreign capital seems to have a higher propensity to export than firms with domestic capital only. But do incentives make a difference? Figure 4.2 shows the export performance of firms that were involved with foreign businesses in one way or other (as in Figure 4.1b) and compares it with those that qualified for tax concessions. Loosely speaking, Figure 4.2a represents NFI *and* FDI, while FDI is singled out in Figure 4.2b. For the automotive sector (in 1989/90), chemicals (in 1990/91) and electrical equipment and electronics (in both years), there is clearly a difference. In the automotive sector, exports from all foreign business-related projects grew

Figure 4.2   Export growth by sector (previous year = 100)

(a) Businesses involved with foreign capital (FDI + NFI)

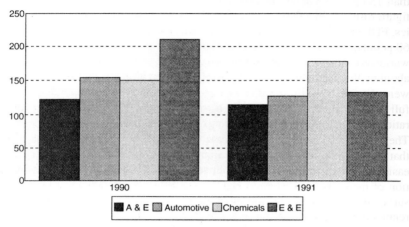

Notes: The dataset is the same as for Figure 4.1. Not all of the businesses
described in the figure were entitled to tax concessions. More information
in text.

Source: *Businesses Eastern Europe*; author's calculations.

(b) Businesses involved with foreign capital (FDI only)

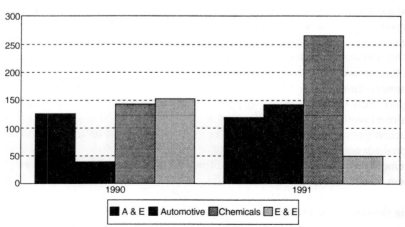

Notes: The data are a subset of the one used for Figures 4.1 and 4.2(a). All the
businesses described in the figure were entitled to tax reductions or tax
holidays. More information in text.

Source: *Business Eastern Europe*; author's calculations.

by 50 per cent, while exports by FDI-related firms fell by 50 per cent in 1989/90. By contrast, exports by the latter in the chemical sector were more than 150 per cent higher in 1991 compared to 1990; the joint FDI and NFI figure rose only by some 80 per cent. In electrical equipment and electronics, FDI and NFI-related export growth was lower in both years (by roughly 60 per cent in 1989/90 and by some 80 per cent in 1990/91). But caution is warranted when interpreting this. One reason is that, when information about neither capitalisation nor the foreign equity share was available, firms were classified as NFI. In actual fact, however, they may have qualified for a full tax holiday. This may exaggerate the distinction between export growth ratios of all foreign business-related *vis-à-vis* FDI(only)-related products. These results do not show that incentives do not work: they only suggest that NFI is important in Hungary, possibly because it has traditionally been easier to implement. From the sample it is not clear whether the differentiation of incentives makes that much of a difference; one would need to do survey research to find that out. It could be, of course, that tax holidays are relatively unimportant in one sector but essential in other sectors to attract foreign capital. This question surely merits further inquiry. As pointed out above, the amendment to the 1988 FDI legislation changed, with effect from 1991, the criteria for tax reductions. In general, projects needed a higher capitalisation to qualify for tax relief. It had to be HUF 50 million with a minimum foreign share of 30 per cent. Foreign firms thus had to come up with about $800 000 (at 1990 exchange rates) to take advantage of the reductions. Preliminary answers as to whether this had an impact on the export propensity of firms operating with foreign capital can presently not be given since 1992 trade data, at the time of writing, are not yet published.[8] What this measure did do was to represent a step towards an equal treatment of foreign and domestic capital, which is a stated goal of the Hungarian government. Until then, small Hungarian entrepreneurs were doubly disadvantaged. First, they competed against foreign investors and their domestic partners whose corporate tax rates were considerably lower than their own. Second, they were barred from making use of their comparative informational advantage relative to foreign investors *vis-à-vis* other East European countries; restrictions on capital outflows made it extremely difficult for them to, say, invest in Romania.[9]

Big (Foreign) Business

Although the government thus tried to accommodate the interests of its new entrepreneurial class, it continued to draw criticism, mostly from conservative quarters, for selling out national property to TNCs whose activities would allegedly not benefit the country (cf. Gabor and Ravasz 1990). A major criticism was that profits from investments were not used to establish additional capacities but to expand control over existing property by raising the foreign equity share and by cornering the market. Foreign investors, so to speak, had a 'market-share' bias and not a 'growth' bias; it was feared that the old state monopolies would be replaced by foreign monopolies (cf. Major 1992, 54). In addition, the proceeds from privatisations were criticised for being put into the financing of the budget and debt service and not into new investment. Again, the latter charge begs the question whether a voucher-type give-away would have turned out differently; surely it would not have generated revenue for the authorities. Privatisation without foreign capital would only have been feasible on the basis of a voucher system, for instance, along the lines of the Czech example, because there was simply not enough private capital in Hungary to cover the existing assets. Private savings were below 10 per cent of the value of state assets when the transformation began. Iván Major points out that even a higher volume of savings may not have made much difference: 'It should also be considered that a significant part of private savings were not intended for later investments. The deepening economic crisis, the dramatic increase of unemployment, and consequently the shaken financial security of the population must have been the main reason for the fast increase in the nominal value of savings' (1992, 53). Therefore, whether assets were sold at knockdown prices is less interesting because the alternative would have been a free give-away, which might have been to the benefit of Hungarian citizens but would certainly have been even more of a 'sale' below value.

An assessment of the charge that TNCs move in to occupy the domestic market while destroying domestic competitors through reckless pricing has to rely on anecdotal evidence (cf. Czauner 1992; Denton 1992). While it is true that foreign investors' interest was concentrated in consumer products and services, it is not true that they only creamed off Hungary's top companies in terms of profitability or hard-currency exports. In fact, the first list offering state enterprises for sale and drawn up for potential foreign investors included both very good performers and record loss makers. In 1990, Sanofi, a member of the Elf Aquitaine group, acquired a majority share in Chinoin Pharmaceutical and Chemical Works Ltd, one of Hungary's top exporting companies. General Electric bought a 50 per cent share in Tungsram, whose non-rouble export sales in 1989 amounted to some $152.5 million. Electrolux bought the Lehel Refrigerator Factory, one of Hungary's top 20 exporters in 1989. But Tate & Lyle acquired a minority share in Hajdusági Sugar, one of the 1988 top loss makers. Group International invested in Csepel Automobile Works, a part of Csepel Works, the number -2 loss maker in 1988. Although it cannot be ruled out that foreign investors acquire Hungarian companies in close competition with their own product range simply to run them down, this is not borne out by the above deal.[10] Csepel, in fact, is supposed to assemble Cummins diesel engines for International.

Clearly, foreign investors often acquire control over the most promising firms in a sector, prop them up financially and technologically, thereby possibly ruining cash-poor domestic competitors. This does not mean that they are always profitable. In 1990, for example, companies with foreign investment in basic metals and casting and in machinery and equipment reported losses of HUF 208.1 million and HUF 1397.9 million, respectively (*East-West Joint Ventures News* 1992, 26). Is this particular form of import competition a reason for dependency nightmares or for the charge propagated by Hungary's extreme right that the country is selling out to Western interests? The answer to this question depends to no small degree on whether or not foreign investors, especially TNCs, are primarily interested in access to the Hungarian market to distribute their products and in cheap labour to use the country as an assembly base, or whether their operations contribute directly or indirectly to a technological modernisation of the economy. It has been shown above that there is reason to believe that foreign capital is not invested to engage only in 'local-for-local' production. The TNCs' impact on the innovative capacity of the host country is more difficult to assess. Ultimately, it depends on being able to measure foreign investors' local upgrading over time. The international evidence on this is, at best, fragmented (see Stopford and Strange 1991, 157, who also elaborate the difference between 'dependent' and 'independent' exporting; see 25–7).

Especially in the automotive sector, investment by TNCs has had visible trickle-down effects. Following General Motors' early involvement, Ford, Daimler-Benz, Fiat, Renault, Suzuki and Audi invested in Hungary. Some of them use supplies manufactured by local companies. The French GM affiliate, AC Prochester, in 1992 set up a joint venture with Bahony Works which had been supplying the former with spark plugs since 1988. In 1992, Bahony received more advanced technology from GM under a leasing agreement and, in 1993, planned to supply 20 million spark plugs and ceramic articles. Similarly, US-based Loranger Manufacturing set up a new factory to supply Ford with ignition system coils and fuel pumps. Philips followed up the building of its video cassette recorder factory with a joint venture a year later in which it now produces plastic components for electric equipment. The new plant's output will be sold to Philips and to car manufacturers. Suzuki took local suppliers as equity partners to offer them a stake in the success of the new factory they built (Denton and Done 1991). Hungary's interest in seeing local suppliers involved in as much component manufacturing as possible fits in with Suzuki's strategy to supply automobiles to the EC under the new rules for local content specified in the Association Agreement between the EC and Hungary. Since local suppliers often lack the funds to restructure their operations to meet Suzuki's quality requirements, and state money is unavailable because of the country's budgetary problems, Japanese bank credits might be made available (Bakos 1992b, 13). In electronics, Samsung is developing its joint venture into Central and Western Europe's main supply base. In 1990, 44 per cent of its production of colour televisions was exported.

Privatisation officials managed to put a limit on the redundancies which normally followed foreign acquisitions; when Feruzzi-Unilever bought a controlling stake in Eastern Europe's biggest vegetable oil processing company, Nömov, the new owners guaranteed to maintain the current level of sunflower purchases from Hungarian growers and not to dismiss more than 10–15 per cent of the workforce. In the summer of 1991, Hungary decided to close some of its aluminium plants because of world surplus capacity. A year later, Alcoa, the world's biggest aluminium producer, set up a joint venture with Hungalu in which it holds a majority share. The US company made a sort of goodwill payment of $50 million and plans to invest $125 million in the company, as well as reinvesting dividends to upgrade technology, protect the environment and increase safety. Although the aluminium industry worldwide is in a difficult position, Hungary's share in world aluminium exports continuously increased in the second half of the 1980s (from 0.9 per cent in 1985 to 1.6 per cent in 1990) and the country's exports grew by almost 60 per cent in 1989/90. Furthermore, 'global' is contagious; Pannonplast Synthetics Ltd is converting its productive units into joint companies with foreign investors from the Netherlands, South Korea and Austria, and thus slowly coming to resemble a TNC itself.

There are examples where even food and apparel multinationals are interested not only in the customer base of the firm they buy an interest in, but also in its original product range. US-based Sara Lee, for instance, one of Europe's largest apparel companies, used its share in the Compack Trading and Packing Company, bought in 1991, to introduce its own brands in the market. But it is also modernising the manufacture of Compack's traditional food products. French Sanofi finances an expansion of the R&D activities of Chinoin Pharmaceutical and Chemical Works in which it acquired a majority share in 1991. Being a French company, Sanofi is in a position to help Chinoin gain access to the Common Market. Market access, in fact, may be the major reason why TNCs are generally welcome in Central Europe.

The situation in microelectronics is more complex. The success of the Hungarian computer industry was owed not just to innovative ingenuity but also to the largely protected market in which it used to operate (cf. Mester 1992). With the protection mostly gone, Hungarian firms now face electronics giants such as IBM or DEC and others. Their survival depends on beating them in niche markets or on teaming up with them in joint ventures. These firms appear to be hit harder by the implications of the new bankruptcy law. On the one hand, they require capital injections to remain viable. IBM, for example, acquired shares in Müszertechnika, the major producer of computers in Hungary, and has development plans for the company. It is obviously easier for IBM to tap capital sources than for its Hungarian partner. On the other hand, it is not clear that foreign investment will help Hungarian establishments to stay in the market as independent suppliers rather than just as retail outlets or assembly plants for Western TNCs. For the time being, given the precarious financial situation of these firms and the parallel problems with public finance, alternatives to accepting FDI do not exist. In Chapter 1 the net resource outflow from Hungary was discussed; FDI eases the negative effects of the capital export. For example, if a country has a neutral trade and transfer balance and FDI inflows cover interest payments, they would enable the country to avoid resource outflows while not running up additional debt. Financing interest payments with equity capital might seem ill-advised in that it resembles raising new credit to pay old debt: a policy the experience of the debt crisis cautions against. But there is another way of looking at this: imports not covered through exports minus interest payments are made possible through foreign equity capital. Thus, they may help to avoid the 'created adjustment' discussed in Chapter 1, allowing the country to run a deficit on the non-interest current account. The latter may then lead to adjustment with growth without running all the risks accompanying protracted recessions. This sketch certainly applies to the situation in Hungary since 1989 (cf. Oblath 1992).

FOREIGN CAPITAL, DEBT MANAGEMENT AND TRADE LIBERALISATION

Hungarian authorities designed incentives so as to attract relatively highly capitalised foreign investors (with presumably easy access to capital), especially in the manufacturing sector. Foreign investors came and, regardless of whether or not the underlying relationship between incentives and FDI is one of cause and effect, the government might well claim that its policy has been successful. In absolute terms, Hungary received more FDI flows than any other country in the region. An important goal of FDI management – stimulation of export activity – seems to have been reached although it is not clear from the analysis that direct equity participation by foreign firms brings superior results in this respect compared with other forms of cooperative arrangements between domestic and foreign companies. The point here is not to disprove that FDI is 'bad', as parts of the Hungarian political spectrum charge. However, in light of the evidence presented, the opposite view is more likely to apply: the involvement of foreign firms has been making a constructive initial contribution to Hungary's opening-up. It is an important task for future research to understand the precise effects of joint ventures, strategic alliances and other cooperative arrangements. The more such research focuses on the activities of individual firms, the more differentiated the picture that emerges is likely to be. Distinctions are important; the idea that TNCs are always *engines for growth*, having only benign effects on the host country, is hardly convincing. More detailed research would provide valuable insights for the design and operation of trade development and investment promotion schemes which are necessary tools for these countries to edge their way into a difficult world market.

At the end of 1993, the incentive package is scheduled to be retired; from 1994, foreign and domestic investors are supposed to receive equal treatment. Foreign investors and consultancies argue, not surprisingly, that this is a mistake ('On Foreign Businesses in Hungary', 1992, 61; see especially the comment by Price Waterhouse's David Young). In late 1992, the Hungarian Association of International Companies was formed. This pressure group represents some 35 per cent of FDI stock in the country; undoubtedly, the government will have to consider the arguments of this lobby. It may well find it advisable to enlist international support, for example at the OECD, to bolster its decision to do away with incentives.

The real problem for the future may be different, however. Tax reductions are given on profits; to enjoy them, therefore, one first needs to make profits. Quite a number of foreign investors in 1992 did not. In April, General Electric interrupted production at Tungsram for two weeks. The company was in its third loss making year and suffered from increased production costs due to the higher than expected inflation in the country. Consequently, General Electric scaled back investments and cut staff further. General Electric had regularly argued for a devaluation of the forint to retain its international competitiveness *vis-à-vis* competitors Osram and Philips. While fearful of cost-push inflation and increased costs of debt financing, the National Bank nonetheless devalued the forint by 5.8 per cent in late 1991. Not only did this come late, but it also aroused the protest of the Austrian Chamber of Commerce which accused Hungary of running an artificially low forint exchange rate and requested import barriers from its own government. General Electric-Tungsram is only one joint venture among many, but it is one of the biggest and most ambitious investment projects in the new Eastern Europe to date. What is happening to General Electric's investment thus is significant beyond the firm itself. Decisions General Electric makes are likely to influence other investors, primarily foreign but also domestic ones. Hence, it is obviously in the Hungarian government's interest to do what it can to promote the profitability of foreign investments in its economy. But in what it can do to this effect, the government is constrained by the very problems treated throughout this work, namely external debt, and the difficulty of attaining competitiveness in Western markets as well as the absence of a more comprehensive Western effort to stabilise the economic and political transformation in ECE. By way of conclusion, the treatment of foreign capital is now tied in with debt management and trade liberalisation in order to establish how FDI management relates to the overall policy of opening up.

Three important variables have changed since foreign capital first moved into Hungary following the liberalisation of the FDI regime: first, the withdrawal of the transfer rouble as a means of payment in intra-CMEA trade in 1991. This led to the collapse of commercial relations between and within ECE and the former Soviet Union. All of a sudden, very sizeable outlets, especially for Hungarian manufactures, were lost. They were replaced by costly barter trade or, worse, nothing at all. Second, the measures intended to bring about the transition from plan to market, notably the phasing-out of subsidies, price liberalisations and so on, caused a contraction of domestic activity much deeper and longer than was expected. Domestic demand was regularly predicted to resume growth, and it regularly failed to do that. According to forecasts by the OECD and the Hungarian government in early 1992, Hungary was to exit from the perennial tunnel by the end of that year. It did not. At the time of writing, growth is predicted for 1993; whether it will happen is uncertain. Even if it does materialise, it is likely to take years before Hungarian GNP reaches its 1989 level. Third, imports were rapidly and almost entirely liberalised within only three years. This meant that import competition was introduced overnight for many firms, including those that faced high start-up costs in terms of investment outlays or training, and which still had to cope with productivity levels below Western standards. In 1989, investors, in tune with everybody else, had entertained much more optimistic expectations of how things would go (cf. Denton 1992).

Consider these problems in turn. Neither the Hungarian government nor the foreign firms in Hungary could do much about the demise of the CMEA trade and payments system. Only a concerted effort by Western governments, in conjunction with the former CMEA members, could have stemmed the decline in commercial activity by providing sufficient liquidity to operate some kind of a substitute multilateral payments system.[11]

Since everybody was wrong about how long-drawn-out the (adjustment-in-) transition would be,[12] the second problem – of reviving domestic demand – is also one about which the Hungarian government would have had difficulty in establishing an 'alternative consensus' with the G-24 and the IFIs. An 'alternative consensus' would have consisted of tying the speed of the transition to the costs it imposed on the production structure and the social fabric. This is normal practice in industrialised countries where governments occasionally need to worry about their re-election. Being an indebted assistance and aid recipient, Hungary was clearly not in a position to develop criteria for how much contraction of demand was acceptable, and to request a corresponding treatment from the IFIs; although one step in this direction would have been, as was suggested in Chapter 1, to follow a different debt management strategy. Only the EC could have come up with a plan to ease the balance of payments position of the Central European countries as it became apparent how dramatically the recession unfolded. In fact, this is what many concerned observers saw as the Community's main task, *Preventing a New East-West Divide* (Clesse and Tökés 1992), by much more aggressively stabilising Central European economies and polities. A Brookings Paper contended that the systemic transformation in the East required systemic reform in the West; the latter is taken to mean institutional steps which facilitate the East's integration into the West European economy (Reinicke 1992). Concretely, this would have meant more immediate and more extensive access to the EC market for the Central Europeans, to which we return below. But most of all it would have required a both more generous and more efficient (alas, more enlightened) handling of credit provision. Instead, as a recent study found, of the credit commitments the G-24 had made to Hungary, only some 16 per cent were disbursed in 1990 (Barre *et al.* 1992). The small amount of assistance that comes in the form of aid (that is, at below market interest rates or grants) is marred by severe shortcomings in distribution, allocation and so on (Wedel 1992). If measured by their success in convincing EC leaders to upgrade Central Europe on the Community's agenda, most of these studies recommending ways and means of widening the EC eastwards were largely written in vain.

That leaves the third problem. There is no question that import liberalisation *in general* was a necessary policy: it exerted competitive pressures on domestic producers and, perhaps more importantly, enabled the incorporation of Western high-quality inputs into Hungarian manufactures (something without which the country was unlikely to develop a competitive export base). However, experience suggests that general import liberalisation may still be accompanied by select, qualified exceptions. For example, presuming that the Hungarian authorities have an interest in seeing General Electric expand investments and production as originally planned rather than cutting investments and staff (not a very wild presumption), they could do the following: since it is next to impossible to regain outlets for lightbulbs in the immediate future in the former CMEA, notably in the CIS, and next to ridiculous to expect that a population plagued by a double-digit recession will massively increase its purchases of lightbulbs, the government could at least ensure that the existing demand for lightbulbs be met by local supply only, namely Tungsram. In effect, the government would need to discriminate against imports of lightbulbs. I am suggesting 'lightbulbs' rather than 'electrical household goods' because there is no reason to restrict imports in general. They should be firm-specific to limit the associated distortionary effects as much as possible. One may argue that firm-specific protectionism is politically not feasible and rather opens the dangerous possibility that old-style state-owned enterprises would file for the same sort of relief. But there is no reason why transitory firm-specific import controls should lead to any more misgivings among domestic firms than firm-specific tax incentives. The government has successfully defended the latter for almost five years. Clearly, firm-specific tariff or non-tariff protection would be temporary, conditional on an improvement of the operating conditions in the environment for (foreign) businesses. Things like this are provided for under the safeguard clauses within the framework of the Association Agreement. The difficulty of trade liberalisation for small countries is, of course, that once undertaken they are difficult to roll back for fear of retaliation by (bigger) trade partners. In fact, Hungarian attempts to protect the emerging local car industry[13] by limiting the import of passenger cars and according import preferences, for example, to a special Ford model, have led to protests from the IFIs. Inasmuch as the IFIs reflect the opinion of their major shareholders, this can also be interpreted as a lesson in 'do as I say and not as I do'. Oye (1992) called the concomitance of discriminatory commercial practices and non-discriminatory rhetoric in developed countries the 'political economy of hypocrisy'. The financial leverage of the IFIs makes it unlikely that this sort of ad hoc protectionism can go on for long. In the absence of some enlightened Western partner willing to accept an interpretation of the Association Agreements on Hungary's terms, the country may have to consider the rather uglier toolbox of low-key managed trade. However, measures such as slowing customs procedures or finding some excuse about unfulfilled safety requirements are no long-term solution for troubled foreign investors because, *vis-à-vis* the EC, Hungary holds the short end of the stick. It is not difficult to imagine a less grim outlook. The idea of asymmetry, whose spirit was codified so imperfectly in the Association Agreements, could take care of transitional problems such as inflation and the impact it has on competitiveness by establishing a differentiated, multi-stage approach to association. In such a plan the ECE countries would form a customs union and charge the EC a higher tariff on imports than their exporters need to pay to sell in the common market (Aghion, *et al.* 1992).[14] Hungarian lightbulbs, then, would be competitive in the domestic market as well as abroad because the price of foreign lightbulbs (via the tariff) would reflect the foreign share in the costs of transition. But, again, only the EC could organise such a scheme and, since it does not, this alternative remains in the realm of imagination.

It is important to learn from the Hungarian experience that it may make sense to combine even across-the-board import liberalisation with temporary exceptions to the rule if viable businesses are threatened. If somebody argues that General Electric has simply not cut enough personnel to be viable or that it should not have invested at all,[15] they definitely miss the (Hungarian) point. Hungary, along with the other Central European countries, depends on the TNCs to help them integrate successfully with the world economy. As long as the Community does not integrate these countries more actively into what could become a continental common market, Hungary is well advised to care about the economic viability of its (large) foreign investment projects.

What ten years of opening up have shown is that cooperative international arrangements can be helpful in facilitating a small country's integration into the world market, but they need not always. Being a nice debtor does not rule out liquidity problems due to massive foreign capital 'desertion'; being a GATT member does not guarantee non-discriminatory treatment; and becoming an associate of the EC two years after the Iron Curtain came down does not insure against running into a steel curtain a few months later. A future common continental market is in many ways a desirable option for the Central Europeans, and their foreign economic strategy should strive towards it. However, small countries cannot enforce integration nor determine how the rules for it are made. Hence, there may be periods – such as the early 1990s – when short-term deviations from integrative policies (such as temporary protectionism), while in seeming contradiction to long-term goals, are in these countries' best interest.

APPENDIX

Table A4.1 Foreign capital in 'special interest' areas, 1989 registration

Foreign Firm	Hungarian Firm	Deal	Foreign Share %	Total Capital*	Output
Tunaverken (S)	Alumina Enterprise Ajka	License	–	–	Wheel brake discs HCH
Pharma (CH)	Chinoin/Medimpex	JV	30.5	66.5	Vitamin concentrates, vitamin
C Kummler and Mattler (A)	Transelektro and others	JV	48.0	5.0	Overhead lines for trolleybuses
Geco (D)	Sopron Carpet Factory/ Chemolimpex	JV	52.0	310.0	Polypropylene-based fibres used in manufacture of carpets
Tektronix (A)	Texo Cooperative	CA	–	–	Oscilloscopes Wellcome
Foundation (UK)	Chinoin/Chemolimpex	JV	50.0	–	Pyrethroid insecticide
Elagru (D)	Szekszárd-Baja Waterworks	JV	50.0	7.2	Compressors
Hi-Med Systems (Can)/ Fomenex (D)	–	JV	32.6	60.5	Computer-controlled medical instruments (e.g., kidney dialysis systems)
John Deere (USA)	Kaposvr Agricultural Machines Manufacturing Cooperative	Licence	–	–	Front-loading equipment using hydraulic parts for mounting on universal tractors
Eltrona (A)	Protokon	JV	30.0	25.3	Assembly of microcomputers
Sibco (S)/Transron (L)	Rona	JV	35.0	0.15	Asbestos-free brake linings
Siemens (D)	JV Sicontact (est. 1974)	Licence	–	–	Computer control systems for computer-aided numerically machine tools
GFTK (D)	Kemikal Building Materials/ Hungarian Transport Construction Association	JV	37.0	46.0	Modified road bitumen
Pyne Gould Business (NZL)	–	JV	60.3	36.5	Cattle breeding
Bären Batterie (A)	Veszprém Collieries	CA	–	–	Batteries
Dow Chemical (USA)	Nitrokemia/Chemolimpex	JV	50.0	$6 m.	Extruded polystyrene foam insulation products

Table A4.1 cont.

Foreign Firm	Hungarian Firm	Deal	Foreign Share %	Total Capital*	Output
International Planning Corporation (CH)	Borsod Chemical Combine/ National Commercial and Credit Bank	JV	26.0	3.8	PVC casings, household plastic articles
Samsung (SK)	Orion Radio Elektrika Vox	JV	50.0	–	Assembly of color tv sets
Fine Products International (L)	Obuda Agricult. and Horticult. Coop./ Machine and Machine-Tool Trading	JV	–	26.0	Packaging machinery
New England Machinery (USA)	–	Subsid.	100.0	$600000	Packaging machines
Hoechst (D)	Kőbánya Pharmaceutical Enterprise	Licence	–	–	Insulin
Hoechst (D)	OMFB/Committee for Technical Dev.	CA	–	–	Herbicides
Pioneer Overseas (A)	Agker/GKI-Szeged Institute	CA	–	–	Hybrid corn seeds
Euribrid (NL)	Red Star Cooperative Farm	JV	80.0	40.0	Hybrid chicken
Schlumberger Industries (F)	Ganz Electricity Meter	JV	75.0	$ 8 m.	Electrical equipment (e.g., one- and three-phase electricity meters)
Comytali (I)	12 farms	JV	30.0	7.0	Hybrid seed corn, green peas, beans
BASF (D)	Tisza Chemical Complex	Licence	–	–	Low-density polyethylene Chris
CA	–	–Integrated circuits and resistors			for ignition systems
Wiener Kabel- und Metallwerke (A)	Hungarian Cable Works and others	JV	45.0	77 (800)	Telephone cables

Table A4.1 *cont.*

Foreign Firm	Hungarian Firm	Deal	Foreign Share %	Total Capital*	Output
MAN Roland (D)	Csepel Machine Tool Works	CA	–	–	CNC boring mills, processing units for printing drums
Felber-Ottmann (A)	Konkord Industrial and Service Cooperative	JV	50.0	2.0	Transmission cables, printed circuit boards, control panels for video cassette recorders and computers
Standard Electric Lorenz (D)	Videoton	JV	50.0	30.0	Digital telephone exchanges
AEG (D)	Iron Industrial and Instrument Manufacturing Cooperative	Licence	–	–	Semiconductors
Gutbrod (D)	Robix	JV	50.0	130.0	2000 6–9 kw tractors
Knorr Bremse (D)	Szim and Mögurt Enterprises	JV	35.0	8.0	Brakes for commercial vehicles

Notes: *a in HUF million unless otherwise specified. Figures in brackets denote increase in capitalisation shortly after initiation of deal
CA = Cooperation agreement
JV = Joint venture. Subsid. = Subsidiary.
Source: Business Eastern Europe

Table A4.2   Foreign capital in 'special interest' areas, 1990 registration

Foreign Firm	Hungarian Firm	Deal	Foreign Share %	Total Capital*	Output
Ziersch (D)	Szim Grinding Machine	CA	–	–	Plane grinders
Akzo (NL)	TVK	JV	51.0	G 37.1 m.	Paints and varnishes
Bolta Industrie und Bauprofile (D)	Rakoczi Ferenc Cooperative Farm/Komplex	JV	56.0	34.0	Car bumpers, cable casings, plastic panelling for furniture
Rhône-Poulenc (F)	Borsod Chemical Works	JV	50.0	10.0	Plant protection agents
Braas & Co (D)/Flair (NL)	Borsod Chemical Works	JV	44.2	520.0	Plastic garden furniture, water pipes for roof structures, heat insulating windows
Bull (F)	Videoton	CA	–	–	Computer systems
Wella (D)	Florin	JV	–	–	Cosmetics
Zub (D)	Szim Machine Tools	CA	–	–	Surface grinding machines
Central Soy (USA)	Agrokomplex	JV	30.0	$ 7 m.	Animal fodder
Walter MHder (D)	–	JV	–	–	Household detergents, paints
Sluis & Groot (NL)	–	CA	–	–	Vegetable seeds
Audi (D)	Bicske Electrical Fitters	CA	–	–	Electrical cables for passenger cars
Leonische Drahtwerke (D)	Bicske Electrical Fitters	JV	–	–	Electrical cables
BASF (D)	Tisza Chemical Complex	License	–	–	High-pressure polyethylene
Motorenwerke Mannheim (D)	Rba Railway Carriage Works	JV	–	–	Diesel engines
Hitachi (J)	Egyedi Gépgyár	JC	–	–	Rolling mill equipment
Alcatel (A)	Hiradstechnika Cooperative	JV	53.0	ECU 1.6m.	Private telephone systems
Theodor Goldschmidt (D)	Székesféhervar Heavy Metal Foundry	Licence	–	–	Slide bearings for vehicles
Seeburger Konservenfabrik (A)	Rábaközi Afesz/Petöfi . Agricult. Coop	JV	50.0	63.2	Pickled vegetables

Table A4.2   cont.

Foreign Firm	Hungarian Firm	Deal	Foreign Share %	Total Capital*	Output
Software Technologies Trading (Isr)	State Construction Enterprise/ Rakamaz Wood and Metall Industry Cooperation	JV	48.0	9.0	Alarm systems
Ruf (D)	Ajka City Council	JV	91.9	48.0	Potentiometers
Ansaldo (I)	Ganz Electric Works	JV	51.0	2 bn	Railway rolling stock
Mannesmann Rexroth (D)	Danuvia	JV	80.0	DM1 (9)m.	Hydraulic control units
Prinzhorn Group (A)	Hungarian Paper Industry	JV	40.0	205.0	Paper packaging and lining materials
Mecman (S)	Egri Finomszerelvénygyár	JV	51.0	–	Dish washing products, detergents, softeners, shoe polishes, cosmetics, glues
Shaver (CAN)	Bbolna Farming Complex/ Kaposfarm	JV	30.0	C$ 1 mn	Cattle breeding

Notes: *In HUF million unless otherwise specified. Figures in brackers denote increase in capitalisation shortly after initiation of deal.
CA = Cooperation agreement. JV = Joint venture. JC = Job cooperation.
Source: Business Eastern Europe.

Notes

Preface

1. Throughout this book, 'billions' are American: a thousand million.
2. Lee also finds that incidences of past debt reschedulings are highly significant for (worsening) credit ratings given to LDC borrowers. But there may be a problem with Lee's dataset which consists of 40 LDCs in 1979–87. The countries are not identified. Since in this period a large majority of LDCs rescheduled and only a handful did not, his sample may have an in-built bias.

Introduction

1. For a brief but comprehensive overview of the necessary reforms and their sequencing, see Williamson (1991).
2. These ideologues do exist. For a particularly confused example, see Gowan (1991–92).
3. For a summary of the reforms to the mid-1980s, see Kornai (1986).
4. Michael Porter (1990) and John Stopford and Susan Strange (1991) have persuasively argued that it is not meaningful to discuss competitiveness as the characteristic of an entire nation. Even sectors may be too broad a categorisation because the nature of competition and the sources of competitive advantage vary a great deal within them. The appropriate unit of analysis, hence, is the firm.
5. For a brief, internal evaluation of structural adjustment programmes, see 'Adjustment with Growth' (1987) and, especially for the design of SAL (structural adjustment loan) evaluations, Corbo and Rojas (1991). For a critique targeted primarily at Bela Balassa's work in this context, see Gibson and Ward (1992).
6. Hungary unified its tourist and commercial exchange rates in 1982. To claim that the state's role in the economy expanded makes sense only if seen in perspective. It certainly did not expand compared to the late 1970s, or in comparison with other CMEA countries. Trade was heavily distorted, but whether it was more so than ten years earlier is arguable.
7. Taiwan would also be part of this group but is not recognised by the Bank.
8. Koh and Lee Tsao Yuan are director and deputy director, respectively, of the Institute of Policy Studies in Singapore.
9. A similar argument with particular emphasis on industrial strategy and development of technology in Korea is made by Pack and Westphal (1986). They support the neoclassical charge that government intervention often produces failures. But they argue that, instead of reiterating this credo time and again, it would be more interesting to investigate the relationship between relative prices for industrial products and the concomitant development of elements of technology. A more recent article in the same vein, by DeLong and Summers (1990), shows that the relative cost of machinery is highly

correlated with economic growth in a large sample of countries and that equipment investment is relatively more significant than structural investment in this respect.

10. Free trade does not mean that there are no subsidies. No subsidies exist when ERP = 0 for both importables and exportables. Such a condition of pure *laissez-faire* is unlikely to exist in any country in the world. Export promotion in a free trade setting, hence, makes up for whatever degree of import substitution the system sponsors, thus balancing the biases for and against exports.

11. See in this context also Stanley Katz's contribution (1991). Katz's interpretation of industrialisation in East Asia is closer to Amsden's and Wade's; interestingly, he was Vice-President of the Asian Development Bank until 1990.

12. There is little disagreement about the management of exchange rates. In Taiwan and South Korea, RER was not overvalued as it was in most Latin American countries. Export successes in the former and failures in the latter are thus consistent with theory and, in this sense, 'getting the prices right' is not an issue of contention. Ironically, however, a recent World Bank study found that RER depreciation is not so strongly correlated with structural adjustment (measured as real GNP – gross national product – growth, inflation, ratio of current account to GNP, ratio of domestic investment to GNP) (Conway 1991).

13. Exceptions to this are the articles by Wing Thye Woo (1990) and Wade (1991). In both, a sharp pencil combines allegiance to neoclassical theory (Woo) and to 'new interventionism' (Wade) with criticism directed at their respective schools of thought. Both pieces also provide excellent reviews of much relevant literature. Written in a similar spirit is Broad, Cavanagh and Bello (1990/91).

14. US support for import substitution in developing countries after the Second World War is analysed by Maxfield and Nolt (1990).

15. Of course, world trade is still expanding although at a much lower rate than in the 1960s. An increasing share of international commerce is affected by various forms of managed trade. This means that, relative to the 1960s, life has become more complicated for newcomers to the world economy.

16. The current mix of values is far from consensual. For a full-flung (in scope though not in substance) critique of post-Cold War arrangements consider the following statement, made by a group close to the Group of 77:

> some Northern proposals for an institutional division of labour with respect to development-related functions assign peace and social concerns to the UN, finance and macroeconomic management to the IMF, development strategies to the World Bank and trade matters to GATT. If these proposals were to be accepted, the Northern vision of the world economy would be beyond effective challenge, intellectual pluralism would be threatened, and alternative views would have difficulty in attaining an institutional foot-hold or international visibility.

And further, 'Total dependence on the Bretton Woods institutions and GATT for facts and figures – and their interpretation – would make it that much easier for the North to resist the arguments and demands of those who may wish to question or criticise the workings of the dominant world system' (South Centre 1992b, 17). The dissent is even more evident in UNECA (1992) or in UNCTAD's *Trade and Development Report 1992* which calls more generally for an internationally coordinated pump-priming to get out of the worldwide recession.

17. Cf. in this context Peter Katzenstein's analysis of small European economies in the 1970s (1983).

18. Charles Kindleberger, in his own field, has termed this 'comparative economic history in the small'. The search for the most important counterfactual in human history is, 'What would have happened in the system if Cleopatra's nose had been one-quarter inch shorter?' (1978, 1). Comparative work on structural adjustment in LDCs and Eastern Europe is found in Köves and Marer (1991; on methodology, see especially the introduction) and Stevens and Kennan (1992).

19. This section builds especially on Berend and Ránki (1974a; 1974b; 1982; 1985). For a very brief overview, see alternatively Berend (1986b).

20. Between 1867 and 1914, 65–70 per cent of all foreign capital in Hungary was Austrian. Towards the end of the century, French and German capital also undertook sizeable investments, especially in mining.

21. Detailed sectoral information on capital accumulation is given in Berend and Ránki (1979).

22. In this respect, Hungary resembles the Danish path to industrialisation.

23. Manufacturing remained largely limited to the primary processing of raw materials. Only 20–25 per cent of machine tools and other industrial equipment were produced domestically. In manufacturing, the electrical industry was the most advanced branch. A detailed sectoral overview is given in Berend and Ránki (1960).

24. This suggests the fallacy of applying dependency theories to commercial relations within the Habsburg Empire. If even Marxist historians do not accept exclusive outside-in explanations, there is likely to be a series of internal factors that help to explain the specifics of Hungary's relationship with Western Europe's industrialised core. For a different interpretation, emphasising pervasive 'displacement competition', see Senghaas (1985, Ch. 6).

25. On average the country became more industrialised in that most manufacturing activities were located in and around Budapest.

26. This was a key factor in Japan, Korea and Taiwan after the Second World War.

1 The Management of External Debt

1. Some bankers claim that they knew this all along. 'There was never a chance that LDC debt was going to topple the world banking system because it was in no one's interest to have it happen – except maybe the press. All that was just editorials and third-rate academicians and headline hunters. But it was never going to happen because the system wasn't going to let it' (John Heimann of Merrill Lynch, quoted in Frieden 1987, 154). If this first-rate banker is right, then many others are not just third-rate but also dumb. If one or two US money centre banks had gone bust, the 'system' would have taken care of it, Heimann says. 'Taking care', in this case, means absorbing the costs. The threat implied in the banks' stance, 'Unless you repay you won't get new money' was credible only insofar as the banks had something to lose.

Alternatively, if it was clear that governments would provide for whatever bail-out was going to become necessary, debtors would have been subject to credible threats only with regard to future flows of official funds. Hence, according to this reasoning, giving in to banks' pressure was not really necessary.

2. That is to say, it never rescheduled debt. Another rare member in this club is South Korea. Altogether, of the 55 countries that rescheduled official debt between 1980 and 1990, only five remained current on their debt obligations. These exceptions are Chile, the Gambia, Malawi, Romania and Turkey (Kuhn and Guzman 1990, 7).

3. Wood (1986, chap. 6) argues that international aid disbursements were themselves a source of the 1982 crisis. Hardening terms on official aid provided incentives for borrowers to shift to non-aid resources, thus escaping the discipline of the aid regime which consequently lost its capacity to influence terms and timing of the borrowers' graduation from concessional to market-based lending. 'The changes in the aid regime in the 1970s ... increased both the appeal and the viability of a range of strategies that, despite their diversity, may be called 'state capitalist'. Ironically, the commercial banks in the advanced capitalist countries made possible statist and nonmarket forms of development that the aid regime had historically obstructed' (ibid, 249). On externally financed state capitalism, see also Frieden (1981). Wood's interpretation, although derived from an analysis of developing countries, is interesting for the situation in Central Europe today in that it suggests that conditionality associated with assistance programmes will work only in the absence of alternative sources of financing. Given the current worldwide capital scarcity, that is presently not a problem. Wood's point should rather be seen as a reminder that extremely harsh conditions on official credits may turn out to be counterproductive – in the logic of the system – at some later point.

4. The history of relations between Eastern European countries and IFIs is reviewed by Assetto (1988), Lavigne (1991, chap. 8), Marer (1988) and Zloch-Christy (1987, chap. 4)

5. The hard-currency surplus was misleading: it was actually a mix of a deficit with the West and a surplus from intra-CMEA trade.

6. Large commercial banks employ economists to assess sovereign risk. Evidently, some of these professionals saw what was coming (namely, that the lending craze of the 1970s would eventually haunt the creditors). But loan officers did not get paid for prudent portfolio management: their bonuses were directly related to the volume of credits they dished out. Most importantly, loan officers were superior to risk analysts in the banks' hierarchy. For (at times, hilarious) accounts of how country risk analysts got shunned by bank management, see Bouchet (1987) and Lissakers (1991). A more sober view of country risk is found in Bird (1986). An instructive document of the banks' unawareness of the impending crisis is Mathis (1981). In this volume, bankers describe international loan portfolio management as though country risks existed only in textbooks.

7. 'Neighbourhood problems' became a recurrent feature of the debt crisis. Brazil, in September 1982, was the first country to feel the spill-over from Mexico's default. Later, Colombia was affected although it had a perfectly undisturbed payment and service record. Until the end of the decade, Colombia had problems in securing voluntary lending.

8.   At the time, international statistics followed Hungarian authorities in report-
     ing a $300 million surplus. In fact, the figure was much lower, but the
     creative use of larger-than-life performance figures helped Hungarian deci-
     sion-makers to paint a more optimistic picture of the situation in Hungary.
     Apparently, they felt that overreporting guaranteed them milder treatment
     from the IMF.

9.   One might, of course, hypothesise that the banks assumed a uniform distribu-
     tion of country risk over the entire area once Poland had declared insolvency.
     That begs the question of why – with the Polish situation not improving at all
     – the banks began differentiating again among debtor countries in 1984/85.

10. To be sure, loan loss reserves exact a price, but here the issue was that official
     creditors averted a default that would have cost the involved banks much
     more than the temporary income reduction that goes along with setting up
     reserves.

11. For a very lucid analysis of the politicisation of the crisis and its implications
     in both the international and the domestic dimension, see Frieden (1987).

12. In 1986, $5 billion was traded which compared to $380 billion of outstanding
     debt. By 1989, the secondary market had grown to a volume of more than
     $60 billion. Brief overviews of old financing techniques and the new, so-
     called 'menu-approach' are given by de Svastich (1986) and Schubert
     (1987). How the Fund sees them is explained in Blackwell and Nocera
     (1988) and Regling (1988) and, in the context of the Brady initiative, in
     Gajdeczka and Stone (1990). A comprehensive overview of financial instru-
     ments is found in BIS (1986). Mike Faber defines the securitisation of
     sovereign debt as follows: 'the art of packaging a set of extremely insecure
     investments so attractively that someone else will be induced to buy them.
     Favoured by the Bank of England as a way of distributing the High Street
     banks' risk to investors at large. The resultant instruments are known as
     "James Bonds" since the chance of full recovery is about 007' (1989, 229).

13. For a fascinating account of how the plan matured within the US administra-
     tion, see Vernon, Spar and Tobin (1991).

14. A popular version of this argument is nicely summarised in 'Sisters in the
     Wood' (1991, 31–39); for a more technical treatment and a brief run through
     the relevant literature, see D.Cohen (1992). The special case of debt forgive-
     ness by official creditors but, not simultaneously, by private creditors, is anal-
     ysed by Dooley (1993).

2   The Management of Industrial Policy and Trade

1.   Possibly, trade deficits reflected a cyclical mechanism. First, a surge in
     Western imports causes an increase in Hungary's non-rouble exports, fol-
     lowed by domestic output growth. Then, resulting higher imports into
     Hungary fail to be balanced by export growth due to domestic supply difficul-
     ties or slackening Western demand (Szakolczai, Bagdy and Vindics 1987, 60).

2.   Kádár suggests that CMEA raw-material based exports to the OECD include
     mostly products of higher-than-average capital intensity. Imports, by con-
     trast, being mostly highly processed, are less capital-intensive. 'In other

words, these countries, despite their relative poverty in capital, help the rich Western countries save investments due to this 'irregular' export specialization' (1984b, 220). An aluminium smelter may be more capital-intensive than, say, a plant producing machinery or equipment, but it is obviously a mistake to equate capital intensity with heavy industry. Highly processed pharmaceuticals are not necessarily less capital-intensive than whatever raw-material based product Kádár may have in mind. At any rate, the consequences of Kádár's argument are not clear. What would a 'regular' export specialisation look like: Western coal against Eastern refrigerators?

3. The error on their part is due to the fact that they base their table on the Hungarian commodity classification which divides all goods into five broad groups (in contrast to the nine SITC categories). The second of these comprises raw materials *and* semi-finished products *as well as* spare parts. The latter two should clearly be recorded as manufactures and not – as in Landesmann and Székely – simply be subsumed under raw materials. The (static) CEPR table is even more misleading when compared to the development of volume indices. Thus, machinery and industrial consumer goods are by far the most dynamic categories of all non-rouble imports. In 1989, they are, respectively, 39.5 per cent and 88.3 per cent higher than in 1980.

4. The Central Committee and the politbureau, in consultation with the Council of Trade Unions, typically discussed guidelines for industrial policy. For a description of other ministries and agencies involved in the preparatory or implementation phase, see Román and Bayer (1987).

5. Havasi also argued that gearing the economy towards export-orientation while pushing for a faster increase of exports than imports required a '*stronger role of central planning*' (Havasi 1981, 13; emphasis in original). Thus, he did not believe that the reformed price system and financial mechanism by themselves would guarantee the structural transformation of the economy.

6. Still in place from the 1970s was the Computer Technology CDP. It aimed at building a domestic industry for small computers and peripherals. It was phased out in 1985 as planned. By the mid-1980s Hungary had a computer industry that produced a few internationally competitive software programmes. Partly due to the Coordinating Committee on Trade with Communist Nations (COCOM) restrictions – at times successfully circumvented with the help of Taiwanese firms – Hungarian hardware development was less successful. Whether the CDP actually helped the rather small-scale entrepreneur-inventors that drove innovation in the industry would be an interesting question to pursue. To my knowledge, internationally accessible literature on this is not available.

7. It is important to realise the difference between industrial policy in a market economy and in a CPE. In the former, at least in theory, externalities in high-tech industries or rents possible in monopolistic competition provide the rationale for industrial policy. For an overview, see the volume edited by Paul Krugman (1988). (In practice, of course, the various manifestations of subsidies, soft credits, protection and so on are applied for reasons that are often totally different from those in the above rationale.) The point here is that industrial policy intervenes in the market without finding anything wrong with the market (institution) as such. In CPEs, on the other hand, the 'imperfection', so to speak, is the system itself.

To the extent that shortcomings in the system of economic management impede the transfer of resources to potentially dynamic sectors or fail to stimulate the rapid adoption of new products and technologies, the system may be viewed as a barrier to the growth of the most promising sectors of the economy. Reforms, whether centralizing or decentralizing, that improve the system's functioning in these areas are then also a form of industrial policy. (Brada and Dunn 1987, 58)

Thus, taking care of the imperfection means dealing with the institution (of economic planning and management) itself.

8. In 1988, Hungary invested about 2.3 per cent of its GDP in R&D. (This fell to 1.7 per cent in 1991.) Measured as per capita spending, this is roughly 4–8 times lower than related expenditure in industrialised countries.

9. The price reform effectively presented firms with an incentive to reduce convertible-currency exports. If prices for exports and their profitability did not rise, domestic prices had to remain at the current level. But by eliminating exports realising only below-average prices, a firm could then increase domestic prices. In any case, progressive taxes on wage increments saw to it that successful exporters were unable to reward their employees. In addition, limited access to financing for export activities and short repayment periods for loans contributed to the poor export performance (Balassa 1988). According to Balassa, the issue was not just one of problematic policy implementation but also of bad policy.

10. For a similar interpretation, see Oblath (1990). In any case, the forint actually appreciated between 1979 and 1984. This was due to an inappropriately weighted currency basket against which Hungary fixed its exchange rate. The US dollar, rapidly appreciating at the time, had a large weight in this basket although Hungarian trade with the USA represented less than 5 per cent of its hard currency trade. See Balassa (1988), and also Csikos-Nagy (1987, 248–9), Gács (1987). In contrast, in the late 1980s the forint appears to be undervalued (Hare and Révész 1992, 248). Boote and Somogyi (1991) give a concise overview of foreign trade and exchange rate reform since 1968. Bácskai (1984) gives an extensive overview of the history of Hungarian exchange rate management.

11. His analysis of Hungary is part of a larger paper in which Brada argues that declining levels of technical efficiency – and not a lack of technological progress – are responsible for negative growth of industrial output in Eastern Europe. The transitional economies are, so to speak, not mainly backward but rather in wrong gear. This assertion is highly relevant for designing transformation strategies.

12. For sectors much *below* average-efficiency, take Japanese or Bavarian farming, or Italian banking, for example. In varying degrees, this is a situation well known from developed market economies that are – by comparison – generally held to be 'systemically efficient'.

3 International Competitiveness

1. Italy's manufacturers of footwear are struggling, in fact, against import competition, notably from South Korea and Taiwan. In 1987, the EC allowed Italy to impose quantitative restrictions (QRs) on exports from these two

countries. In addition, Korea honoured a voluntary export restraint (VER) agreement with Italy (Kelly *et al.* 1988, 84–5).

2. The formula for calculating RCAs is

$$RCA_{ij} = (x_{ij}/X_{it})/(x_{jw}/X_{tw})$$

where

x_{ij} = value of country i's export of j
X_{it} = value of total manufacturing exports of country i
x_{jw} = value of world exports of industry j
X_{tw} = value of total world manufacturing exports

Cf Yeats (1985).

3. That the index has serious shortcomings even if used only as an ordinal measure is discussed, along with other issues, in Yeats (1985).

4. SITC 1 (beverages and tobacco) contributed only 0.5 per cent, in value terms, to Hungary's hard currency exports in this period. In what follows, I only look at SITC groups 0 (food) and 5–8 (manufactures). These commodities made up two-thirds of Hungary's hard currency exports in 1988.

5. 541: –34.2 %; 001: –55.4 %; 851: –41.0 %; 561: –53.7%; 821: +52.2%.

6. But even before the dissolution of CMEA, Hungary's exports did not develop in step with either imports or output. From 1987 to 1988, imports in current forints of basic (final) pharmaceutical products increased by 15.1 (18.1) per cent, and output by 20.2 (14.7) per cent. Exports only grew by 11 (2.4) per cent. See UNECE (1991a).

7. With the exception of plastics, the production of chemicals also fell in constant terms. However, while growth of world output of chemicals slowed down in general towards the late 1980s, it actually turned negative in 1989 in the whole of Central Europe. In contrast, moderate to very high growth rates were realised by European NICs such as Turkey (6.2%), Spain (5%), and Ireland (21.3%). Thus, the Central European decline does not reflect general demand conditions but appears more of a homemade problem (UNECE 1991a).

8. One assumes that at a given point in time a country's shares in world exports are 'normal' and should remain constant over time.

9. From SITC rev. 2 to SITC rev. 3. Unfortunately, most countries did not manage to implement the new SITC code immediately, hence there are no commodity tables for 1988.

10. The most comprehensive discussion of EC anti-dumping is Vermulst (1987). EC rules for imports from the CPEs are found in the *Official Journal* L195/1 (1982).

11. The Commission's argument is a bit like saying that anti-dumping investigations of Taiwanese typewriters did not impede the export growth of Taiwanese screwdrivers. For a brief review of policy issues associated with anti-dumping, see Matsumoto and Finlayson (1990), and, more specifically, Messerlin (1989).

12. Allowances for progress in reforms or GATT membership were generally not made (Hirsch 1988).

13. Hindley (1992) discusses anti-dumping in the context of the Association Agreements between the EC and a number of Central and Eastern European countries. He argues that contingent protectionism is a possible rather than an actual threat for Central European exports. Developments in EC steel policy in

late 1992, only months after Hindley's paper was written, show that it is difficult to make good predictions in this field, (this although Hindley was aware of intense industry lobbying during the negotiation of the Agreements).

14.   Hirsch suggests that this is also true for the CMEA as a whole.

Rather more surprising is the phenomenon that several CPEs, all members of Comecon, appear to be competing in identical product markets. One would have expected Comecon members to coordinate to some extent their export policies and thus avoid, or at least reduce, the double penalty of cutting prices in the process of seeking entry (which dumping is all about) and paying fines for doing so in the form of anti-dumping duties. (1988, 470)

Hirsch then goes on to conclude that the decline in the proportion of investigations against CMEA suggests that those countries have somehow learnt to outwit anti-dumpers. A simpler but no less convincing reason for the relative decline is that these measures remain in place for a couple of years, so a decline in new investigations may go hand in hand with a larger trade flow actually affected by the stock of old and new rulings.

15.   Artificial corundum is a very hard and strong industrial abrasive. It is used to make, for example, grinding and polishing wheels, and is also employed in the manufacture of special heat-resistant materials.

16.   External constraints are international market or political pressures. Both types of constraint were relevant for Hungarian adjustment policy. Domestic constraints include the influence of social groups (for example, the heavy-industry lobby) and the operation of (public) institutions and agencies. The latter point has been analysed elsewhere and is not treated here. See, for example, Comisso and Marer (1986) or, applied to Korea, Haggard and Chung-In Moon (1990).

17.   See, for example, Köves's treatise against proponents of de-linking, *Turning inward or turning outward* (subtitle, 1985; esp. the introduction). For a typical political pro-adjustment piece, see Birö (1980) or Faluvégi (1980). In contrast, see Berend (1980) for an article arguing that Hungary was not yet fit for the encounter with the world market.

4   The Management of Foreign Direct Investment

1.   This newly found enthusiasm is also reflected in *Transnational Corporations*, a new journal sponsored by UNTCMD. For an example of one such enthusiastic piece on how TNCs help national economic restructuring, (indirectly) stabilise infant democracy and enable domestic producers to become TNCs themselves, see Kline (1992). For a much more sober analysis of TNCs, but already part of the 'new literature' on FDI, see the very useful volume edited by Moran (1986), especially the contributions by Grieco and by Encarnation and Wells.

2.   In order of magnitude of FDI receipts: China ($3.5 billion); Malaysia ($2.9 billion); Mexico ($2.6 billion); Thailand ($2.3 billion); Portugal ($2.1 billion); Argentina ($2.0 billion); Brazil ($1.3 billion).

3.   A rare and in-depth study of very complex technology transfer deals between US TNCs and a few Eastern European countries is Liebrenz (1982).

4.   For a Hungarian appraisal, see Balkay (1984) and the contributions to 'Foreign Direct Investments and Joint Ventures in Hungary: Experience and

Prospects' (1990). More specifically on TNCs, see the description by Simai (1988). Andras Inotai (1990) has tried to summarise the historical lessons from changing government-TNC interaction for Central Europe. He argues that broader economic policies have a more significant impact on the decisions of TNCs than the legal, financial and institutional framework. Unfortunately, the volume is so far available only in Hungarian and thus not accessible to me. However, due to its early publication, Inotai does not give a first appraisal of the effects of increased FDI after 1988 in Central Europe which is what I am trying to do here.

5. Of all foreign capital in the manufacturing sector in 1989, 38.4 per cent went into engineering and transport equipment projects; 11.9 per cent into the food sector; 6.5 per cent into textiles, apparel and leather; 19.5 into chemicals, rubbers and plastics. In 1989, Western joint ventures repatriated some $20 million profits (out of $80 million in total profits).

6. Data on FDI are not well covered in international statistics. UNECE runs a database gathering information on FDI in ECE. However, the only merit of this database is that it compiles national data which otherwise would be more complicated to access. But not much else happens in Geneva. The distribution of FDI is broken down by industrial sector rather than by commodity output. Hence, UNECE cannot undertake any analyses comparing foreign equity investment with trade developments because the respective data are not comparable. They essentially rely on the information received from national sources. These, however, may obviously be incomplete or inaccurate. In Hungary, for example, trade data has recently exposed a gap between commodity (customs)-based and payments-based trade statistics.

7. For this reason I did not include any processed food products in the dataset. The number of producing units in the food sector is relatively higher than in the rest of industry. It would thus be impossible to relate a product with any confidence to a particular producer. The same applies, in principle, to agricultural products, although not to agricultural equipment. They are nonetheless included to illustrate the growth rates of the areas into which FDI has flown within agriculture so far.

8. For the sort of firms discussed here, this is rather unlikely. The incentive scheme abandoned in the amendment had applied to joint ventures with at least a 20 per cent participation or HUF 5 million which, at 1990 exchange rates, is less than $100 000. Firms that took advantage of this were often Western retailers or Hungarian firms who faked Western participation (by setting up a mailbox firm abroad and then having it invest a small sum drawn from their own foreign exchange) in order to reduce their corporate tax rates.

9. Imre Boros of Kulturbank, a Hungarian investment bank, pointed this out to me.

10. Such a suspicion led the Central European Investment Company to sell a minority share in the bus manufacturer Ikarus to a Russian-Canadian consortium rather than to one of the numerous Western bidders (Denton 1991).

11. One of the most vocal advocates of such a scheme was van Brabant (1990). The idea was generally not well received by Central Europeans who feared that a Central European Payments Union would resemble a sort of old-Comecon Club.

12. Mario Nuti has observed the cognitive dissonance between the predictions consultants and advisers made and the recessions that followed. He distinguishes

'incredulity (things are not as bad as they look), complacency (things are as bad as they look but this is exactly how they should be), advocacy of gradualism (the course is correct but its speed is excessive)' (1992, 3). Nuti's argument is that things are as bad as they look because of policy failures, notably, among others, the lack of incentives for managers and mismanagement of the state sector.

13. Fiat in Poland and Volkswagen in the former Czechoslovakia have sought and received guarantees for protection against import competition as well.

14. The CIS as a transition latecomer, according to this proposal, would charge the EC higher tariffs than the Central European countries, but be given GSP treatment by both.

15. In 1989, the World Bank was convinced of the viability of the project because it ensured General Electric's acquisition of Tungsram shares with $30 million under the Multilateral Investment Guarantee Agency programme.

References

'A Debtor's Dream', 1988. *The Economist*, 10 September, 81.

'Adjustment with Growth', 1987. Reprinted from *Finance & Development*.

Aggarwal, Vinod and Pierre Allan, 1992. 'Polish Debt Negotiation Games: 1981 Present' (mimeo). Paper presented to the Pan-European Conference in International Relations, September, Heidelberg.

Aghion, Philippe, Robin Burgess, Jean-Paul Fitoussi and Patrick Messerlin, 1992. 'Towards the Establishment of a Continental European Customs Union', in *Trade, Payments and Adjustment in Central and Eastern Europe*, eds John Flemming and J.M.C. Rollo, 157–80. London: Royal Institute of International Affairs.

Aldcroft, Derek H., 1977. *From Versailles to Wall Street 1919–1929*. London: Allen &Unwin.

Allen, Mark, 1982. 'Adjustment in Planned Economies', *IMF Staff Papers* 29: 398–421.

Amsden, Alice, 1989. *Asia's Next Giant: South Korea and Late Industrialization*. New York: Oxford University Press.

Antal, L., 1979. 'Development – with Some Digression', *Acta Oeconomica* 23, nos 3–4: 257–73.

——, L. Bokros, I. Csillag, L. Lengyel and G. Matolcsy, 1987. 'Change and Reform', *Acta Oeconomica* 38, nos 3–4: 187–213.

Armendariz de Aghion, Beatriz, 1993. 'Analytical Issues on LDC Debt: A Survey', *World Economy* 16, no. 4: 467–82.

Assetto, Valerie J., 1988. *The Soviet Bloc in the IMF and the IBRD*. Boulder, CO: Westview.

Bácskai, Tamás, 1984. 'Hungarian Rate of Exchange Policy', *New Hungarian Quarterly* 25 (Winter): 117–48.

Bairoch, Paul, 1976. 'Europe's Gross National Product: 1800–1975', *Journal of European Economic History* 5, no. 2: 273–340.

——, 1982. 'International Industrialization Levels from 1750 to 1980', *Journal of European Economic History* 11, no. 2: 269–333.

Bakos, Gábor, 1992a. 'Free Trade Zone in Central Europe?' (mimeo). Paper presented at the International Studies Association Convention, March, Atlanta.

——, 1992b. 'Japanese Capital in Central Europe' (mimeo). Hitotsubashi University, Department of Economics, Tokyo.

Balassa, Bela, 1988. 'The "New Growth Path" in Hungary', in Brada and Dobozi (1988).

Balázs, Katalin, Paul Hare and Ray Oakey, 1990. 'The Management of Research and Development in Hungary at the End of the 1980s', *Soviet Studies* 42, no. 4: 723–41.

Balkay, Bálint (ed), 1984. 'International Transfer of New Technologies and Problems of Adjustment in Small Open Economies', *Trends in World Economy*, no. 50.

Balvany, Iris, 1988. 'Hungary and the Third World: A Specific Approach', in *East-South Relations in the World Economy*, ed. Marie Lavigne, 225–35. Boulder, CO: Westview.

Bareau, Paul, 1983. 'The Lessons of an Earlier Debt Crisis', *The Banker* (December): 35–9.

Barre, Raymond, William H. Luers, Anthony Solomon and Krzysztof J. Ners, 1992. *Moving Beyond Assistance*. New York: Institute for East-West Studies.

'The Bear Necessities', 1982. *The Economist*, 20 March, 70–1.

Bell, Geoffrey, 1982. 'Debt Rescheduling – Can the Banking System Cope?', *The Banker* (February): 17–24.

Bélyácz, I., 1984. 'Investment Policy and Structural Transformation in Hungary', *Acta Oeconomica* 33, nos 3–4: 273–91.

Berend, Iván T., 1980. 'The Hungarian Economy and the World Market in the 20th Century', *Acta Oeconomica* 24, nos 1–2: 1–20.

——, 1981. 'Reflections on the Sixth Hungarian Five-Year Plan (1981–1985)', *Acta Oeconomica* 26, nos 1–2: 17–27.

——, 1986a. *The Crisis Zone of Europe*. Cambridge: Cambridge University Press.

——, 1986b. 'The Historical Evolution of Eastern Europe as a Region', *International Organization* 40, no. 2: 153–70.

——, 1990. *The Hungarian Economic Reforms 1953–1988*. Cambridge: Cambridge University Press.

Berend, Iván T. and György Ránki, 1960. *The Development of the Manufacturing Industry in Hungary* (1900–1944). Budapest: Akadémiai Kiadó.

—— [1965]. 'The Role of Foreign Capital in Hungary after the First World War', in Berend and Ránki (1979).

—— [1972]. 'Economic Development in Hungary between the Two World Wars', in Berend and Ránki (1979).

——, 1974a. *Economic Development in East-Central Europe in the 19th and 20th Centuries*. New York: Columbia University Press.

——, 1974b. *Hungary. A Century of Economic Development*. Newton Abbot: David & Charles.

——, 1979. *Underdevelopment and Economic Growth*. Budapest: Akadémiai Kiadó.

——, 1980. 'Foreign Trade and the Industrialization of the European Periphery in the XIXth Century', *Journal of European Economic History* 9, no. 3: 539–84.

——, 1982. *The European Periphery and Industrialization 1780–1914*. Cambridge: Cambridge University Press.

——, 1985. *The Hungarian Economy in the Twentieth Century*. London: Croom Helm.

Biersteker, Thomas J., 1990. 'Reducing the Role of the State in the Economy: A Conceptual Exploration of IMF and World Bank Prescriptions', *International Studies Quarterly* 34, no. 4: 477–92.

Bird, Graham, 1986. 'New Approaches to Country Risk', *Lloyds Bank Review*, no. 162: 3–16.

Birö, G., 1980. 'Ungarns internationale Wirtschaftsbeziehungen an der Schwelle der achtziger Jahre' (Hungary's International Economic Relations on the Threshold of the 1980s), *Acta Oeconomica* 24, nos 3–4: 263–76.

Bank for International Settlements (BIS), 1986. *Recent Innovations in International Banking*. Basle: BIS.

Blackwell, Michael and Simon Nocera, 1988. 'The Impact of Debt to Equity Conversion', *Finance & Development* (June): 15–17.

Bod, Peter Ákos, 1989–90. 'Market Strategy of the Hungarian Enterprise', *Eastern European Economies* 28, no. 2: 153–71.

Bodó-Vértes, Ágnes, 1984. 'Results of the Co-operation Strategy in the 70's – Exemplified by the Production Co-operation between Machine Tool Manufactures in the

FRG and Hungary', in *Organization and Interaction Patterns in Hungarian Industry*, eds András Rába and Kar-Ernst Schenk, 189–213. Stuttgart: Fischer.

Bognár, József, 1988. 'Decision-Making and Instruments for Socialist Foreign Trade', in Saunders (1988).

Boote, A.R., 1992. 'Assessing Eastern Europe's Capital Needs' (mimeo). Working Paper 92/12, IMF, Washington, DC.

—— and Janos Somogyi, 1991. 'Economic Reform in Hungary since 1968', IMF Occasional Paper no. 83, IMF, Washington, DC.

Borensztein, Eduardo, 1989. 'The Effect of External Debt on Investment', *Finance & Development* (September): 17–19.

——, 1991. 'Will Debt Reduction Increase Investment?', *Finance & Development* (March): 25–7.

Boschmann, Niña, 1991. 'The Philippines: The IMF's Intractable Regular', In *The Poverty of Nations*, eds Elmar Altvater, Kurt Hübner, Jochen Lorentzen and Raúl Rojas, 182–92. London: Zed.

Bouchet, Michel Henri, 1987. *The Political Economy of International Debt*. New York: Quorum Books.

Brada, Josef C., 1988. 'Industrial Policy in Eastern Europe', in Brada, Hewett and Wolf (1988).

——, 1989. 'Technological Progress and Factor Utilization in Eastern European Economic Growth', *Economica* 56 (November): 433–48.

Brada, Josef C. and Istvan Dobozi (eds), 1988. *The Hungarian Economy in the 1980s: Reforming the System and Adjusting to External Shocks*. London: JAI Press.

Brada, Josef C. and Robin L. Dunn, 1987. 'Industrial Policies in East and West Europe Compared', in Saunders (1987).

Brada, Josef C., A. Hewett and Thomas A. Wolf (eds), 1988. *Economic Adjustment and Reform in Eastern Europe and the Soviet Union*. Durham, NC: Duke University Press.

Brada, Josef C. and John M. Montias, 1984. 'Industrial Policy in Eastern Europe: A Three-Country Comparison', *Journal of Comparative Economics* 8, no. 4: 377–419.

Bradford Jr, Colin I., 1987. 'Trade and Structural Change: NICs and Next Tier NICs as Transitional Economies', *World Development* 15, no. 3: 299–316.

Bradshaw, York W. and Zwelakhe Tshandu, 1990. 'Foreign Capital Penetration, State Intervention, and Development in Sub-Saharan Africa', *International Studies Quarterly* 34, no. 2: 229–51.

Broad, Robin, John Cavanagh and Walden Bello, 1990/91. 'Development: The Market is not Enough', *Foreign Policy*, no. 81: 144–62.

Buchan, David, 1983. 'Hungary Finds it Hard to Keep the Lid on the Economy', *Financial Times*, 2 November, 2.

——, 1985. 'The Industrial Sector's Manufacturing Skills are Earning Hard Currency in the West', *Financial Times*, 14 May, 22.

Business Eastern Europe, various issues.

'Can we Help You, Sir?', 1988. *The Economist*, 23 September, 93–4.

Cardoso, Eliana A. and Albert Fishlow, 1989. 'The Macroeconomics of the Brazilian External Debt', in Sachs (1989a).

Carneiro, D. Dias, 1988. 'Brazil and the IMF: Logic and Story of a Stalemate', in Griffiths-Jones (1988c).

Celâsun, Merik and Dani Rodrik, 1989. 'Turkish Experience with Debt: Macroeconomic Policy and Performance', in Sachs (1989a).

Chung-In Moon, with assistance of Chul-Ho Chang, 1989. 'Trade Friction and Industrial Adjustment: The Textiles and Apparel in the Pacific Basin', in Haggard and Chung-In Moon (1989).

Clarke, Roger (ed). 1989. *Hungary: The Second Decade of Reform*. Harlow: Longman.

Clesse, Armand and Rudolf Tökés (eds), 1992. *Preventing a New East-West Divide: The Economic and Social Imperatives of the Future Europe*. Baden-Baden: Nomos.

Clute, Robert and Scott Turner, 1992. 'Sub-Saharan Structural Adjustment Programs: Have They Succeeded?' (mimeo). Paper presented to the International Studies Association Convention, March, Atlanta.

Cohen, Benjamin J., 1989. 'Developing-Country Debt: A Middle Way', Essays in International Finance no.173, Princeton University, Princeton, NJ.

Cohen, Daniel., 1992. 'The Debt Crisis: A Post Mortem', Discussion Paper no. 692, (CEPR), London.

Colclough, Christopher, 1991. 'Structure versus Neo-Liberalism: An Introduction', in *States or Markets? Neo-Liberalism and the Development-Policy Debate*, eds Christopher Colclough and James Manor, 1–25. Oxford: Clarendon Press.

Colitt, Leslie, 1983. 'Taking on More Responsibility', *Financial Times*, 10 May, 16.

——, 1984. 'The Ways Hungarians Earn Hard Currency', *Financial Times*, 26 September, 6.

Collins, Susan and Won-Am Park, 1989. 'External Debt and Macroeconomic Performance in South Korea', in Sachs (1989a).

Collins, Susan and Dani Rodrik, 1991. 'Eastern Europe and the Soviet Union in the World Economy' Washington, DC : Institute for International Economics.

Comisso, Ellen and Paul Marer, 1986. 'The Economics and Politics of Reform in Hungary', International Organization 40, no. 2: 421–54.

Commission of the European Communities, 1990. '7th Annual Report of the Commission on the Community's Anti-Dumping and Anti-Subsidy Activities', COM (90) 229 final. Brussels.

Conway, Patrick, 1991. 'An Atheoretic Evaluation of Success in Structural Adjustment', PRE Working Paper no 629, World Bank, Washington, DC.

Corbo, Vittorio, 1991. 'World Bank-Supported Adjustment Programs: Lessons for Central and Eastern Europe', in Corbo, Coricelli and Bossak (1991).

DeLong, J. Bradford and Lawrence Summers, 1990. 'Equipment Investment and Economic Growth', Working Paper no. 3515, National Bureau of Economic Research, Cambridge, MA.

——, Fabrizio Coricelli and Jan Bossak (eds) 1991. *Reforming Central and Eastern European Economies: Initial Results and Challenges*. Washington, DC: World Bank.

Corbo, Vittorio and Patricio Rojas, 1991. 'World Bank-Supported Adjustment Programs', PRE Working Paper no. 623, World Bank, Washington, DC.

'Crisis? What Crisis?' 1992. *The Banker* (September): 11–14.

Csaba, László, 1989. 'The Recent Past and the Future of the Hungarian Reform: An Overview and Assessment', in Clarke (1989).

Csejtei, Mária, 1992. 'Opportunities Awaiting', *Hungarian Economic Review* (October): 52–5.

Csikos-Nagy, Béla, 1987. 'Export-Oriented Policies Under Severe Import Regimes: A Case Study for Hungary', in Saunders (1987).

Czauner, Péter, 1992. 'Multinationals Target the Hungarian Market', *Hungarian Economic Review* (October): 56–9.

De Fontenay, Patrick, 1982. 'Hungary: An Economic Survey'. IMF Occasional Paper no. 15, IMF, Washington, DC.

Denton, Nicholas, 1990. 'Forum on Course to Lead Hungarian Government', *Financial Times*, 30 March, 3.

——, 1991. 'Soviet Group in Joint Venture for Hungarian Buses', *Financial Times*, 2 May, 4.

——, 1992. 'Hungarian Investors Think Again', *Financial Times*, 14 September, 3.

—— and Kevin Done, 1991. 'Suzuki to Set Up Car Assembly Plant in Hungary', *Financial Times*, 25 April, 3.

De Svastich, Peter, 1986. 'A Market Approach to Debt Reduction', *The Banker* (September): 35–40.

Devlin, Robert, 1989. *Debt and Crisis in Latin America*. Princeton, NJ: Princeton University Press.

Dooley, Michael, 1993. 'An Analysis of Burden Sharing among Creditors of Economies in Transition', in Uvalić, Espa and Lorentzen (1993).

Dornbusch, Rüdiger, 1990. 'Economic Reform in Eastern Europe and the Soviet Union: Priorities and Strategy' (mimeo). Paper presented to the Conference on The Transition to a Market Economy in Central and Eastern Europe, November, OECD, Paris.

Douglas, Sara U, 1989. 'The Textile Industry in Malaysia', *Asian* Survey 29, no. 4: 416–38.

'Eastern Europe: A Cautionary Note', 1990. *World Financial Markets* , no. 1: 12–16.

East European Markets, various issues.

east-west, 1992, no. 521, 26 February.

East-West Joint Ventures News , 1989, no. 2.

——, 1990, no. 6.

——, 1992, no. 11.

'East-West Traders Raise the Curtain', 1984. *The Economist*, 7 January, 64–5.

Édes, Bart W., 1992–93. 'Import Liberalization and Industry Protection', *Russian & East European Trade and Finance* 28, no. 4: 30–56.

Eichengreen, Barry and Peter H. Lindert (eds), 1989. *The International Debt Crisis in Historical Perspective*. Cambridge, MA: MIT Press.

Encarnation, Dennis J. and Louis T. Wells Jr, 1986. 'Evaluating Foreign Investment', in Moran (1986).

EUROSTAT, Monthly EEC External Trade (Combined Nomenclature) [CD–Rom].

Faber, Mike, 1989. 'Beware of Debtspeak', In *Third World Debt. The Search for a Solution*, ed. Graham Bird, 218–35. Hants: E. Elgar.

——, 1990. 'Renegotiating Official Debts', *Finance & Development* (December) 19–21.

Fairlamb, David. 1987. 'Eastern Europe Comes in from the Cold', *The Banker* (February): 48–50.

Faluvégi, L., 1980. 'Conditions of Hungarian Economic Development and Financial Policy', *Acta Oeconomica* 24, nos. 3–4: 213–32.

Fekete, J., 1980. 'Crisis of the International Monetary System – Impact of World Economic Changes on Hungarian Economic Policy', *Acta Oeconomica* 24, nos 3–4: 233–50.

Financial Research Ltd, 1991. 'Jelentések az Alagútbol' [Reports from the Tunnel]. June, Budapest.

Fischer, Stanley, 1989. 'The Key Question is the Bargaining', in *Alternative Solutions to Developing Country Debt Problems*, eds Rüdiger Dornbusch, John N. Makin and David Zlowe, 75–8. Washington, DC: American Enterprise Institute.

'Foreign Direct Investments and Joint Ventures in Hungary: Experience and Prospects', 1990. *Trends in World Economy*, no. 64.

Freeman, Christopher, 1988. 'Technology Gaps, International Trade and the Problems of Smaller and Less-Developed Economies', in Freeman and Lundvall (1988).

—— and Bengt-Åke Lundvall (eds), 1988. *Small Countries Facing the Technological Revolution*. London: Pinter.

Frieden, Jeffry A., 1981. 'Third World Indebted Industrialization: International Finance and State Capitalism in Mexico, Brazil, Algeria, and South Korea', *International Organization* 35, no. 3: 407–30.

——, 1987. *Banking on the World. The Politics of American International Finance*. New York: Harper & Row.

Gabor, Andrea and Kroly Ravasz, 1990. 'Unhappy Hunting Ground', *International Management* (September): 61–3.

Gabrisch, Hubert and Jan Stankovsky, 1989. 'Special Forms of East-West Trade. Part III. Higher Forms of Economic Cooperation', *Soviet & Eastern European Foreign Trade* 25, no. 2: 6–117.

Gács, János, 1986. 'The Conditions, Chances and Predictable Consequences of Implementing a Step-by-Step Liberalization of Imports in the Hungarian Economy', *Acta Oeconomica* 31, nos 3–4: 231–50.

——, 1987. 'Import Substitution and Investments in Hungary in the Period of Restrictions (1979–1986)', in *Investment System and Foreign Trade Implications in Hungary* , eds András Rába and Karl-Ernst Schenk, 155–87. Stuttgart: Fischer.

——, 1989. 'Changes in the Structure of Production and Foreign Trade of the Hungarian Industry in the Period of Restrictions (1978–1986)', *Acta Oeconomica* 40, nos 1–2: 79–103.

——, 1990. 'Foreign Trade Liberalization (1968–1990)', in Marrese and Richter (1990).

Gajdeczka, Przemyslaw, 1988. 'International Market Perceptions and Economic Performance: Lending to Eastern Europe', *Eastern European Politics and Societies* 2, no. 3: 558–76.

—— and Mark Stone, 1990. 'The Secondary Market for Developing Country Loans', *Finance & Development* (December): 22–5.

Geipel, Gary L., A. Tomasz Jarmoszko and Seymour E. Goodman, 1991. 'The Information Technologies and East European Societies', *East European Politics and Societies* 5, no. 3: 394–438.

Gelb, Alan H. and Cheryl W. Gray, 1991. *The Transformation of Economies in Central and Eastern Europe*. Washington, DC: World Bank.

Gereffi, Gary and Donald Wyman. 1989. 'Determinants of Development Strategies in Latin America and East Asia', in Haggard and Chung-In Moon (1989).

Gerschenkron, Alexander, 1966. 'Economic Backwardness in Historical Perspective', in *Economic Backwardness in Historical Perspective*, 5–30. Cambridge, MA: Belknap of Harvard University Press.

Gibson, Martha Liebler and Michael D. Ward, 1992. 'Export Orientation: Pathway or Artifact?' *International Studies Quarterly* 36, no. 3: 331–44.

Gomulka, Stanislaw, 1986. 'The Incompatibility of Socialism and Rapid Innovation', in *Growth, Innovation and Reform in Eastern Europe*. Brighton: Wheatsheaf.

Gowan, Peter, 1991–92. 'Old Medicine, New Bottles', *World Policy Journal* 9. no. 1: 1–33.

Greskovits, Béla, 1987. 'The Hungarian Credit Programme to Stimulate Exports', In *Investment System and Foreign Trade Implications in Hungary*, eds Andrs Rba and Karl-Ernst Schenk, 189–228. Stuttgart: Fischer.

——, 1988. 'Western Technological Policies and the Approach of Hungarian Industrial Policy', *Acta Oeconomica* 39, nos 1–2: 95–109.

Grieco, Joseph, 1986. 'Foreign Direct Investment and Development: Theories and Evidence', in Moran (1986).

Griffiths-Jones, Steffany, 1988a. 'Conclusions and Policy Recommendations', in Griffiths-Jones (1988c).

——, 1988b. 'Debt Crisis Management, an Analytical Framework', in Griffiths-Jones (1988c).

—— (ed), 1988c. *Managing World Debt*. Brighton: Harvester Wheatsheaf.

Gueullette, Agota Anna, 1988. 'Hungarian Policy on Imports of Licenses and the Assimilation of Transferred Know-How', *European Economic Review* 32: 611–17.

——, 1989. 'Financing the Acquisition of Western Technology in the Context of the Hungarian Reform', *Soviet Studies* 41, no. 4: 592–601.

Guisinger, Stephen, 1986. 'Host-Country Policies to Attract and Control Foreign Investment', in Moran (1986).

Haggard, Stephan, 1989. 'Introduction: The International Politics of Industrial Change', in Haggard and Chung-In Moon (1989).

——, 1990. *Pathways from the Periphery. The Politics of Growth in the Newly Industrializing Countries*. Ithaca, NY: Cornell University Press.

Haggard, Stephan and Robert Kaufman, 1989. 'The Politics of Stabilization and Structural Adjustment', in Sachs (1989a).

Haggard, Stephan and Chung-In Moon (eds), 1989. *Pacific Dynamics*. Boulder, CO: Westview.

——, 1990. 'Institutions and Economic Policy: Theory and a Korean Case Study', *World Politics* 42, no. 2: 210–37.

Halpern, László, 1992. 'Microeconomic Factors of Trade Reorientation in Hungary (1981–90)' (mimeo). Paper presented to the Annual Meeting of the European Economic Association, June, University of Dublin.

Hanson, Philip and Keith Pavitt, 1987. *The Comparative Economics of Research Development and Innovation in East and West: A Survey*. Chur Switzerland Harwood.

Hare, Paul, 1988. 'Industrial Development of Hungary since World War II', *Eastern European Politics and Societies* 2, no. 1: 115–51.

—— and Tamás Révész, 1992. 'Hungary', *Economic Policy* (April): 227–64.

Haus, Leah, 1992. *Globalizing the GATT*. Washington, DC: Brookings.

Havasi, F, 1981. 'The Sixth Five-Year Plan of the Hungarian National Economy (1981–1985)', *Acta Oeconomica* 26, nos. 1–2: 1–16.

Helleiner, Gerald K., 1991. 'Protectionism and the Developing Countries' (mimeo) Department of Economics, University of Toronto.

——, 1992. 'Introduction', in *Trade Policy, Industrialization and Development: New Perspectives*, ed. Gerald K. Helleiner, 1–32. Oxford: Clarendon Press.

Hindley, Brian, 1992. 'Exports from Eastern and Central Europe and Contingent Protection', in *Trade, Payments and Adjustment in Central and Eastern Europe*, eds John Flemming and J.M.C. Rollo, 144–53. London: Royal Institute of International Affairs.

Hirsch, Seev, 1988. 'Anti-Dumping Actions in Brussels and East-West Trade', *World Economy* 11 (September): 465–84.

Hoen, H.W. and H.-J. Wagener, 1989. 'Hungary's Exports to the OECD: A Constant Market Shares Analysis', *Acta Oeconomica* 40, nos 1–2: 65–77.

Holliday, George D., 1984. 'Transfer of Technology from West to East: A Survey of Sectoral Case Studies', Part II of *East-West Technology Transfer*. Paris: OECD.

Horváth, László, 1988. 'Marketing and Innovation Strategy in a Major Hungarian Enterprise – Taurus', in Saunders (1988).

Hrndcír̆, Miroslav, 1993. 'Barriers to Trade and Revival of Economic Growth in Czechoslovakia', in Uvalic, Espa and Lorentzen (1993).

Hughes, Gordon and Paul Hare, 1991. 'Competitiveness and Industrial Restructuring in Czechoslovakia, Hungary and Poland', *European Economy* Special Edition no. 2: 83–107.

Hughes, Gordon and David M.G. Newbery, 1986. 'Protection and the LDCs', *Economic Policy* 1, no. 2: 409–53.

Hungarian Central Statistical Office. (HCSO) 1991. *Statistical Yearbook 1989–1990*. Budapest: HCSO.

——, *Statistical Yearbook of External Trade*, various volumes. Budapest: HCSO.

'Hungary – Memorandum of Economic Transformation and Medium-Term Policies', 1991. (Annex to Letter of Intent with IMF, confidential document).

'Hungary's Case,' 1982. *The Economist*, 20 March, 16.

IMF, 1987. 'Theoretical Aspects of the Design of Fund-Supported Adjustment Programs', IMF Occasional Paper no. 55, IMF, Washington, DC.

——, 1991. *International Capital Markets. Developments and Prospects*. Washington, DC: IMF.

——, *International Financial Statistics*, various volumes. Washington, DC: IMF.

'Initiatives by the Hungarian Government Concerning the Negotiations with the Group of "24"' (mimeo). n.d. (late 1989).

Inotai, András, 1986. 'Die RGW-Länder im internationalen Handel von Maschinenbauprodukten' (The CMEA Countries in the International Trade of Machinery Products). *Osteuropa-Wirtschaft* 31, no. 4: 307–22.

——, 1987. 'The Present and Future of Economic Relations between Hungary and the EC', *Hungarian Business Herald*, no. 1: 28–32.

——, 1988. 'International Competitiveness and Imports', *Acta Oeconomica* 39, nos 1–2: 45–60.

——, 1990. *A Mukodotoke a Vilaggazdasagban* (Direct Capital in the World Economy). Budapest: Kossuth Könyvkiadó.

Institute of International Finance, 1990a. *Annual Report*. Washington, DC: IIF.

——, 1990b. 'Republic of Hungary. Special Report' (mimeo). June, Washington.

'International Credit Market Developments', 1982. *World Financial Markets* (August): 7–11.

Janos, Andrew C., 1982. *The Politics of Backwardness in Hungary 1825–1945*. Princeton, NJ: Princeton University Press.

——, 1989. 'The Politics of Backwardness in Continental Europe, 1780–1945', *World Politics* 41, no. 3: 325–58.

Joint Ventures in Hungary with Foreign Participation, 1991. Budapest: Magazin Kiadó.

Kádár, Béla, 1980. 'Some Strategic Aspects of Structural Policy in Hungary', *Acta Oeconomica* 24, nos 3–4: 277–88.

——, 1983a. 'Changes in the World Economic Environment and Hungarian Industry', *Acta Oeconomica* 30, no. 1: 111–27.

——, 1983b. 'World Economic Situation of the 1980s and Conclusions on the Development of the Hungarian Economy', *Acta Oeconomica* 30, nos 3–4: 291–311.

——, 1984a. 'The External Economic Framework and the Conditions of Accelerating Hungarian Growth', *Acta Oeconomica* , nos 1–2: 89–104.

——, 1984b. *Structural Changes in the World Economy*. London: Frances Pinter.

——, 1985. 'Hungarian Industrial Development in the Light of World Economic Changes', *Acta Oeconomica* 34, nos 3–4: 241–62.

——, 1990–91. 'What We Inherited', *Soviet & Eastern European Trade* 26, no. 4: 3–24.

Kaminski, Bartlomiej, 1988. 'External Dimension of Balance of Payments Adjustment in Eastern Europe', *Osteuropa-Wirtschaft* 33, no. 2: 122–39.

Kaser, M.C, 1985. 'Introduction', in Kaser and Radice (1985), vol. 1.

—— and E.A. Radice, 1985. *The Economic History of Eastern Europe 1919–1975*. vol. 1. Oxford: Oxford University Press.

Katseli, Louka, 1992. 'Foreign Direct Investment and Trade Interlinkages in the 1990s: Experiences and Prospects of Developing Countries', Discussion Paper no.687, CEPR, London.

Katz, S. Stanley, 1991. 'East Europe Should Learn from Asia', *Financial Times*, 24 April.

Katzenstein, Peter J., 1983. 'The Small European States in the International Economy: Economic Dependence and Corporatist Policies', in *The Antinomies of Interdependence*, ed. John Gerard Ruggie, 91–130. New York: Columbia University Press.

Kelly, Margaret, Naheed Kirmani, Miranda Xafa, Clemens Boonekamp d Peter Winglee, 1988. 'Issues and Developments in International Trade Policy', IMF Occasional Paper no. 63, IMF, Washington, DC.

Kerpel, Éva and David G. Young, 1988. 'Hungary to 1993. Risks and Rewards of Reform', Special Report no. 1153, *The Economist* Intelligence Unit, London.

Kindleberger, Charles P., 1978. *Economic Response. Comparative Studies in Trade, Finance, and Growth*. Cambridge, MA: Harvard University Press.

——, 1989. *Maniacs, Panics, and Crashes*, 2nd edn. London: Macmillan.

Kiss, Judit, 1993. 'Debt Management in Eastern Europe', Working Paper no. 15, Institute for World Economics of the Hungarian Academy of Sciences, Budapest.

Kline, John M., 1992. 'The Role of Transnational Corporations in Chile's Transition: Beyond Dependency and Bargaining', *Transnational Corporations* 1, no. 2: 81–95.

Klodt, Henning, 1990. 'Technology-Based Trade and Multinationals' Investment in Europe: Structural Change and Competition in Schumpeterian Goods', Paper presented to the Conference 'Multinationals in Europe and Global Trade in the 1990s', September, American Institute for Contemporary German Studies, Washington, DC.

——, 1991. 'Comparative Advantage and Prospective Structural Adjustment in Eastern Europe', *Economic Systems* 15, no. 2: 265–81.

Koh, Tommy and Lee Tsao Yuan, 1992. 'Hong Kong and Singapore Are Hard Acts to Follow', *International Herald Tribune*, 29 July, 4.

Kornai, János, 1986. 'The Hungarian Reform Process: Visions, Hopes, and Reality', *Journal of Economic Literature 24* (December): 1687–737.
———, 1993. 'Postsocialist Transition: An Overall Survey', *European Review* 1, no. 1: 53–64.
Kovács, András, 1984. 'The Relationship between Producer and Foreign Trade Enterprises: Observations on Cooperation between an Impex and its Producers', *Soviet & Eastern European Trade* 20, no. 2: 69–87.
Köves, András, 1985. *The CMEA Countries in the World Economy: Turning Inwards or Turning Outwards*. Budapest: Akadémiai Kiadó.
——— 1990. 'A New Situation in Hungarian–Soviet Trade: What Is to Be Done?', in Marrese and Richter (1990).
——— and Paul Marer (eds), 1991. *Foreign Economic Liberalization. Transformations in Socialist and Market Economies*. Oxford: Westview.
Krasznai, Z. and M. Laki, 1982. 'Conditions and Possibilities of Cooperation in Production and Trade with Western Firms in Hungary', *Acta Oeconomica* 29, nos 1–2: 149–66.
Krugman, Paul (ed), 1988. *Strategic Trade Policy and the New International Economics*. Cambridge, MA: MIT Press.
———, 1989. 'Private Capital Flows to Problem Debtors', in Sachs (1989a).
Ku, Susan, 1990. 'Much Ado about SMEthing', *Free China Review* (May): 66–7.
Kuczynski, Pedro Pablo, 1989. 'Brady and Beyond', in *Debt Equity Swaps in the 1990s*, vol. 1, ed. Steven M. Rubin, 3–10. *The Economist* Special Report no. 1203, London.
Kuhn, Michael G. and Jorge P. Guzman, 1990. 'Multilateral Official Debt Rescheduling. Recent Experiences', IMF World Economic and Financial Surveys, IMF, Washington, DC.
Laird, Sam and Alexander Yeats, 1990. *Quantitative Methods for Trade-Barrier Analysis*. London: Macmillan.
Landesmann, Michael and István Székely. 1991. 'Industrial estructuring and the Reorientation of Trade in Czechoslovakia, Hungary and Poland', Discussion Paper no. 546, CEPR, London.
Lányi, Kamilla, 1990. 'Visible and Invisible Trade Regulation and Deregulation', in Marrese and Richter (1990).
Lavigne, Marie, 1991. *International Political Economy and Socialism*. Cambridge: Cambridge University Press.
Leamer, Edward E. and Robert M. Stern, 1970. *Quantitative International Economics*. Chicago, IL: Aldine.
Lee, Sun Huk, 1993. 'Are the Credit Ratings Assigned by Bankers Based on the Willingness of LDC Borrowers to Repay?', *Journal of Development Economics* 40: 349–59.
'The Left, the Right and the Third World', 1992. *The Economist*, 14 March, 103–4.
Lehman, Howard P. and Jennifer L. McCoy, 1992. 'The Dynamics of the Two-Level Bargaining Game', *World Politics* 44, no. 4: 600–44.
Leipold, Alessandro, Mohamed A. El-Erian, Ajai Chopra, John Clark, Paul Mylonas and Louis Pauly, 1991. 'Private Market Financing for Developing Countries', World Economic and Financial Surveys, IMF, Washington, DC.
Lewis, John P., 1986. 'Overview: Development Promotion: A Time for Regrouping', in *Development Strategies Reconsidered*, eds John P. Lewis and Valeriana Kallab, 3–46.

Li, Kui Wai, 1991. 'Positive Adjustment against Protectionism: The Case of Textile and Clothing Industry in Hong Kong', *The Developing Economies'* 29, no. 3: 197–209.

Liebrenz, M.L., 1982. *Transfer of Technology. US Multinationals and Eastern Europe.* New York: Praeger.

Lin, Ching-Yuan, 1989. *Latin America vs East Asia.* London: M.E. Sharpe.

Lindert, Peter H., 1989. 'Response to Debt Crisis: What is Different about the 1980s?', in Eichengreen and Lindert (1989).

—— and Peter J. Morton, 1989. 'How Sovereign Debt Has Worked', in Sachs (1989a).

Lissakers, Karin, 1991. *Banks, Borrowers, and the Establishment: A Revisionist Account of the International Debt Crisis.* New York: Basic.

Lórincze, Péter, 1988. 'Economic Relations between Hungary and the United States', in Brada and Dobozi (1988).

Maass, Peter, 1992. 'East Europe Capitalizes on Brainpower', *International Herald Tribune*, 21 January.

Mádi, C., 1990. 'Transfer of Technology – Hungary in the Eighties', *Acta Oeconomica* 42, nos 1–2: 141–68.

Major, Iván, 1992. 'The State's Role in Attracting Foreign Investment Capital', *Hungarian Economic Review* (August): 52–7.

Marer, Paul, 1986. *East-West Technology Transfer. Study of Hungary 1968–1984.* Paris: OECD.

——, 1987. 'Can Joint Ventures in Hungary Serve as a "Bridge" to the CMEA Market?', Working Paper no. 87/276, European University Institute, San Domenico di Fiesole.

——, 1988. 'Centrally Planned Economies in the IMF, the World Bank, and the GATT', in Brada, Hewett and Wolf (1988).

Marin, Dalia, 1986. 'Import-Led Innovation. Technical Advance in Austrian Textiles', Research Memorandum no. 231, Institute for Advanced Studies, Vienna.

Marrese, Michael, 1990. 'Hungarian Foreign Trade: Failure to Reform', in Marrese and Richter (1990).

—— and Sándor Richter (eds), 1990. *The Challenge of Simultaneous Economic Relations with East and West.* London: Macmillan.

Marton, Katherin, 1993. 'Foreign Direct Investment in Hungary', *Transnational Corporations* 2, no.1: 111–34.

Matejka, Harriet, 1988. 'Trade and Cooperation between the Community and the CMEA: The Significance of the Joint Declaration of June 25th, 1988' (mimeo). Paper presented at the European University Institute, San Domenico di Fiesole.

Mathis, F. John (ed.), 1981. *Offshore Lending by U.S. Commercial Banks,* 2nd edn. Washington, DC: Bankers' Association for Foreign Trade.

Matsumoto, Ken and Grant Finlayson, 1990. 'Dumping and Antidumping: Growing Problems in World Trade', *Journal of World Trade Law* 24, no. 4: 5–19.

Maxfield, Sylvia and James H. Nolt, 1990. 'Protectionism and the Internationalization of Capital: U.S. Sponsorship of Import Substitution Industrialization in the Philippines, Turkey and Argentina', *International Studies Quarterly* 34, no. 1: 49–81.

McDougall, Rosamund, 1990. 'Last Ones under the Curtain', *The Banker* (July): 20–4.

Mendelsohn, M.S, 1983. 'International Debt Crisis: The Practical Lessons of Restructuring', *The Banker* (July): 33–8.

Menzel, Ulrich, 1991. 'Das Ende der "Dritten Welt" und das Scheitern der groen Theorie. Zur Soziologie einer Disziplin in auch selbstkritischer Absicht' (The End of the "Third World" and the Failure of Grand Theory. Self-Critical Remarks on the Sociology of a Discipline), *Politische Vierteljahresschrift* 32 (March): 4–33.

Messerlin, Patrick A, 1989. 'The EC Antidumping Regulations: A First Economic Appraisal', *Weltwirtschaftliches Archiv* 125: 563–87.

——, 1992. 'The Association Agreement between the EC and Central Europe: Trade Liberalisation vs. Constitutional Failure?' (mimeo). Institute d'Études Politiques de Paris.

——, 1994. 'CEEC's Trade Laws in the Light of International Experience', (Unpublished manuscript).

Mester, Sándor. 1992. 'A Challenge to Survive', *Hungarian Economic Review* (October): 49–51.

Meth-Cohn, Delia *et al.*, 1994. 'Foreign Investment Survey', *Business Central Europe* (April): 35–50.

Ministry of Finance, 1991. 'Act on Investments of Foreigners in Hungary', *Public Finance in Hungary*, no. 75. Budapest: Perfekt.

Montagnon, Peter, 1986. 'Hungary to Renegotiate $210m Bankers Facility', *Financial Times*, 18 February, 30.

Moran, Theodore H. (ed.), 1986. *Investing in Development: New Roles for Private Capital?* Washington, DC: Overseas Development Council.

Naray, Peter, 1989. 'The End of the Foreign Trade Monopoly. The Case of Hungary', *Journal of World Trade* 23, no. 6: 85–97.

National Bank of Hungary, *Annual Report 1990*. Budapest: National Bank of Hungary.

Nelson, Joan M., 1989. 'Overview: The Politics of Long-Haul Economic Reform', in *Fragile Coalitions: The Politics of Economic Adjustment*, ed. Joan M. Nelson and Contributors, 3–26. Washington, DC: Overseas Development Council.

Nötel, R., 1974. 'International Capital Movements and Finance in Eastern Europe 1919–1949', *Vierteljahresschrift für Sozial-und Wirtschaftsgeschichte* 61: 65–112.

——, 1986. 'International Credit and Finance', in Kaser and Radice 1986 (1985), vol. 2.

Nuti, Domenico Mario. 1992. 'Economic Inertia in the Transitional Economies of Eastern Europe' (mimeo). EC Commission, Brussels.

Nyerges, János, 1986. 'Hungary's Experiences in GATT', in *East-West Economic Relations in the Changing Global Environment*, eds B. Csikós-Nagy and D.G. Young, 196–204. New York: St Martin's Press.

Nyers, Rezső, 1988. 'National Economic Objectives and the Hungarian Reform Process in the 1980s', in Brada and Dobozi (1988).

—— and M. Tardos, 1979. 'What Economic Development Policy Should we Adopt?' *Acta Oeconomica* 22, nos 1–2: 11–31.

—— and M. Tardos, 1984. 'The Necessity for Coordination of the Economy and the Possibility of Development in Hungary', *Acta Oeconomica* 32, nos 1–2: 1–19.

Oblath, Gábor, 1990. 'Trade Policy Recommendations', in Marrese and Richter (1990).

——, 1992. 'Hungary's External Debt: Past Trends, Constraints and Policy Options', (mimeo). Paper presented to the Conference "Impediments to the Transition", January, European University Institute, San Domenico di Fiesole.

OECD, 1989. *Series C. Trade by Commodities*. Paris: OECD.

——, 1991. Hungary. *Economic Surveys* (July).

——, 1992. *Bank Profitability. Statistical Supplement. Financial Statements of Banks 1981–1990*. Paris: OECD.

——, *Financial Market Trends*, various volumes. Paris: OECD.

——, *Series C. Trade by Commodities*, various years. Microfiche.

'Off the Leash', 1990. *The Banker* (September): 18.

Official Journal, various issues.

Olea, Miguel A., 1989. 'The Latin American Debt Crisis: The Debtor's View', in *Third World Debt. The Search for a Solution*, ed. Graham Bird, 70–7. Hants: E. Elgar.

Olechowski, Andrzej and Alexander Yeats, 1982. 'The Incidence of Nontariff Barriers on Socialist Country Exports', *Economia Internazionale* 35, no. 2: 227–45.

Oman, Charles P., 1986. 'New Forms of Investment in Developing Countries', in Moran (1986).

'On Foreign Businesses in Hungary', 1992. *Hungarian Economic Review* (December): 59–62.

'Opportunity East', 1992. (mimeo). Summary of a Conference organised by the EC Commission and the OECD, April, Brussels.

Ostry, Sylvia, 1993. 'The Threat of Managed Trade to Transforming Economies', Occasional Paper no. 41, Group of Thirty, Washington, DC.

Oye, Kenneth A, 1992. 'The Politics of Bilateral and Regional Openness', in *Economic Discrimination and Political Exchange*. Princeton, NJ: Princeton University Press.

Pack, Howard and Larry E. Westphal, 1986. 'Industrial Strategy and Technological Change', *Journal of Development Economics* 22: 87–128.

Paulat, Vladislav J., 1954. 'Investment Policy and the Standard of Living in East-Mid-European Countries', *Journal of Central European Affairs* 14: 38–64.

Pauly, Louis W., 1990. Institutionalizing a Stalemate: National Financial Policies and the International Debt Crisis', *Journal of Public Policy* 10, no. 1: 23–43.

Perez, Carlota, 1988. 'New Technologies and Development', in Freeman and Lundvall (1988).

'Pioneers of capitalism', 1992. *The Economist*, 4 April, 79–80.

Piontek, Eugeniusz, 1987. 'Anti-Dumping in the EEC – Some Observations by an Outsider', *Journal of World Trade Law* 21, no. 4: 67–94.

'Poland to Resume Talks with the Banks', 1993. *International Herald Tribune*, 30/31 January, 11.

Pollard, Sidney, 1986. *Peaceful Conquest. The Industrialization of Europe 1760–1970*. Oxford: Oxford University Press.

Popper, Stephen, 1988. 'The Diffusion of Numerically Controlled Machine Tools in Hungary', in Brada and Dobozi (1988).

Porter, Michael E., 1990. *The Competitive Advantage of Nations*. London: Macmillan.

Poznanski, Kazimierz Z., 1987. *Technology, Competition, & the Soviet Bloc in the World Market*. Berkeley: University of California.

——, 1988. 'Economic Determinants of Technological Performance in East European Industry', *Eastern European Politics and Societies* 2, no. 3: 577–600.

Rácz, István, 1993. 'Transition in East-Central Europe: The Investment Criterion', in Uvalić, Espa and Lorentzen (1993).

Ránki, G., [1968]. 'On the Economic Development of the Austro-Hungarian Monarchy', in Berend and Ránki (1979).

Ray, Dennis M., 1992. 'Perspectives on Urban Economic Development', *Entrepreneurship, Innovation, and Change* 1, no. 1: 27–56.

Regling, Klaus P., 1988. 'New Financing Approaches in the Debt Strategy', *Finance & Development* (March): 6–9.

Reinicke, Wolfgang H., 1992. *Building a New Europe*. Washington, DC: Brookings.

Rejtő, G. 1983. 'A Debate in Hungary on the Possibilities of Cooperation with Western Firms (1982–83)', *Acta Oeconomica* 31, nos 3–4: 327–40.

'Renewed Appetite', 1984. *The Banker* (December): 90.

Reti, Pál, 1988. 'Technological Change by Central Control: The Case of the Hungarian Electronics Industry', in Freeman and Lundvall (1988).

Rhodes, William R., 1992. 'The Disaster that Didn't Happen', *The Economist*, 12 September, 17–21.

Richardson, J. David, 1971. 'Constant-Market-Shares Analysis of Export Growth', *Journal of International Economics* 1, 227–39.

Riecke, Werner, 1992. 'Managing Foreign Debts and Monetary Policy During Transformation', (mimeo). Paper presented to the Conference 'Hungary: An Economy in Transition', February, CEPR, London.

Rollo, Jim and Alasdair Smith, 1993. 'EC Trade with Eastern Europe', *Economic Policy* (April): 139–81.

Román, Zoltán and Kurt Bayer, 1987. 'Structural Policy in Hungary and Austria', in Saunders (1987).

Ruggie, John Gerard, 1983. 'Introduction: International Interdependence and National Welfare', in *The Antinomies of Interdependence*, ed. John Gerard Ruggie, 1–39. New York: Columbia University Press.

Sachs, Jeffrey (ed.) 1989a. *Developing Country Debt and the World Economy*. Chicago, IL: University of Chicago Press.

——, 1989b. 'Making the Brady Plan Work', in *Debt Equity Swaps in the 1990s*, vol. 1, ed. Steven M. Rubin, 11–22. *The Economist* Special Report no. 1203, London.

Sapir, André. 1994. 'The Europe Agreements: Implications for Trade Laws and Institutions', (mimeo). Paper presented to the Workshop 'Trade Laws and Institutions for Emerging Market Economies', March, CEPR, Brussels.

Saunders, Christopher T. (ed.), 1987. *Industrial Policies and Structural Change*. London: Macmillan.

—— (ed.), 1988. *Macroeconomic Management and the Enterprise in East and West*. London: Macmillan.

Schriber, G., 1992. 'Host Country Incentive Measures – A Western Company View', *East-West Joint Ventures News*, no. 11: 14–17.

Schubert, Martin, 1987. 'Trading Debt for Equity', *The Banker* (February): 18–31.

Schulmann, Horst, 1992. 'How to Compete for Scarce Capital', *The Banker* (September): 8–9.

Sealy, Tom, 1983. 'High Technology Hard Hit by West's Sanctions', *Financial Times*, 10 May, 18.

Senghaas, Dieter, 1985. *The European Experience. A Historical Critique of Development Theory*. Leamington Spa: Berg.

Senior Nello, Susan, 1990. 'Some Recent Developments in EC-East European Economic Relations', *Journal of World Trade* 24, no. 1: 5–24.

Siklos, Pierre L, 1991. *War Finance, Reconstruction, Hyperinflation and Stabilization in Hungary, 1938–48*. London: Macmillan.

Simai, Mihály, 1988. 'Hungary and the Transnational Corporations', in *Transnational Corporations and China's Open Door Policy*, eds Weizao Teng and N.T. Wang, 165–70. Lexington, MA: Lexington Books.

'Sisters in the Wood', 1991. *The Economist*, 12 October, 1–54 (Survey of the IMF and the World Bank).

'So Have We Learnt Our Lesson?', 1988. *The Economist*, 30 July, 78–80.

South Centre, 1992a. *Enhancing the Economic Role of the United Nations*. Geneva: South Centre.

——, 1992b. *The United Nations at a Critical Crossroads*. Geneva: South Centre.

Stallings, Barbara, 1992. 'International Influence on Economic Policy: Debt, Stabilization, and Structural Reform', in *International Constraints, Distributive Conflicts, and the State*, eds Stephan Haggard and Robert R. Kaufman, 41–88. Princeton, NJ: Princeton University Press.

Stevens, Christopher and Jane Kennan (eds), 1992. *Reform in Eastern Europe and the Developing Country Dimension*. London: Overseas Development Institute.

Stopford, John and Susan Strange with John S. Henley, 1991. *Rival Firms, Rival States. Competition for World Market Shares*. Cambridge: Cambridge University Press.

Storf, Otto, 1992. 'The Future of East-West Financial Relations and the Responsibility of the Banks', (mimeo). Paper presented to the Conference 'Impediments to the Transition', January, European University Institute, San Domenico di Fiesole.

Strange, Susan, 1974. 'IMF: Monetary Managers', in *The Anatomy of Influence*, eds Robert W. Cox and Harold K. Jacobsen, 263–97. London: Yale University Press.

——, 1985. 'Protectionism and World Politics', *International Organization* 39, no. 2: 233–59.

——, 1988. *States and Markets. An Introduction to International Political Economy*. London: Pinter.

Swain, Nigel, 1992. *Hungary. The Rise and Fall of Feasible Socialism*. London: Verso.

Szakolczai, György, Gábor Bagdy and József Vindics, 1987. 'The Dependence of the Hungarian Economy on the World Economy: Facts and Consequences', *Soviet & Eastern European Foreign Trade* 23, no. 1: 54–88.

Tardos, M. 1981. 'Options in Hungary's Foreign Trade', *Acta Oeconomica* 26, nos 1–2: 29–49.

Thomson, Stephen and Stephen Woolcock, 1993. *Direct Investment and European Integration*. London: Royal Institute of International Affairs.

Tovias, Alfred, 1991. 'EC-Eastern Europe: A Case Study of Hungary', *Journal of Common Market Studies* 29, no. 3: 291–315.

—— and Sam Laird, 1991. 'Whither Hungary and the European Communities?', PRE Working Paper 584, World Bank, Washington, DC.

'Turning the Screw', 1983. *The Banker* (July): 77.

Tussie Diana, 1991. 'The Impact of Indebtedness in the Uruguay Round: A Case Study of Argentina', (mimeo). Paper presented to the International Studies Association Convention, March, Vancouver.

Tyson, Laura D'Andrea, 1986. 'The Debt Crisis and Adjustment Responses in Eastern Europe: A Comparative Perspective', *International Organization* 40, no. 2: 239–85.

206   *References*

——, Sherman Robinson and Leyla Woods, 1988. 'Conditionality and Adjustment in Hungary and Yugoslavia', in Brada, Hewett and Wolf (1988).

UN, *Industrial Statistics Yearbook* , various volumes. New York: UN.

——, *International Trade Statistics Yearbook*, various volumes. New York: UN.

UNCTAD, 1990 (and other years). *Handbook of International Trade and Development Statistics*. Geneva: UN.

——, 1992. Trade and Development Report 1992. New York: UNCTAD.

UNECA (Economic Commission for Africa), 1992. *Alternative Framework to Structural Adjustment Programmes for Socio-Economic Recovery and Transformation*. Addis Adaba: UNECA.

UNECE (Economic Commission for Europe), 1982. *Economic Bulletin for Europe* 34, no. 4. Oxford: Pergamon Press.

——, 1990. *Economic Bulletin for Europe* 42. New York: UN.

——, 1991a. *Annual Review of the Chemical Industry 1989*. New York: UN.

——, 1991b. *The Livestock and Meat Market*. New York: UN.

UNIDO, 1985. *Handbook of Industrial Statistics 1984*. New York: UN.

——, 1991 (and other years). *Industry and Development. Global Report 1990–91*. Vienna: UN.

UNTCMD (UN Transnational Corporations and Management Division), 1992. *World Investment Report 1992. Transnational Corporations as Engines of Growth*. New York: UN.

Uvalic\$, Milica, Efisio Espa and Jochen Lorentzen (eds), 1993. *Impediments to the Transition in Eastern Europe*. Florence: European University Institute.

Valencia, Matthew and Peggy Simpson, 1994. 'Shedding the Stigma', *Business Central Europe* (April): 13–14.

Van Brabant, Jozef M., 1990. *Remaking Eastern Europe – On the Political Economy of Transition*. Dordrecht: Kluwer.

Van den Bossche, Anne-Marie, 1989. 'GATT: The Indispensible Link between the EEC and Hungary?', *Journal of World Trade* 23, no. 3: 141–55.

Van Wijnbergen, Sweder, 1991. 'The Mexican Debt Deal', *Economic Policy* (April): 13–56.

Varga, G. 1984. 'The Long-Run Development of Hungarian Industry (Outlines of an Approach to Industrial Policy)', *Acta Oeconomica* 32, nos 1–2: 91–112.

Vermulst, Edwin A., 1987. *Antidumping Law and Practice in the United States and the European Communities. A Comparative Analysis*. Amsterdam: North-Holland.

Vernon, Raymond, Debora L. Spar and Glenn Tobin, 1991. 'International Debt and the Creation of the Brady Plan', in *Iron Triangles and Revolving Doors*. New York: Praeger.

'Virtue Rewarded', 1992. *The Economist*, 31 October, 88.

Wade, Robert, 1990. *Governing the Market*. Princeton, NJ: Princeton University Press.

——, 1991. 'East Asia's Economic Success. Conflicting Perspectives, Partial Insights, Shaky Evidence', *World Politics* 44, no. 2: 270–320.

——, 1992. 'State and Market Revisited', *The Economist*, 4 April, 81.

Wallace, William, 1989. 'The Context of Reform', in Clarke (1989).

—— and Roger A. Clarke, 1986. *Comecon, Trade and the West*. London: Frances Pinter.

Walsh, Vivien, 1988. 'Technology and the Competitiveness of Small Countries: Review', in Freeman and Lundvall (1988).

Wang, Zhen Quan, 1993. 'Foreign Investment in Hungary: A Survey of Experience and Prospects', *Communist Economies & Economic Transformation* 5, no. 2: 245–54.

Wedel, Janine R, 1992. 'The Unintended Consequences of Western Aid to Post-Communist Europe', *Telos*, no. 92: 131–8.

Westlake, Melvyn, 1991. 'Bulls buoyed by Brady Bonanza', *The Banker* (October): 50–4.

Whitehead, Laurence, 1989. 'Latin American Debt: An International Bargaining Perspective', *Review of International Studies* 15, no. 3: 231–49.

Williamson, John. 1991. *The Economic Opening of Eastern Europe*. Washington, DC: Institute for International Economics.

Wing Thye Woo, 1990. 'The Art of Economic Development: Markets, Politics, and Externalities', *International Organization* 44 (Summer): 403–29.

Winiecki, Jan, 1988. 'East European Economies: Forced Adjustment Forever?', Seminar Paper no. 413, Institute for International Economic Studies, Stockholm.

Wolf, Thomas A., 1985a. 'Economic Stabilization in Planned Economies', *IMF Staff Papers* 32: 78–131.

——, 1985b. 'Exchange Rate Systems and Adjustment in Planned Economies', *IMF Staff Papers* 32: 211–47.

Wood, Robert E., 1986. *From Marshall Plan to Debt Crisis*. Berkeley: University of California Press.

World Bank, 1991. *World Debt Tables* vol. 1, Analysis and Summary Tables. Washington, DC: World Bank.

——, *World Debt Tables*, various volumes. Washington, DC: World Bank.

——, *World Development Report*, various volumes. Washington, DC: World Bank.

World Economy Research Institute, 1992. *Poland. International Economic Report 1991/92*. Warsaw: Warsaw School of Economics.

Wszelaki, Jan, 1951. 'The Rise of Industrial Middle Europe', *Foreign Affairs* 30: 123–34.

Yeats, Alexander J., 1985. 'On the Appropriate Interpretation of the Revealed Comparative Advantage Index: Implications of a Methodology Based on Industry Sector Analysis', *Weltwirtschaftliches Archiv* 121: 61–73.

Yoffie, David B., 1989. 'The Newly Industrializing Countries and the Political Economy of Protectionism', in Haggard and Chung-in Moon (1989).

Young, David, 1989. 'Hungary – Debt versus Reform', *World Today* 45 (October): 171–75.

Zloch-Christy, Iliana, 1987. *Debt Problems of Eastern Europe*. Cambridge: Cambridge University Press.

Index

208